CHEATING TIME

Science, Sex and Ageing

Roger Gosden

CHEATING TIME

Science, Sex and Ageing

MACMILLAN

First published 1996 by Macmillan

an imprint of Macmillan General Books
25 Eccleston Place London SW1W 9NF
and Basingstoke

Associated companies throughout the world

ISBN 0 333 62823 3

9 8 7 6 5 4 3 2 1

A CIP catalogue record for this book is available from
the British Library

Typeset by CentraCet Limited, Cambridge
Printed and bound in Great Britain by
Mackays of Chatham PLC, Chatham, kent

This book is dedicated to the memory of Professor
Charles-Édouard Brown-Séquard (1817–1894),
a pioneer in the quicksands of sex-hormone
and ageing research. His excessive attachment
to pet theories and inadequate methods have been
endlessly ridiculed, but I admire this visionary of
medical science, not least for his indefatigable
efforts and sacrifices.

Contents

CONTENTS

Preface

Shortly after turkey and trimmings I began to ponder what to write in this preface. I was still uncomfortably aware of my mother's rich pudding and wondered whether I would have survived so long if Christmas came round more often. As far as I can tell, her secret recipe involves blending every sweet, rich and alcoholic ingredient in sight and leaving the brew to mature for as long as possible.

Her son was tempted to do likewise with this book. The subject of ageing, especially when spiked with sex, is as intriguing and irresistible as any pudding. But it can be spoiled by too many additions and by overcooking. Most people are grateful for portions of science just big enough to swallow, and do not like to be overstuffed with facts – always a danger when a hopeful scientist sets out to write about his or her pet subject.

This book was written for everyone who is curious about ageing of the body, or what scientists prefer to call 'senescence'. There are few subjects as complex or more diverse in the whole of biology, which would seem reason enough to confine myself to the aspects I know best, namely the reproductive system and the menopause. That was how the book was born. But, as it began to take shape, other subjects gradually crept in. I was unable to build one story without leaning on another because the manifold aspects of ageing are indivisible. I decided to risk the broader – and harder – path, and hoped readers would not lose sight of the wood for the trees. The reader must judge whether I have succeeded.

I have done my best to produce a work that can be understood at a single reading by anyone with a smattering of biology or medical science. I hope that others who are sufficiently interested in the subject and willing to grapple with a few unfamiliar ideas will find it rewarding too. My models for writing have been the best scientific journalists in the newspaper business as well as that admirable weekly the *New Scientist*, on which I cut my scientific teeth as a schoolboy. Following their example, I have aimed to be comprehensible rather than comprehensive. This is not a textbook to be dipped into: rather, the reader is invited to test the waters from beginning to end.

To change the metaphor, writing this book has proved to be like climbing a mountain – a much longer haul than I bargained for at the outset. Part 1 describes the sort of terrain to be tackled, explaining what ageing is and what it is not, who ages and who is 'immortal'. It admittedly pulls up short of some of the more technical details, though salient ones are mentioned. Chapter 5 is a watershed in so far as it spells out the reasons why ageing exists at all. From that high ground, the whole landscape of age changes in the body can be appreciated. Biologists generally find reasonable answers to the 'why' questions of existence when they turn to evolutionary theory, and this is equally true for ageing. The time course for the decay of living cells is not fixed by the laws of physics but is affected by the same forces that have shaped our bodies. This implies the possibility of change.

Thereafter, I explore the realms of reproductive biology and medicine. This is not simply because that is where I am most at home, though that is true, but because the reproductive organs are among the first parts of the body to show their age. Changes in sex-hormone levels have important effects on virtually all parts of the body. At one time these hormones were thought to be elixirs of life, but now they and their offshoots in the form of hormone replacement therapy or HRT have come to be regarded with suspicion. I give a fairly full account of the old misconceptions, because some of them proved to be fruitful errors.

Some people may be apprehensive about what they might find in this book as its subject touches our mortal existence. Ageing is regarded as a morbid subject, and we will all suffer from some of its more malign effects – if we are lucky to live long enough. Regrettably, we are not able to defeat ageing yet, but we are learning to cheat time in all sorts of ways. Seen from a scientific perspective, the landscape is not quite as depressing as was once thought, and it is not pipedreaming to believe that the tide of age will be edged back.

A few people may baulk at the sexual overtones of the book, but I don't offer any apology. Reproduction and ageing are inseparable, like the two sides of a coin. Besides, there is nothing particularly prurient in this book, only bare facts and biological theories. But, like politics and religion, sex and ageing are matters that are too important to be taken utterly seriously. In my attempts to lighten the gloom, I hope that the basic messages have not been masked by anecdotes or by descriptions of the droll theories and trials of overzealous scientists.

Some of my colleagues will no doubt be puzzled about my reasons for having written this book. After all, I could, and perhaps should, be spending the time on experiments and with my students in the laboratory. Close friends will no doubt jest that publication marks the high-water mark of a mid-life crisis! I have to admit that this project is a pet indulgence, but in this respect it is not unlike a lot of experiments. Most scientists are led more by curiosity than by high-minded hopes of improving the lot of mankind.

The book has been written partly to satisfy myself. The discipline of collecting and organizing a large body of information from many sources, and not only in science, has been illuminating and has helped to crystallize in my mind some of the profound biological questions. I used to feel confident that I knew my research field but, as I had to explain it afresh and unstrait-jacketed by conventional university lectures, I realized how circumscribed a specialist's view can become. But most of all I now realize how lucky I was when, as a young undergraduate, I stumbled upon the subject that could absorb me for the rest of my days.

If this book fails either to interest or to enlighten others I accept full blame, because mine is no dry-bones of a subject. Perhaps the only topic in the whole of science that carries more human interest than sex *or* ageing is sex *and* ageing. Advances are constantly being made, and some indication of the public appetite for knowledge can be gauged by the level of media coverage. My hope is that readers will be able to share something of the challenge and the fun I have had in writing this book. If I succeed in illuminating my subject and dispelling some myths, without undermining a sense of wonder at the natural world, the uphill struggle will have been worthwhile.

Roger Gosden
School of Clinical Medicine
University of Leeds
West Yorkshire
July 1995

Acknowledgements

Writing for the general reader does not come naturally to most scientists and doctors, and I am no exception. The task would have been impossible without my helpmate, Carole. Some authors are grateful to their spouses for patience and cups of tea, but my debt to her is much greater. She has not only acted as my first critic and confidante, but also assisted with the composition of early drafts and has done an enormous amount of editing work. She kept the book simmering away in the background when I ran into conflict with my other work. Such conflicts are perhaps the chief reason why few researchers find time to undertake a project like this before they retire or expire.

I am delighted that the three people who have been my closest advisers are all women, though this was more by chance than a deliberate choice. The other two were my editor at Pan Macmillan, Georgina Morley, and my agent, Maggie Pearlstine. Without Maggie's belief in this book and her faith in the author's ability to do the subject justice, the project would have been stillborn. All three have helped me to see the biology of ageing from the woman's point of view whenever possible, and have curbed any careless remarks I might have slipped in. Also, a mysterious Reader has helped me to avoid drifting into unnecessary detail or labouring pet subjects, but the mask of anonymity prevents me from a proper acknowledgement. During the closing stages my secretary, Vivienne Ingham, provided the same enthusiastic and loyal assistance with the manuscript that she gives to the rest of my office work.

Science has never been much of a respecter of either miles or national boundaries, and two of my colleagues in far corners of the globe have had more influence on my scientific thinking than almost anyone else. No one has taught me more about the nature of ageing than Caleb Finch (University of Southern California), and the sharp wit and eye for detail of Malcolm Faddy (University of Queensland, Australia) have helped me avoid many a pitfall. Most of all, their infectious enthusiasm has encouraged me along the discovery trail, which often gives a traveller a bumpy ride. They have been generous and patient enough to read the whole manuscript, and made incisive comments, but any remaining errors are my responsibility alone.

Unfortunately I cannot mention everyone who has contributed to this work, so I have listed those who, knowingly or otherwise, have been helpful providers of information or encouragement: Steve Austad (Idaho), David Baird (Edinburgh), Merriley Borrell (Minneapolis), Alex Comfort (Cranbrook, Kent), James Drife (Leeds), Robert Edwards (Cambridge), David Hamilton (formerly Glasgow), Bruce Hobson (Edinburgh), Tom Johnson (Colorado), Tom Kirkwood (Manchester), Andrew Messenger (Sheffield), Jane Morris (Edinburgh), James Nelson (San Antonio), Roy Oliver (Dundee), Malcolm Pike (Los Angeles), Edwin Reavley (Edinburgh), Marilyn Renfree (Melbourne), Anthony Rutherford (Leeds), Roger Short (Melbourne), Sherman Silber (St Louis), Peter Temple-Smith (Melbourne), Robert Winston (London). Thanks to one and all.

The text is peppered with the names of some of the leading scientists and doctors who have contributed to the tale I shall tell. The list is far from complete, and I should have liked to acknowledge everyone. As it is, I have been constrained by the need for economy and have chosen to mention only those who have influenced me most.

Finally, I should like to thank my sons, Matt and Tom, for patiently enduring their father's preoccupation with his wordprocessor and greying hairs. After I have left the scene and this book is long forgotten, I hope they will still be here to prove that at least my genes have cheated time.

Introduction

Next to the Edinburgh Royal Infirmary stands the rather grandly named Simpson Memorial Maternity Pavilion, where one of my sons was born. James Young Simpson, the Professor of Midwifery in the 1860s, is now remembered as a great pioneer, but in his day he was responsible for a storm of controversy.

A few friends regularly met at his home in Queen Street on Saturday afternoons to discuss medical matters and indulge in a little parlour science. A bottle of chloroform was passed round for inhaling, rather like the habit of sharing a snuffbox. After rousing from forty winks, the company agreed that the results were agreeable, and Simpson soon introduced chloroform anaesthesia to the labour wards of the hospital. This compassionate act unexpectedly drew the wrath of theologians and some of his medical colleagues. They dogmatically accused him of being impious because it had been ordained that women should give birth in pain as a punishment for Eve's sin. Edinburgh – home of the author of *Dr Jekyll and Mr Hyde* – has always been a schizophrenic place, a bastion of conservatism as well as a seedbed for radicals.

I had never imagined myself being cast in the role of a dangerous radical, but, however innocent or arcane at first, scientific work can catapult the unwary researcher out of his ivory tower into the mainstream of public life. Lurid headlines about my attempts at

Edinburgh University to reset the biological clock in women ushered in the 1994 New Year. The *Los Angeles Times* reported, 'Use of Fetuses' Eggs for Fertility Sparks Furor'. Back home in Scotland, the *Daily Record* declared that I was 'The Doctor Who'd Make Babies from the Dead'. Dr Frankenstein, it was said, was alive and working in Edinburgh!

Public interest had already been kindled by an announcement that a British woman of fifty-nine had given birth to twins after receiving eggs from a donor in Italy. The scarcity of eggs for donation and the high cost of treatment reassured detractors that few late pregnancies could be established – until research on ovarian transplants was announced. A transplant of youthful eggs from a young cadaver or a foetus might rejuvenate the ovaries of older women by topping up the egg store and putting the menopause into reverse. It would enable women to get pregnant at whatever age they chose and in the time-honoured way rather than with the help of a bevy of doctors and IVF technology.

It is still too soon to predict the value of transplants, but the idea provided plenty of food for thought in 1994. Some people were curious to know how long women could have normal periods after the operation, and what upper limit should be set for motherhood, if any. Others felt that this was another unwelcome instance of natural processes being interfered with, and that treatment with tissue from the dead was abhorrent. Many wondered whether children growing up with elderly parents would be set at a disadvantage. Questions were asked in Parliament, and an amendment was tacked on to the Criminal Justice Bill forbidding foetal eggs from being used for fertility treatment. One MP even accused me of 'womb-robbing', which invited unsavoury comparisons with Dr Robert Knox, who bought corpses from body-snatchers for his anatomy classes in Old Edinburgh.

Another difficulty I had was the history of sex-gland therapy as a cure-all for old age. The idea of winding back the biological clock is a perennial hope, and organ products have long been prized ingredients in 'elixirs of life'. The idea that the sexual parts of the body carry the secrets of long life has been popular since the first mountebanks and quack doctors plied their trades. In living memory, ovaries and, even more frequently, testicles have been used in operations to attempt to rejuvenate women and men. Dr Serge Voronoff, one of the pioneers of monkey-gland grafts, claimed that they were '*les sources de la vie*'. He thought that weakness and disease in old age begin as soon as sex-hormone levels wane, though the fact of the matter turned out to be more complicated. Before pure hormones became available in the 1930s, the best way of boosting levels in the bloodstream was by grafting an organ from a young donor.

One of the curious facts about human fertility is that it tapers off after a short period of flowering and while we are still in our prime. The sex organs age prematurely, and perhaps faster than any other organs in the body. The hormonal changes that result echo around the body as side-effects such as menopausal symptoms and various diseases. The old myth that sexual ageing leads to general ageing has a germ of truth in it. The couple who are having difficulty conceiving, the woman with breast disease and even the man with the bald head are all victims of this process, and are understandably outraged at the early downturn of fortune. From the biological perspective, it seems perverse that biology halts our ability to pass down our genes so early.

This book was originally drafted to explain why our sexual parts deteriorate and to suggest some remedies. But, at an early stage, it became apparent that a piecemeal explanation would not suffice and I would have to tackle the larger tapestry of life and old age. Reproduction is not just another function of the body, like breathing or sweating, but is writ large in the rationale of life. Sufficient numbers of individuals must live long enough to try their luck at mating, otherwise the species is doomed. Consequently, the milestones of puberty and ageing occur at times that are specific for each species of animal or plant; the whole story is called the life history. Each history has its own logic and has been shaped in the evolutionary past by natural selection, just as the size of the body, the colour of plumage and other characteristics have.

Evolution has served for biologists as Newton's laws have done for physics – it is a tree on which to hang many of the facts of life. This was another great controversy that Edinburgh had a hand in, if only through causing the young Charles Darwin to flee from the horrors of human surgery and the tedium of anatomy classes under Knox's rival, Alexander Munro Tertius, to the arms of naturalists and men in holy orders in Cambridge. So pervasive has his theory of natural selection become that an evolutionary explanation is sought for every natural phenomenon, though ageing has only lately come under its sway. Biologists no longer surrender the phenomenon of ageing to physicists, and repudiate the simple view of ageing as organic decay and a necessary fact of being alive. Ageing is turning out to be rather more interesting and elastic than had been supposed. Its pace and character are not immutably fixed but depend on an evolutionary tension between the drive to produce offspring and the need for self-preservation. This theory calls to mind the old tale that procreation and degeneration are opposite sides of the same coin, which was originally behind sex-gland therapy.

People in Britain are living twice as long as in Victorian times, and, as life expectation creeps up in most parts of the world, ageing is becoming a key subject for politicians and public policy-makers to debate. The shift in population age has, of course, nothing to do with evolutionary change, nor with any conquest of the ageing process itself. The globe is greying because public-health measures and mass vaccination have successfully rid much of the world from epidemic diseases that used to scythe away young people. Nowadays, survival to the biblical quota of three score and ten or four score years is almost assumed as a right, but the maximum lifespan has probably not changed from time immemorial.

The threats to health and survival in childhood have mainly been external ones, but those for older people are internal and biological and the bread-and-butter of most medical research. Heart disease, cancer, Alzheimer's disease, Parkinson's disease, diabetes and osteoporosis are rarely found in young people, and if they could be eradicated as effectively as smallpox we could all hope to live even longer and better. The Nobel Prizewinner Sir Peter Medawar pointed out that 'The prolongation of a good life, happy and healthy, is fully in keeping with the spirit of medicine and is in a sense the very consummation of all that medical research has worked towards, *for all advances in medicine increase life expectancy*' (emphasis added). When he wrote that, he was bravely coping with the after-effects of a stroke and may have had in mind the effects of the humble aspirin in avoiding another blood platelet crisis. Bit by bit we are pushing back the onslaught of degenerative diseases, but there seems to be no lasting conquest in sight.

Everyone is comfortable with the efforts to prune back the effects of the ageing process, but fewer people applaud attempts to pull it up by the roots. This is an odd reaction, because ageing underlies most health problems and is a modern scourge on the enjoyment of life. One of the most disturbing discoveries we ever make is in childhood when loved ones get old and decrepit and die, and another is in mid-life when we realize that the human lifespan is briefer than we had perceived from the anterior end of life. Yet our longevity is still widely regarded as in the lap of the gods, rather as labour pains were in Simpson's day, with the implication that it should be left alone.

Evolutionary theory challenges this view because it contends that ageing came in by the back door, uninvited but unopposed. The ills that sweep in behind have no biological purpose. If this argument fails to convince readers that we can, and perhaps should, consider tinkering with our biological roots, perhaps another will. It is a fallacy to assume that the ills of ageing are problems only for the elderly and can safely be ignored while we are 'young'. Sexual and reproductive problems are not the only effects of ageing to show up early, and the roots of many a disease and disability in riper years are planted by our physiology, habits and environment at early ages. What is more, some 10 per cent of serious inborn genetic diseases have symptoms of premature ageing. Ageing is not just an unpalatable supper served up late in the day, but is never very remote and should concern us all.

One of the reasons why onlookers often look down their noses at ageing research is that its record has not always been impressive or noble. No other subject became so encrusted with eccentric notions and bizarre cures, nor has had as much cold water poured over it. The science of ageing became known as 'gerontology', literally meaning the study of old *men*. The figure of a silver-haired boffin vainly trying to halt the ravages of time seems as farcical as Canute's attempts to hold back the tide, and the quest for an elixir of life was the ultimate folly. Medieval alchemists could be excused on grounds of ignorance, but crafty practitioners in this century who attracted celebrities to their rejuvenation clinics damaged the reputation of gerontology in its infancy. Some people will pay almost any sum in the faint hope of regaining lost youth, which twists the purer objectives of science and is a temptation to commit fraud. Not surprisingly, many students have been deterred from testing the murky waters of gerontology. What has happened to the old man of the sciences?

Modern gerontology has had to overcome suspicion and prejudice to take its place among respectable sciences, and in some quarters is still hardly regarded as a respectable subject in its own right. Many doctors still view ageing as a matter of wear and tear plus the effects of disease, while others are more circumspect in judgement and pessimistic about progress. Lewis Wolpert at London's Middlesex Hospital recently said that 'Not many scientists work on the problem of ageing even though its importance cannot be doubted ... The problem is, at this stage, just too difficult, and gifted scientists with their skill in choosing the right problem recognize this. Only when an experimental approach to solving the problem becomes available will more scientists enter the field.' Given the immense progress in his own field of developmental biology, it is perhaps understandable that he should regard gerontology as a shady backwater.

Others trivialize the complexity, if not the significance, of ageing. At first glance our bodies seem to have much in common with our automobiles – like machines, they need fuel to work and they have built-in obsolescence. As a student, I was only too familiar with the problems of extending the working lifespan of an ancient motor bike or car. An engine or gearbox transplant could reinvigorate an old banger for a while, but rust would get it in the end. We are now doing comparable preventive care and repair work where necessary for our bodies. Healthy habits are now the order of the day, and almost any major organ (short of the brain) can be replaced with a transplant or a prosthesis to extend life. At the same time, the cosmetic industry panders to a society which sets almost as high a value on looking and feeling young as on being healthy.

But gerontology is more than skin-deep and disease is not its main focus, as in conventional medical research. Rather than tackling mechanical faults and rust one by one, it enquires whether a long-lasting model might be made in the first place. A slower pace of ageing would preserve the bloom of youth and fertility and postpone degenerative diseases. The complexity of cells and a disreputable start may call the enterprise in doubt, but researchers have already found ways of prolonging the lives of some animals, and are busy trying to discover the mechanisms and whether the exercise can be repeated in other species.

Progress will be slow until the nature of the underlying process of ageing has been understood. Without an appreciation of basic principles we would not have witnessed moon landings and nuclear power and any conquest of genetic diseases would be unthinkable. At one time it could be claimed with little exaggeration that there were as many theories of *how* ageing occurs as there were gerontologists. Many more students, especially in America, are now making geron-tology a career choice, and the confusing plethora of theories is being whittled down by the keen edge of empirical selection. But there is only one explanation of *why* ageing exists in the first place, and that is cause for greater optimism than ever before. On this hangs the answer to the question of whether it will ever be possible to control biological time.

This progress explains why ageing research is commanding newspaper headlines once again, and a major breakthrough could be around the corner. There now seems no reason in theory why the present ceiling on the human lifespan cannot be lifted at least a little

– which might be discomfiting news to some people. Peter Medawar put it this way: 'It is the great glory and also the great threat of science that anything which is possible in principle – which does not flout a bedrock law of physics – can be done if the intention to do it is sufficiently resolute and long-sustained.' Predicting the pace of progress for those who hope for it and others who fear it is more tricky, and unlikely to be as accurate as a British weather forecast.

The quest to temper the ageing process would seem to warrant a suitably impressive overture to this book. But progress is often made from unexpected quarters, and biology has a tradition of transferring lessons learned from one species to another. This story does not therefore begin in a hi-tech laboratory with people in white coats jockeying for the human longevity genes, but in the Australian outback. An obscure marsupial 'mouse' demonstrates better than most laboratory experiments that ageing is not fixed and immutable, which implies that humans too can cheat time.

Part One

The Seeds
of Time

CHAPTER 1   **Mating Madness**

> ... the common origins of sex and of death by aging
> survives among our feelings in a hazy, primitive fashion
> and is ready to haunt the mind
>
> J. T. Fraser: *Time – the Familiar Stranger*

• The Quest for *Antechinus*

The austral spring had just begun and, as I trudged along muddy
tracks in the wooded foothills of the Great Dividing Range in
Australia, the roar of streams in spate reminded me of the Scottish
Highlands. But the vegetation was completely different in those wet
sclerophyll forests. Great tree ferns grew to seven metres tall, crimson
bottlebrush flowered in wet gullies and gum-trees soared towards an
azure sky. Here and there under the delicate canopies of eucalyptus
were trees that had died of old age or from lightning strikes many
years earlier. The foresters, who had left a few of them standing as
wildlife refuges, call them 'stags' because their naked boughs stretch
out like huge antlers. The trunks were pock-marked from attacks by
insects and birds, and some of the larger holes probably harboured
nests of the creatures I was seeking. I knew that searching by day was
bound to be fruitless: females would emerge from their holes only
under cover of darkness to catch insects and grubs, but not a single
male would join them. Adult males had become extinct in the wild in
August, the season of mating madness.

I was visiting Australia late in 1993 to do some theoretical work
on the human menopause with Malcolm Faddy, a colleague at the
University of Queensland. The weekend provided a long-awaited

3

opportunity to explore the habitat of an animal that is rarely seen outside its native country. Brown marsupial mice, or *Antechinus stuartii* to be more accurate, are justly famous down under as the 'little critters that root themselves to death'. Since the probability of seeing a male antechinus in the wild was almost zero, I contacted Peter Temple-Smith at Monash University in the Melbourne area. He has been studying antechinuses for several years, and his knowledge of their biology is second to none.

One of the delights of working in science is that perfect strangers who otherwise have nothing in common will often strike up an immediate rapport as soon as they discover a shared interest. On this occasion, the mere mention of antechinus over the telephone was enough to draw an enthusiastic invitation to visit Peter's laboratory. On my arrival, he ushered me upstairs from his office to the vivarium, though the strong animal odour was already leading me by the nose.

Peter had captured a few wild antechinuses during the winter months, shortly before the breeding season. Each animal was housed in bachelor quarters. There was a cardboard tube in the cage to serve as a nest box, a bottle of drinking-water and a food dish. The menu that day was dried cat-food. Freshly minced liver was provided as a treat once a week – very different to the vegetarian fare of wild mice back home, but then antechinuses are rather exotic.

Peter tried to coax a sleepy male out of its nest tube, but the creature was much more alert than we had bargained for and shot right out of the cage and on to the floor. After several bold but futile goalie dives, the tall, bearded biologist decided to resort to the Elliott traps. These folding triangular aluminium contraptions are used to catch animals under licence for ecology research in the field. They are baited with peanut butter, oats and honey, which the animals find irresistible. Once the unwary eater gets into the trap, a door snaps shut behind. The animals come to no harm and can be weighed, examined and labelled. When they are released again some individuals become 'trap-happy' and take advantage of a free lunch at every opportunity.

Bait was not needed to catch our escapee, who was only too

eager to retreat into the safety of darkness. Peter triumphantly put his hand into the trap and pulled out the squirming animal, which immediately buried its teeth into his finger. Had this been a true mouse its sharp incisors would have drawn blood, but antechinuses have only small teeth for biting insect prey. They are popularly known as 'marsupial mice', although this is something of a misnomer because they are not closely related to rodents. Carnivores by nature, they would be better called marsupial shrews.

Antechinuses are members of a group called dasyurids, the best-known member being the fierce-looking Tasmanian devil. They are found between New Guinea and the southern tip of Australia in a wide range of habitats. So abundant are brown antechinuses during the mating season that they are regarded as pests in some regions. Friends complained that they invade their country home, nesting in coat pockets and kicking up a rumpus on the tin roof at night.

The animal in Peter's hand had a long naked tail and a dark brown pelt with an attractive yellow underbelly. He was larger than a mouse, with a long pointed snout and great bulging eyes. More surprisingly, his genitals were in reverse order: two testicles in front and the penis behind! This arrangement down under is the rule for marsupials but its advantages are more apparent in kangaroos, which might otherwise bruise their delicate members when bouncing across the bush.

Having heard so much about antechinuses and having come so far to see them, the moment of first encounter was thrilling, especially when I reflected on the possibility that this might have been the only adult male left alive in the world. While the rest of his generation had expired after mating in August, he had been saved by enforced celibacy. With a little help from a biologist, he had cheated time! When the extraordinary life history of antechinuses first came to light it was received by the scientific world with some disbelief. No other warm-blooded vertebrate, apart from a handful of related species, exhibits such a clear link between reproduction and mortality. Nor is there a better example of programmed ageing.

After returning the animal to the nest box, we examined a female in the next cage. She was a little smaller and less inclined to bite. Otherwise she looked the same, until she was turned upside down to reveal a set of eight nipples. But there was no true pouch in this marsupial. Had she been nursing young she would have had a wriggling mass of naked bodies clinging on precariously. As with other marsupials, new-born pups are tiny and weigh just half a gram. Despite this immaturity, their fore-quarters and reflexes are sufficiently well developed to help them crawl to the nearest nipple and hold on for dear life. Sometimes there are more pups than nipples available, which is unfortunate for late arrivals because no mother will wet-nurse the surplus babies of another.

All antechinuses are born within a few days of each other in September. This is the beginning of spring in the Southern Hemisphere when insects are becoming more abundant after a period of winter scarcity. The young cling to their mothers for their first two months of life. She is vulnerable at this time, and emerges from the nest hole only when absolutely necessary, to feed and drink. By late November the babies are sufficiently well developed to allow her to leave them behind while she goes hunting. The weight of the litter has by this time increased ten-fold, to equal her own, and by the time they are weaned some weeks later the babies have grown three times bigger still.

This is a much longer period of filial dependence than in most animals of this size. Mice and rats, for instance, are weaned a month after birth, and can become parents themselves a month later. They can live for two or more years as adults. However, antechinuses take much longer to reach puberty, but the adult phase in males is extraordinarily short.

Andrew Cockburn is an ecologist at the Australian National University in Canberra who studies the movements of antechinuses in their natural environment. He traps wild animals and attaches miniature radio-transmitters to their backs before releasing them. Researchers are led to the nest sites by the periodic bleeping of a radio receiver, each animal being identified by its own particular frequency. The movements of the young from the nest can then be followed until the animals drop.

He found that, after scattering from the natal nest, the males travel some distance to join other colonies. As the nights grow longer and cooler the advantages of huddling together in groups of twenty or thirty individuals are obvious. But these cordial relations evaporate once the reproductive system starts to awaken at the end of winter and sex-hormone levels begin to rise. The survival of the species is then served more by aggression and an insatiable libido than by communal peace.

For animals living near the equator it matters less when they breed because seasonal fluctuations in food abundance and weather are minimal. Those at higher latitudes, however, must deliver their offspring when food is most plentiful, to maximize their chances of surviving. Large animals with long pregnancies tend to mate in the autumn, while small ones with shorter pregnancies wait until the spring. The need to synchronize breeding condition in males and females is paramount, and is another reason why biological clocks are so important. As far as we know, antechinuses are like other animals that have a biological timepiece in their brains to measure the daylength – or rather nightlength.

• Biological Clocks

In many species the trigger for switching on reproduction is the perception of a seasonal shift in daylength, although some species respond (more romantically perhaps) to moonlight. Air temperatures can affect fertility too but, because the weather can be capricious, they are less reliable indicators of the best time to breed. The precision of some biological clocks can be astonishing. The spawning of some coral polyps in the Great Barrier Reef is an unforgettable spectacle from the air – a huge pink slick drifting near the surface of the ocean. The biggest storm of spawning occurs on the fifth night after the first full moon in midsummer when millions of polyps release pinhead-sized eggs within minutes of each other. The strategy of putting all the eggs into one basket, so to speak, by committing everything to a once-a-year episode of mass reproduction is less risky than it seems. Far more eggs and larvae are produced than predators could possibly consume at a sitting, so some are bound to survive. What appears to human eyes as wasteful has served these species admirably well.

Subtropical species are not the only ones with an eye on the calendar. One of my Edinburgh colleagues, Gerald Lincoln, has been lucky enough to combine laboratory work with field trips to study red deer on the Isle of Rhum off the west coast of Scotland. He got to know some of the beasts by name. One dignified stag, called 'Aristotle', had shed his antlers on the same day plus or minus one every year for ten years. By casting off the old pair, he could grow a larger set for the next autumnal rut. But antlers do not know when to be shed more than leaves choose when to fall. Their cycles of growth and death are controlled by hormonal fluctuations.

Corals and deer live much longer than antechinuses, and if breeding is unsuccessful they can try again the next year. The date of the annual sexual congress of antechinuses is critical because these animals have only one opportunity in a lifetime to reproduce. The females all come into sexual 'heat', or oestrus, within a few days of each other, and pheromones probably help to ensure that both sexes are keeping in time. These chemicals are nature's aphrodisiacs and are released from glands whenever an individual is in season, to attract members of the opposite sex.

The biological clock in most mammals is the pineal gland, which is attached to the back of the brain. Back in evolutionary history it was sensitive to light and acted as third eye, but now has acquired a new role as keeper of biological time. (Descartes thought it was the home of the soul, because, unlike most other structures in the brain, it is unpaired and no one can have more than one soul!)

We now know that the pineal gland releases the hormone melatonin during the hours of darkness. This happens in most animals, and helps to keep physiology in step with the daily rhythm of activity and rest. In humans it causes drowsiness (signalling to the traveller's body that it is bedtime in Melbourne even if morning in London), and some of the symptoms of jet lag may be due to a delay in resetting melatonin release. Five milligrams of pure melatonin taken on the night of arrival after a flight from Australia may help to beat those blighted days. Whatever the other roles of melatonin – and many have been suggested – it is certainly important for fertility in animals that breed seasonally, and keeps mating partners in synchrony. The word 'hormone' was coined from the Greek, meaning 'to excite'; but not all hormones are stimulants, and melatonin has turned out to be a 'downer'. It reduces the release of two fertility hormones from the pituitary gland, which lies under the brain.

Melatonin trickling out of the pineal gland is carried by the bloodstream to the floor of the brain, the hypothalamus, and the underlying pituitary gland. So important is the pituitary – once thought to be a mere mucus-secreting gland – that it has been called the conductor of the orchestra of hormone-secreting glands. The two hormones it produces for fertility are luteinizing hormone and follicle-stimulating hormone, or LH and FSH for short. They are identical in both sexes, and are also called gonadotrophins, because they act exclusively on the gonads – the ovaries and testicles – to stimulate production of sex hormones and either eggs or sperm. The main sex hormones are oestrogens in females and androgens in males, the chief androgen being testosterone.

The longer the hours of darkness, the more melatonin is released from the brain to suppress fertility. As the days lengthen at the end of the Australian winter, less melatonin is released and the sex organs of the antechinuses start to awaken and the early signs of puberty emerge. By late July, levels of male sex hormones have reached their peak, transforming docile juvenile antechinuses into fierce adolescents with unparalleled appetites for copulation.

Mating antechinuses behave like stags during the rutting season. They don't carry weapons on their heads for clashing with rivals, but they use their teeth to full effect in trials of strength and for subduing females. Sooner or later the battle scars become obvious and the creatures look anorexic and haggard. They are balding, and have tattered ears and chewed tails.

Females do not come off completely unscathed after each round of courtship. A male mounting from behind may grab an ear or hang on to the female's coat with his jaws. Once secure, he begins a series of vigorous thrusts that continues for up to twelve hours, with the occasional rest to take breath. After mating with one female he quickly goes in search of another, and has no scruples about cuckolding other males. One particular male in captivity was seen to mate with sixteen females in succession, two of them twice, and each for the full period – until he expired *in flagrante delicto*.

The drama of the last days of *Antechinus stuartii* has stimulated some exaggeration about its hormone levels. Its blood testosterone level is no higher than in other adult animals, including men, but there is an important distinction. In most species only 3 per cent of all circulating testosterone is biologically free to act on cells. Most of the hormone binds to blood proteins – and in particular to sex hormone binding globulin, which we shall abbreviate SHBG. These proteins, which are made in the liver, act like chaperones to prevent too many hormone molecules straying into cells where they may cause overstimulation. This arrangement ensures that a large store of inactive testosterone in the blood can be called into action at any moment. Antechinuses are unusual because they have no SHBG in their blood and so males are exposed to testosterone at almost full, intoxicating strength.

Males rarely break between bouts of mating to sleep or groom themselves, and they even forget to eat and drink. They are utterly single-minded, and their behaviour becomes increasingly frenzied, as if they are running out of time. They are! After several days of this mating marathon they begin to totter in the treetops. Sooner or later they collapse and fall to the forest floor like autumn leaves. Within two or three weeks of reaching puberty, every male has had his day and the habitat is inherited by females.

After such ardent efforts on the part of their consorts, we might expect that every female antechinus would have been well and truly impregnated; but this species has one more surprise in store. Many of the females had not ovulated when they were mated and so could not fall pregnant before the males died. This may seem to be a perverse arrangement, but the males rest in peace because their sperm are safely stored in the females' fallopian tubes until eggs are released from the ovaries.

Sperm normally have a lifespan of only a few days in the female body after ejaculation. In antechinuses, however, they survive for fourteen days, which leaves a sufficient margin until the eggs are finally ovulated. This is longer than for most species, but far from the record, which is held by bats which store their mates' semen through-out the winter months of hibernation or even longer. Ever ambitious to break records, humans have gone a step further by using freezing technology which offers the theoretical possibility of indefinite stor-age. A few women have even requested insemination with the sperm of a long-dead husband to continue his genetic line.

Species that play the Russian-roulette form of reproduction have to be sure of winning the game even though the pay-off is postponed until after the gun has gone off. They have evolved a risky strategy that succeeds because their environment is fairly stable and seasonal food abundance is predictable. If something upset their biological clocks or an environmental catastrophe occurred one August, the world population of *Antechinus stuartii* might be wiped out at a stroke.

Another compensation for this risky game plan is antechinuses' fertility. To be successful, males have to be confident in the quality of their sperm, most of which are healthy and vigorous. Peter Temple-Smith found that somewhere between 15 and 100 per cent of antechinus's sperm reach the site of fertilization in the upper reaches of the female tubes. Only 0.01 per cent of sperm from that paragon of fertility the rabbit achieve their goal, and even fewer in humans. Not surprisingly, antechinus eggs are almost always fertilized, and very few are lost at later stages of pregnancy. Since reproduction is so extraordinarily efficient, the species has no need to produce enormous amounts of sperm. Males make only one sperm for every thousand in other animals of similar size. What is more remarkable is that production of new sperm collapses even before the first act of mating has taken place, and the males have to make do with what they have stored in their tubes. It is possible to tell whether a male has passed this stage of no return by the colour of his scrotum – the sexually mature male becomes literally black-balled.

Sperm cells are produced in the testes rather like blood cells in bone marrow. The parental or so-called stem cells divide asymmetrically into two such that one of the products is a replacement stem cell while the other is a sperm cell. The strategy is rather like living on the interest of an investment which is never withdrawn from the bank. In humans, stem cells in the testes and bone marrow ensure that vast numbers of fresh sperm and blood corpuscles are produced daily into a ripe old age. In antechinuses, the stem cells in the testes die off shortly after they have begun to divide, leaving the animals with a limited store of mature sperm to be portioned out during each round of mating. The male is therefore in the same straits as his mate, who cannot replenish her eggs. He has to become as thrifty with his gametes as she is with hers.

In no other mammal, to my knowledge, does the male totally and permanently lose his ability to make new sperm before mating. But, for a creature with zero prospects of surviving for more than a couple of weeks, this hardly matters. And, since it takes several weeks to make a new sperm cell, it is pointless putting any further effort in that direction. The male that Peter Temple-Smith had rescued from *les femmes fatales* was not therefore 'keeping his powder dry' because he was already on his way to becoming sterile. Even if he had survived to the next breeding season, he would be incapable of fathering offspring because his sperm stores would eventually go stale. In many respects antechinuses are programmed to have short lives.

• The Price of Passion

Why should these animals pay such a heavy price for what is a natural and necessary activity? Some are eaten by predators, because in their sexual ardour they become careless in a world of hungry owls, foxes and feral cats; others die of wounds inflicted by rivals. But not all the causes of death are so obvious, and we need to use the methods of forensic medicine to uncover them.

A post-mortem examination shows that the corpses are lean and wasted. Inside the shrunken stomach and intestines we find bleeding ulcers, and there is a heavy infestation of parasites. Most wild animals harbour some worm and insect parasites, this being a particular hazard for social animals living in nests, but a combination of regular grooming and a vigilant immune system normally keeps most of them at bay. But in the final weeks of an antechinus's life the parasite problem mushrooms. Fleas are abundant, if comparatively harmless. Lice are more pernicious because they attack the skin and eyes and transmit *Babesia*, a microbial parasite of blood cells, rather as mosquitoes transmit the malarial parasite to humans. Lungworms choke bronchial tubes, causing pneumonitis and breathing difficulties, and the liver becomes infected with the bacillus *Lysteria*, better known for its fondness for soft cheese and pâté. This generalized collapse of self-maintenance and defence is reminiscent of AIDS in humans, but the tragedy for antechinuses (if it can be called that) is brought on by hormones rather than a virus.

Some biologists say that the animals die of rapid ageing, while others argue that they suffer from a stress reaction which has gone out of control. In a sense, both are right, and the dichotomy is artificial. According to Caleb ('Tuck') Finch, an eminent gerontologist at the University of Southern California, the word 'ageing' should encompass everything that increases the risk of dying with time. It excludes all the epidemic diseases of youth and other disorders that strike with equal frequency at all ages, but includes all the changes that harm cells and organs over a period of time. Infertility is included in this list because it is a sort of genetic death of an individual, closing the chapter in which contributions can be made to the next generation.

Such a definition of ageing may sound like a catch-all, but then ageing is not a specific disease. Since the word is often popularly used just to indicate the passage of time, whether or not physical changes have occurred, most gerontologists prefer to use the word 'senescence'. Either way, antechinuses undergo rapid ageing or senescence, and stress turns out to be the main cause in this instance. The stress concept was originally conceived by Hans Selye of McGill University and quickly slipped into popular usage. Most people regard stress as the response we make to circumstances in which expectations of what we can do exceed our capacity to deliver. Not only can stress precipitate an emotional crisis: if unremitting, it can also lead to disease and shorten life.

Physiologists have always used the concept rather sparingly, regarding short-term stress as a beneficial internal change which helps the body to survive a threat. We know when a stress reaction is taking place because it involves the adrenal glands. These thumbnail-sized glands, which lie beside the kidneys, release a number of hormones, the best-known being adrenalin (called epinephrine in North America) which heightens mental alertness, accelerates the heart rate and makes sugar available for the vital organs. All these are beneficial changes when a response to emergency situations such as a fright or flight from danger is demanded.

The adrenals have a significance out of all proportion to their size, and a loss of one of their hormones needed for conserving salt rapidly proves fatal. In 1856 a French professor called Charles Édouard Brown-Séquard, who figures later in the book, discovered that guinea-pigs died quickly if their adrenal glands were removed. He thereby confirmed a report published the previous year by a British physician, Thomas Addison, who noticed that patients dying of 'bronzed diabetes' always had damaged adrenal glands. Addison's disease was frequently a complication of tuberculosis in those days, and the novelist Jane Austen succumbed to it at the early age of forty-two, long before it was recognized.

When stress is prolonged, the adrenals release other types of hormone called corticosteroids, which are chemically related to the sex hormones. Synthetic forms of these steroids are familiar in many a household medicine cabinet as medications for asthma and inflammatory skin reactions, and their warning labels indicate that they should be treated with respect. Like adrenalin, corticosteroids help to preserve the vital functions of the body when under threat. They command the bones to transfer calcium to where it is needed and the muscles to convert proteins into glucose to sustain an overtaxed brain and heart. Not surprisingly, continued hormone stimulation eventually leads to problems. Bones become fragile, muscles waste away and diabetes develops. The body bloats with salt and water, the skin becomes thinner and wrinkled and hair falls out. Worse still, corticosteroids suppress the immune system, diverting resources set aside for the battle against parasites and cancer to meet the more acute threat to survival. Male antechinuses do not live long enough to have to contend with cancer, but the hormonal changes set them on course for slow suicide.

Their adrenal glands enlarge to make more corticosteroids because the brain sends a chemical signal to the pituitary gland to release the hormone corticotrophin (ACTH) to act upon them. This state resembles Cushing's syndrome in which patients produce excessive amounts of either the pituitary or the adrenal hormone from a tumorous gland. Antechinuses are cushingoid in so far as their adrenal glands are running at full capacity during the rut; even an injection of a large dose of ACTH is unable to squeeze out any more steroid. Under healthier circumstances there is a mechanism in the brain which prevents the system from becoming overheated. Rising levels of corticosteroids acting on nerves in the brain shut down the release of ACTH, rather like a thermostat switching off a home heating system when the set temperature is reached. But the hormone controller in the brain of a rutting male antechinus is decrepit and fails to sense warning signals; the pituitary therefore continues to pour out ACTH, making matters worse and eventually proving fatal.

Most corticosteroids are attached to a blood protein called corticosteroid binding globulin, or CBG, which keeps their biological activity in check, but in the rut they are almost at full strength. On top of the absence of SHBG, the levels of CBG in antechinuses fall to just 20 per cent of normal under the influence of testosterone, and no longer provide adequate protection against excess hormone stimulation. Antechinuses are therefore doubly compromised, and the hormonal changes which began at puberty are responsible for accelerating ageing and hastening death.

When celibacy is forced on animals in the laboratory the chances of survival are improved because conflict with other males is prevented; but the most dramatic extension of lifespan is achieved by castration before the onset of sexual maturity. Deprived of their sex hormones, and of the urge to mate and fight, the animals can live twice as long – a privilege normally reserved for females. Males are expendable, because they do not contribute to rearing the young. It may be better that they are out of the way altogether because food is still scarce in early spring when competition might jeopardize nursing mothers. Males would also bring their parasite burden into the nests, and might redirect their aggressive tendencies from rivals to mothers and babies.

In most species the female is the longer-lived gender but the two- or three-fold difference in antechinuses is quite exceptional. The more 'dangerous' hormone, testosterone, is present in female antechinuses too, but only at very low concentrations, and most is converted in their bodies to the female sex hormone, oestrogen. Females have fewer parasites and remain relatively calm while the males are gripped by mating madness, but they are at risk from marauding males of another species, *Antechinus swainsonii*. This species is much larger than *A. stuartii*, but conflict is normally avoided because it is usually active only by day. In the mating season, however, it stays up all night. Apart from occasional rape-killings, the females generally emerge at the end of the breeding season in good health, having lost only a few tufts of hair along with their virginity. They may live for another year, and the best of them will breed a second time.

• Sex and Death

However fascinating the life history of animals, we will always be more concerned about the sexual behaviour and life expectation of our own species. We might well ask whether a marsupial shrew can tell us anything about our own biology. The life history of *Antechinus* is an extreme example of a connection between sex and death, but we would be mistaken to dismiss the creature as 'primitive'. Marsupials are an extremely successful group whose members have brilliantly solved the challenge of surviving and breeding in some of the harsher environments on earth. What is even more interesting is that the brown antechinus has close relatives that adopt the more familiar mode of serial breeding with slow ageing – the lifestyle of our own species and of virtually all other mammals. This mode is called 'iteroparity', and is thought to be the ancestral pattern in mammals, from which antechinuses have seen fit to deviate to what is known as 'semelparity', meaning 'breeding only once'. This change probably occurred relatively recently in evolutionary history, and mutations in a few key genes may have been enough for antechinuses to switch from serial breeding to big-bang reproduction.

From the perspective of a typical mammal, the semelparous pattern of life and death may seem strange. Yet, if we cast our biological net wider to include invertebrates and even plants, iteroparity is not quite the dominant lifestyle we had imagined. Many other successful living things have inherited the same lifestyle as *Antechinus*, and, in each case that has been studied, hormones turn out to be the trigger for both reproduction and ageing.

The fruiting bodies of annual plants produce hormone-like substances that cause senescence in the rest of the plant. To take a garden example, if spinach is deflorated the rest of the plant survives much longer, rather like an antechinus after castration. Among animal species, two cephalopod molluscs, the Mediterranean octopus and the cuttlefish, lose weight and die soon after spawning. A hormone from their optic glands renders them anorexic and, since their digestive tract degenerates, they cannot use food anyway. If the gland is removed before the onset of maturity, they live two or three times longer and not only eat better but age more slowly. Rapid senescence also awaits the amorous male tarantula spider. Contrary to popular belief, he is not usually killed by the larger and longer-lived female but suffers death through starvation and decay. The female lives on for decades and mates with much younger partners.

The most familiar examples of big-bang reproduction and ageing are found among the migratory salmonid fish. Pacific salmon of both sexes normally live in the ocean for about four years before returning to spawn in the stream where they spent their nursery days. Their intrepid determination to reach this destination is legendary but, soon after releasing eggs and sperm in quiet headwaters, both males and females keel over and die. The act of spawning is not exhausting in itself. The river estuary was in fact their point of no return, and ageing began as soon as they entered freshwater and stopped feeding. But their death does not signal total abandonment of their offspring in a biological sense. Their rotting bodies enrich the pure waters with nitrogen, causing them to bloom with algae so that the young parr can graze in a water meadow.

Pacific salmon have an excess of corticosteroids towards the end of life, which leads to brain decay. Had they become less demented, perhaps they would have had second thoughts about their journey in the first place. The hormones also encourage coronary heart disease and abnormalities of other internal organs. In their final hours the salmon become covered in fungal growths which they had formerly resisted, indicating a failing immune system. They too are victims of stress and, like male antechinuses, can be saved from an early death by castration – provided the operation is done before they come into breeding condition.

Only a few of the salmon family are strictly semelparous. The rainbow trout does not die after spawning, though it still has the 'death programme' written in its genes. Steroid injections hasten senescence as much in the trout as in its migratory relative, and they have comparable effects in almost every other vertebrate animal too. So semelparity and iteroparity may not be completely different reproductive strategies that have evolved along separate tracks. And, though life history is genetically determined, ageing is not the inexorable process we had thought, and hormones play a role in shaping the life plan for ageing as well as for reproduction.

No man ever died of semelparity like a salmon or an antechinus, but myths and superstitions have given credence to sexual intimations of mortality. One incident in 1899 fired the imagination of the French public as much for its sexual symbolism as for its political significance. Félix Faure, sixth President of the Third Republic, had a mistress who was married to a well-known painter. One day, when fifty-eight years old, he took Spanish fly, a powder made from a bright green beetle that has a reputation as an aphrodisiac. But an archbishop arrived unexpectedly at the Élysée Palace, and the effects of the stimulant were wearing off by the time this visitor had left. Faure took a second dose before returning to the bedroom. The next recorded incident was that he had a seizure. After his mistress had been discreetly whisked away and his dignity had been restored, members of the family were summoned to his deathbed. The following day the French newspapers reported with characteristic aplomb that the President had 'died in the exercise of his functions'. A conspiracy theory was hatched connecting his mysterious death with the infamous Dreyfus affair, but the public guessed that Monsieur le Président had paid a price for his passion.

There are enough anxieties about health for those of riper years without adding unnecessary worries about the safety of sexual relations. Coroners say that 'death in the saddle' is not an unknown *modus moriendi*, but the risks of passion in older couples are far less than the odd colourful anecdote might lead us to believe. After all, almost any activity – from carrying a shopping-bag to straining at stools – is more hazardous for people of advanced age. Sexual intercourse puts only a mild strain on physiology, and abstinence is unnecessarily cautious even for a weak constitution.

Nevertheless, the fact of being sexual creatures affects our chances of a long life in many ways, if not the actual course of ageing. Females of most species outlive the males. Eunuchs are reputed to survive as long, or perhaps longer, than women. Common ailments like heart disease and arthritis are respecters of gender. The suspicion that sex hormones are at least partly to blame for these differences is strengthened by evidence that anabolic-steroid abuse by some athletes and body-builders is harmful. What is more, most of us will suffer with a disease involving our reproductive system at some stage of our lives. Some of the most serious such diseases affect the breast and the prostate glands. We have seen that sex hormones switch on a genetic programme of self-destruction in antechinuses, and we do well to consider our own sexual chemistry.

Sex has carried morbid overtones in biological theory for a long time. At the turn of the century there was a great deal of speculation about the causes and origins of ageing. Many scientists came to view it as the price to be paid for having a complex body. Single-celled animals seem to be able to grow for ever, whereas more advanced forms exhibit a variety of life-history patterns, usually with a definite span. The sex cells were thought to share the special privilege of protozoa in remaining free of time-dependent decay, otherwise babies would be born as 'old' as their mothers. Reproduction had to flower if the species was to survive, but the bodies that carried the eggs and sperm could be cast aside in favour of vigorous new individuals.

This old idea is ever popular. The founder of the International Society for the Study of Time, J. T. Fraser, recently declared, 'Death by aging was an evolutionary development that took place long after life began, and was a necessary corollary to sexual reproduction.' We shall see that this view is not strictly tenable, yet Fraser gives a vital lead. Unless ageing is merely a consequence of the inexorable laws of physics, evolutionary theory should be able to offer a rational explanation for its existence, and to account for the particular costs of sexual reproduction as well. There must have been powerful reasons why antechinuses and Pacific salmon age more rapidly and die earlier than related species. What appears to our eyes to be bad for the individual must be in the interests of perpetuating the species. This was the hard conclusion that Darwin drew in his theory of natural selection, and which horrified his friend Alfred, Lord Tennyson, who wrote:

> Are God and Nature then at strife,
> That Nature lends such evil dreams?
> So careful of the type she seems,
> So careless of the single life.

Adult existence is a very brief affair for male antechinuses, compared with common mice and shrews which reach puberty earlier and last longer. Apes and humans have not even reached puberty until several lifespans of these small animals have passed. Each species has its own timetable of events, yet each of these life histories is successful in so far as the type has survived for millions of years. Each has acquired a successful cocktail of genes to cope with the circumstances in which it finds itself. The history of life on earth has been one of constant experimentation to solve the problems of surviving and reproducing in a hostile and changing environment. In the next chapter we shall see just how long animals and plants can live, and it turns out that they vary as much in this respect as they do in body size and shape.

CHAPTER 2

A Dog's Life

And so, from hour to hour, we ripe and ripe,
And then from hour to hour, we rot and rot;
And thereby hangs a tale.

Jaques in Shakespeare's As You Like It

• Brief Lives

My family passed our summer holidays with my grandmother who lived at the seaside on the Isle of Wight. The blue remembered hills of childhood seemed timeless compared with the hectic pace of life nowadays. She spent every free moment bent over her needlework in the soft chair by the chimney-nook. Nothing seemed to change in her world; each of her days was like the previous one for as long as I could remember.

As childhood slipped into the anxious years of adolescence, our visits were glorious retreats into a womb of the past where time did not matter and we could please ourselves. Nan radiated a sense of continuity; she became an icon of permanence in a changing world. To my eyes she had always seemed elderly. I could not imagine her as a young woman, and the Edwardian period when she was growing up seemed as remote to me as the Roman occupation of Britain. Only in the final few years of her long life did I notice that she had changed from one visit to the next.

I could hardly say the same about her Irish terrier, Lassie. She was born after me, but by the time I was ten, and still in short trousers, she was already past a safe age for having puppies. She no longer begged to go out for a run along the beach, nor was she interested in retrieving sticks or playing other games. She wanted to be left to doze in peace in the sun. Lassie was becoming an old lady, like Nan. Each visit I noticed a bigger change in the dog than the year before, until one summer I was horrified to find her basket empty. Before I had reached the age of sixteen and plucked up the courage for my first date, this dear dog's life had run its full course.

When this sad reflection passed through my mind, I took some comfort in the fact that she had at least enjoyed a longer life than my pets back home in a London suburb. My mice and rabbits had received as much care and attention as I could afford, yet they had died of natural causes after only a few years. An elfin cemetery at the bottom of the garden bore witness to the rodent generations that had passed during the course of my childhood. The neighbours dismissed my feelings for the 'vermin' as unduly sentimental, and my parents reassured me that plenty more were waiting for kindly owners at the pet shop. Nevertheless, I was puzzled and frustrated that their lives were so brief. Why should humans enjoy the privilege of seventy or eighty years of life when a mouse can have but two or three and a rabbit only a few more? Does the tape-recording of life run in fast-forward mode for animals, I wondered?

I recall my dissatisfaction with the explanations offered by teachers and other supposedly wise adults. 'Animals are inferior to humans and wear out quicker,' I was told by one. Another quickly dismissed the question by 'God just made them that way'! I concluded that the answers were unknown – and possibly unknowable. Perhaps most young people have asked themselves such questions. But I have never stopped asking them, and have had the good fortune of being able to pursue them in paid employment.

• The Second Law

When I began my career, few biologists took research into ageing seriously. It still surprises me that, despite a universal fascination with ageing, so little attention has been paid to the really big question of *why* it occurs at all. Unfortunately, the whole field is still clouded by ignorance and prejudice. Even worse, some scientists still think the subject is hardly worthy of serious attention and dismiss ageing as simply a consequence of the laws of physics.

Sceptics usually quote the Second Law of Thermodynamics, as if the mere mention of this grand theory is enough to end debate. There is no question that this law is one of the bedrocks of science. The physicist Sir Arthur Eddington regarded it as the most fundamental of the laws. It predicts that the universe is inexorably moving from its present state towards complete disorder, or 'maximum entropy'. The universe which came into being in a big bang will go out in a whimper or 'heat death'. Evidence of the Second Law in action is everywhere and inescapable – from the formation of red giants from dying stars to the decomposition of organic matter in the garden compost heap. This cosmology is deeply pessimistic, and might well have caused some students to flee from the apparent bleak heart of science to a refuge in the humanities! The Second Law gives us the direction of time's arrow and explains why the history of the universe does not go backwards. The decay of the inanimate seems to be mirrored in living things. According to an ancient Chinese proverb, 'The Yangtse never runs backwards . . . man recaptures not his youth.'

But here is a paradox. Every living animal or plant seems to flout the Second Law. Quite obviously, structural decay does not begin at the moment of birth. Most living things start as a 'simple' egg and get progressively larger and more complex until they reach maturity. The simplest creatures and plants re-create endless, flawless copies of themselves. Others begin with a fertilized egg cell which for each individual is genetically programmed to produce diversity in the body – liver cells, brain cells and so on. Each cell contains the same genes as every other one, bearing the coded messages that are deciphered to produce the proteins that make up our individual physical characteristics, but only a few genes are active at one time. This is rather similar to the way in which a computer runs a few programs which are selected from the vast memory store on the hard disk. Not all of the 'genetic memory' in a cell is accessed at the same time. The triumphant progress of the embryo towards the production of a complicated body with division of labour between its many parts is achieved by means of selecting only the appropriate genes for action.

The fossil evidence of the history of life on the planet is another apparent contradiction of the Second Law. Organisms of increasing complexity have emerged over a long course of time, even though the majority have undergone extinction. So, whether we look at the beginnings of life from the primeval slime or from an egg of a modern species, we see structures of greater complexity and size developing with time. How do they do it? Do living things violate physical laws? Is there a mystical driving-force, like the extended fingers of Michelangelo's God animating Adam on the fresco in the Sistine Chapel?

Let me state at once that any fundamental inconsistency between biology and physics is unthinkable, for that would undermine the whole of the life sciences. Another physicist, Erwin Schrödinger, published a popular explanation of the conundrum in his famous little book *What Is Life?* He pointed out that, so long as entropy increases in the universe *as a whole*, a little more order here or there can be tolerated. The living world is free from the danger of entropy – or decay – only so long as energy is available for building the body and maintaining it in good order. Animals obtain their energy in chemical form as food, while green plants do so using solar radiation for photosynthesis.

The Second Law applies only within closed systems which are cut off from external sources of energy. Closed systems cannot refresh themselves, nor can living cells survive indefinitely in isolation. Even resting spores eventually deteriorate if left in a vacuum. Cells are open systems and need to tap energy and new materials from outside to keep going. They can continue to exist only at the expense of their environment. The paradox is that they have to keep changing to remain the same. In theory, they could do this for ever, just as the streams and fountains in the terraced gardens at the Villa d'Este at Tivoli have played since Renaissance times.

Some parts of the body renew themselves faster than others,

according to need. Cells lining the intestines are engaged in the demanding business of digesting and absorbing food, and receive a lot of chemical insults from the diet at the same time. They need to be completely changed every third day. The lining of the womb is replaced every twenty-eight days in a non-pregnant woman before menopause, and blood cells responsible for carrying oxygen and carbon dioxide are renewed three times a year. Even the apparently unchanging skeleton is in a constant state of flux.

Most proteins are short-lived, but the most abundant one of all – collagen – is exceptional. The small fibres within collagen gradually cross-link over a period of months or years, and so they have been used as molecular clocks for measuring biological time. A moderate degree of cross-linking is good for strength but, if this goes on unchecked, the loss of flexibility can prove harmful. Someone has calculated that, after two hundred years of cross-linking of the fibres, a kangaroo's tail would be too stiff to be serviceable. Needless to say, no animal lives that long.

Only one or two regions of our bodies are sufficiently static to be subject to the Second Law. Most of the proteins in the dentine layers of our teeth were formed before birth and are like the coal strata laid down in the earth during the Carboniferous era, for teeth have their own form of 'carbon dating'. Proteins are made of amino acids linked together like strings of coloured beads. Some amino acids can exist in either of two forms distinguished by the direction in which they bend light, but cells can make proteins only from the left-handed or 'L' variety. This form spontaneously changes into the right-handed or 'D' form at a very slow and steady rate. Most proteins do not persist long enough for detectable amounts of the D to accumulate, but in the long-lived dentine the ratio of L to D gives a measure of the age of the tooth and, hence, its owner.

Teeth provide a rare example of an age change within the body that is thermodynamically driven, though it carries no known disadvantages. Teeth decay through bacterial action and grinding in the act of chewing, but this is not strictly biological senescence. When a child's set of teeth is ravaged by caries, we don't regard the teeth as 'aged', because the damage is a product of external and preventable influences. This sort of harm can occur continuously throughout life, whereas genuine age changes are often programmed in some way or accumulate with time after puberty – especially towards the end of the lifespan. If pressed for an opinion, most gerontologists would state that teeth age only in so far as we are unable to replace a worn-out secondary set with another one.

Most of us will outlive our teeth, but their erosion can be so serious in some animals that it fixes a limit on the lifespan. An enterprising dentist once developed dentures for sheep, but most animals have to manage with what they were born with. The incisors or biting-teeth are not usually a problem, because they grow throughout life in rabbits and some other animals. This advantage carries the slight risk that if one is broken its opposite number will grow round and prevent feeding, and may even penetrate the brain. The working life of the molars is more often the problem, because they act as grindstones and cannot be renewed for ever.

Elephants eat more than 100 kilograms of rough vegetable matter every day. The heavy work of mastication for twelve to eighteen hours out of every twenty-four is done by a single pair of elongated molars on each side. As soon as one set wears down, another erupts to replace it. Most elephants have six sets, the last appearing at about sixty years of age. The wearing out of this last set determines how long an animal can feed, and therefore live, which is a maximum of about seventy years. A few individuals have a seventh set, which gives them a chance of living a little longer. Teeth may seem an odd choice to illustrate ageing, but we shall see other examples of organs and of animals which appear to be programmed simply because renewal of essential parts is impossible.

Some of the best examples are found among insects. A caterpillar emerging from its pupa as a butterfly has few cells that are able to divide. After battering by raindrops, pecking by birds and disentangling itself from webs, it loses legs, antennae and scales so that it is no longer airworthy. None of these structures is replaceable, and the insect's low-protein diet does not help, though this diet is better than nothing. Mayflies are unable to feed at all after hatching because mouth parts are absent and the gut is too vestigial to make use of food. Swarming over a river or lake during nuptial flight, mayflies soon exhaust the limited energy store in their fat bodies and fall back into the water from which they emerged a few hours or days earlier. Their life history, like that of the male marsupial mice and the Pacific salmon, is programmed for a big bang of reproduction with little regard to personal survival.

With few exceptions, animals and plants that have adopted this semelparous lifestyle are small and short-lived. They spend the greater part of their lives growing to maturity and waiting for the right moment to emerge in flaming passion for just long enough to produce descendants. Only in some species of bamboo is the waiting period long. It may take a stand of bamboo 120 years to flower just once before dying, sometimes creating local food shortages for pandas.

Most mammals and all birds are iteroparous and can have more than one try at reproduction. The vast majority of warm-blooded animals age more slowly than the typical semelparous species and enjoy a longer life, even if its span is enormously variable. Some survive no more than a year or two, while others live for decades. There is no easy explanation. Schrödinger was not the last physicist to venture into the realms of biology, but so far every attempt to explain ageing on physical principles alone has been a dismal failure. Why, after the miraculous development of a new individual from a fertilized egg, should the body fail in the apparently simpler task of maintaining itself? If cells can replace and repair themselves, why not continue for ever? It is far from self-evident why 'first we ripen and then we rot'.

• A Bestiary of Ageing

In some respects, the maximum lifespan – or longevity, as we call it – seems a singularly useless piece of information. By definition, it is the exception in the population and not something the majority can aspire to. The record-breaker is the individual who has avoided death by accident or disease for longest. Science, on the other hand, aims to generalize and to converge on the typical case. Even so, the exception can sometimes point to a rule. For instance, the desert rat or jerboa is faced with a problem of conserving water. It solves it by producing a very strong urine. Since it has kidney loops that are far longer than in common rats, we quickly conclude that this must be where urine is concentrated in the kidneys of all mammals. Comparative biology is one of the grand old traditions of zoology, and we shall see how it provides some hints as to why ageing occurs and how.

One reason for estimating longevity is that it is a definite biological characteristic of a species that remains much the same in populations around the world and from one generation to the next. This means that it has a genetic basis and in humans is inherited along with the other characteristics of our species – size, bipedalism, hairiness, and so on. Longevity is an indicator of the 'vitality' of a species, which is another strong reason for looking at it. The bodies of long-lived species stand up better to wear and tear and are likely to be more successful at outsmarting cancer cells and parasites.

Gerontology appeals to the eclectic scientist because the discovery of a species that is exceptionally long or short lived could point to an anatomy, physiology or behaviour that is particularly durable or otherwise. What begins as a natural-history exercise could open the door to laboratory research and even to tracking down the genes responsible for controlling longevity.

Finding out how long animals live, let alone how long they could live in the best of circumstances, is harder than it might seem. In theory, it only requires keeping a cohort of young individuals under ideal conditions from birth until they drop; but in practice there are all sorts of pitfalls – not least time and cost. Long-lived animals usually exceed the three to five years of the average research grant, and may even surpass the lifespan of the researcher. And, as any pet-owner knows, keeping large animals is expensive.

We might expect that the most abundant animals would provide the most reliable figures, but this is mistaken. Few farm animals survive long, for purely commercial reasons, and large numbers are slaughtered even before puberty. It is only the occasional pet that has been allowed to last until it drops, and these cases are not always well authenticated. As far as we know, the upper age limit is about twenty for sheep and thirty for pigs and cows.

Companion animals have the distinction of more accurate records, partly because pedigree dogs have their birth dates and genealogy registered by the Kennel Club, and the National Stud does the same for thoroughbred horses. These sources are potentially rich in information, and are attractive to the gerontologist who wants to combine science with a sporting interest. Records show that cats live to twenty-eight but man's best friend pegs out by twenty. The record for a horse was forty-six, though a former barge-horse called Billy has been claimed to live to sixty. Not for nothing do we speak of 'donkey's years'.

What relation these figures have to those of such animals' wild forerunners is hard to say. The lifespans may not have become higher through domestication, because a price is paid for producing animals to order and flouting the hard master of natural selection by inbreeding to preserve selected characteristics. Most genes are carried in pairs, so that the effects of one harmful mutation may be counteracted by a healthy partner. This cannot occur in highly inbred animals, which have identical pairs, and so genetic diseases can creep in. If long life in a dog is most important, you would be well advised to choose a hybrid or mongrel.

Gerontologists have had to turn to captive animals and birds and zoo specimens to estimate the maximum lifespan of wild creatures. Unfortunately, information is usually scant or unreliable because either the birth dates were not recorded or the numbers were too small or the animals ailed because optimal husbandry conditions were not known. Misconceptions also arose from the temptation to lay too much emphasis on anecdotal sources. In the seventeenth century the celebrated English naturalist John Ray, observing that a caged linnet lived to fourteen and a goldfinch to twenty, wrote:

Of all the sanguineous and hot animals birds are the longest lived. And there is no doubt but birds that enjoy their liberty, living at large in the open air, and using their natural and proper food, in gathering of which they also exercise their bodies, live much longer than those that are imprisoned in houses and cages.

Ray was a careful observer, yet only partially correct. Birds live longer than mammals of the same size, but claiming that they live longer in the wild state than in captivity was rash. He had an idealized view of the natural state, and succumbed to the temptation of speculating too freely, which has plagued gerontology from the start. Francis Bacon had a more accurate impression a century earlier:

Touching the length and shortness of life in living creatures, the information which may be had is but slender, observation is negligent and tradition fabulous. In tame creatures their degen-crate life corrupteth them; in wild creatures their exposing to all weathers often intercepteth them.

Life in the wild is rather less romantic than Ray had assumed. It is a tough battle against starvation, predators and parasites – which is bound to be lost sooner or later. Even predators at the top of the food chain cannot afford to relax. The cheetah is a specialized feeder on gazelles, and these are so fleet of foot that even a slight physical handicap in a cheetah can lead to death by starvation. Most wild animals die young, and it is a very rare individual that lives to bask in the golden sunshine of ripe old age or to the point of decrepitude.

This is true even of our familiar garden birds. Most gardeners have a soft spot for robins, because they sing for more months than any other garden bird and follow the spade in search of an easy meal. We may like to think that it is the same bird year after year in our garden, but this is unlikely because most small wild birds have tragically short lives. David Lack ringed young robins in the Oxford area to find out just how long they survived. One bird made it to eleven years old, but this was exceptional and the average lasted only a year. We are largely unaware of the tremendous slaughter that is going on around us all the time.

Lest we get sentimental, it is worth remembering that if all robins managed to survive to age eleven we might well have a less rosy opinion of them. Their powers of increase are prodigal, and a simple calculation is enough for a Hitchcockian horror story to unfold. Suppose a single pair of robins produced five chicks of each sex in their first year. Further, suppose that in each successive year all the parents and offspring reproduced at this rate, which is compound interest at 500 per cent. What, then, would be the population growth if they all survived? By five years a substantial flock of nearly 8,000 birds would have descended from the single pair, and after another five there would be 24 million! The corresponding figures for rats and mice are even more alarming because, although they are shorter-lived, each pair can produce litters of ten pups every five weeks for much of the year. The caged rodent remains a beloved pet only by virtue of being single and forced against its will into unnatural celibacy.

It is only in a state of domestication or captivity with a regular diet and shelter from predators that the lifespan of a species can hope to reach its full potential. As usual, the zoologist Peter Medawar was able to sum up the situation succinctly: 'Senility is an artefact of domestication, something discovered and revealed only by the experiment of shielding an animal from its natural predators and the everyday hazards of its existence. In this sense, no form of death is less "natural" than that which is so-called.' This must have been true for our own ancestors. Few lived to a ripe old age, and traumatic injury, parasitic diseases and starvation were common causes of death, as they still are in wild animals. Survival to the biological limits of the lifespan is a comparatively modern development for us and for the few species we choose to protect.

• The Three Graces

Cataloguing the maximum lifespans of animals may seem more like a task for the compilers of *The Guinness Book of Records*, but it is a very necessary one for gerontology. Few scientists have tackled the job more enthusiastically than Alex Comfort, who is better known as the author of *The Joy of Sex*, though it was his books on ageing that first sparked my interest in gerontology. Over the years, this London gerontologist collected records of animal lifespans for literally hundreds of species, and was one of the first to make any sense of them.

One fact that stands out clearly is that it is advantageous in the longevity stakes to be big, and this is equally true for wild and domesticated animals. Elephants are the longest-lived terrestrial animals bar one. They are followed by large farm animals, cats and dogs, and rabbits, rats and mice – in that order (see the table on pages 34–5). The trouble with quoting hard-and-fast figures is that sooner or later they will be contradicted, and records tend to edge up as more data come in. As any dog-fancier knows, mastiffs, Great Danes, bloodhounds and German shepherds live little more than ten years, whereas smaller breeds, such as Pekinese and terriers, commonly survive to fifteen or more. This need not turn the predictions from body size upside down if we remember that the rule applies only when species, not breeds, are compared. Even so, the rule is not inflexible. Whales are the largest living animals, but they are fast growers and do not live as long as we might expect. The extraordinary longevity of humans is an even bigger flaw in the argument.

Since birth registration was introduced nationally in England and Wales in 1837, we know more about the longevity of our own species than about any other. In earlier times, it was easier to get away with rounding up figures to exaggerate age, or even more blatant deceit than that. It was said that 'Many Old Men use to sett the Clock of their Age too Fast, and growing ten years in a Twelvemonth, are presented fourscore; yea, within a Year or two after, climb up to an hundred'.

Maximum recorded lifespans of some vertebrate animals

Group/Species	Maximum lifespan in years
Mammals	
Primates	
Rhesus monkey	>35
Chimpanzee	>50
Human	120
Carnivores	
Domestic dog	20
Domestic cat	28
Brown bear	37
Large domestic animals	
Sheep	20
Pig	27
Horse	46
Indian elephant	>70
Rodents	
House mouse	4
Black rat	5
Bats	
Pipistrelle bat	11
African fruit bat	22
Little brown bat	>32
Marsupials	
Marsupial mouse	2
Virginia opossum	3
Birds	
European robin	11
Lapwing	16
Common swift	21
Feral pigeon	30

Maximum recorded lifespans of some vertebrate animals (*cont.*)

Group/Species	Maximum lifespan in years
Herring-gull	49
Fulmar petrel	45
Vasa parrot	54
Andean condor	75
Parrot	>90
Reptiles	
Chinese alligator	52
Galapagos tortoise	>175
Amphibians	
Common European frog	>12
Common toad	36
Fish	
Guppy	5
Perch	25
Pacific rockfish	120

One in ten thousand of us will become a centenarian, and the furthest reach of the human lifespan is about 120. No warm-blooded animal has been found to live longer. Since we are a little heavier than sheep and somewhat lighter than pigs, we should live no longer than about twenty-five years. The privilege of living past what size alone would dictate is shared by our cousins in the primate family. Rhesus monkeys have lived to over thirty years in captivity, and chimpanzees occasionally exceed forty even in the wild. So longevity is not simply determined by body size, and the spotlight has to be turned on other factors.

All primates share a set of distinctive characteristics – none more obvious and significant than a big brain. According to the late George Sacher, brain weight is a much better predictor of the longevity of a species than body weight. This makes sense, because the brain takes time to grow, and there is no point in becoming well endowed with grey matter unless living long enough to enjoy the advantages of using it. A big brain also implies a more sophisticated use of information from sense organs, which grow larger. Their owner is then better equipped to exploit its environment and outwit its enemies. These advantages push up the average survival time, but it is less obvious why they should affect the maximum lifespan of the species. The simplistic argument that a bigger brain can produce more of an invigorating hormone no longer washes, because it could be equally true of any organ – including the spleen, which humans can do without. Size may be a useful predictor, but it means little in itself.

To the duo of body and brain size can be added a third omen of longevity, which has been drawn to attention by the records of bats. They may seem an unlikely group to shed light on anything, but their powers of flight seem to overrule their small-size disadvantage. No one knows quite how long these animals can live in captivity, but ringing studies in the wild have provided some astonishing records. Imagine the shock when a thirty-year-old American researcher found that a little brown bat roosting in a cave was older than himself. Even the tiny pipistrelle, the species most commonly seen in the British countryside, can live for eleven years, which is three times the longevity of a rodent of the same size. Had the marvel of bat longevity been known long ago it would no doubt have been used to bolster superstition and fear about this much-maligned creature, but it may one day help to dispel some myths.

The privilege of a long life seems to go hand in hand with flight in birds and other aerial vertebrates too. Blackbirds, finches, starlings and robins all fall into the ten-to-twenty-year longevity bracket, which is about three times the span of a rodent the same size. A caged chaffinch has lived twenty-nine years, and wild barn swallows can enjoy more than twenty summers despite making intrepid migrations every year. Even the 'flying' squirrel (which is a glider) lives twice as long as its grounded cousin, the chipmunk. Taking to the air by whatever means provides an excellent way of escape from predators and for reaching food denied to those going on foot. It also carries the bonus of a more robust constitution.

Not that birds disobey the body-size rule of thumb. Pigeons, ducks and plovers generally survive longer than small garden birds, which, in turn, beat the eight-year lifespan of the humming-bird. At the opposite end of the scale the longevity of large parrots is the stuff of fables. If you choose a parrot as a pet (please don't) you may have a companion for life. The largest raptors enjoy equally long lives, and condors can aspire to more than seventy years.

The extraordinary powers of survival of many sea birds are rather less well known. The herring-gulls and fulmar petrels which are common around British coasts can live for forty years or more. George Dunnet has been studying fulmars in the Orkney Islands to the north of Scotland since the 1950s when he began his ornithological career, and some of the birds were still nesting with undiminished vigour at the end of the '80s. What is more, the birds had not changed appearance over a period of forty years. Alas, the same could not be said of old George! These birds age so slowly that one wonders whether they do so at all. Our shores are not heaving with the birds because they don't choose their partner until they are at least ten years old, and they then breed only at a slow rate.

Many game birds do not live as long as we might expect from their size. Most pheasants, brush turkeys and peacocks have pegged out by about ten years old even when they live outside hunting-areas. Japanese quail live only half as long. Ostriches and emus ought to be top of the longevity league, but they lost some of the flying start their ancestors had when they sacrificed the power of flight to take up running instead. Forty years for these species may seem long, but this is no more than a gull's quota and far less than a parrot's. These differences hint at the role that vulnerability plays in the evolution of longevity, but that is a matter for another chapter.

This brief tour of the animal kingdom shows that patterns of lifespan in nature or captivity are anything but simple. The main conclusion to emerge is that it is advantageous to be large, big-brained and able to fly. Biology has not managed to combine this triad very successfully because there is a physical limit of about ten kilograms for any body to take off using muscle power alone. Besides, for reasons that are less clear, our feathered friends have never been known for being anything but bird-brained. The only big-brained aerial primate existed in Greek myth, and came to grief.

What is surprising about this survey is that the particular branch of the evolutionary tree of life on which a species perches has little, if anything, to do with longevity. There is no sign that evolution is steadily pushing up the limits of physical endurance. The emergence of a major new structure during evolution, such as the backbone or the placenta, does not signal a leap forward in potential lifespan. For all we know, warm-blooded animals may have been stuck at their present ceiling ever since they first appeared on earth. The specifics of genetic make-up and physiology count for much more than 'status' in the conventional hierarchy of species.

There is no reason in principle why longevity should not get shorter rather than longer. Evolution of a shorter lifespan in *Antechinus stuartii* was an acceptable price to pay if it helped individuals to produce more healthy offspring. With a few exceptions, mammals are not particularly long-lived as animals go. Half the mammalian order consists of rodents and their relatives, and all of them have short lives. Our ancestors were reptiles and, further back, fishes, and their living descendants often enjoy longer lives for their size than mammals. It may be only wishful thinking, but it is possible that there are giant tortoises trundling around the Galapagos Islands that Charles Darwin encountered on his epic voyage in the *Beagle* in 1835. The realm of cold-blooded animals and the plant kingdom both show that evolution sets no particular premium on longer life as more complex forms of life evolved.

When data are hard to come by, it is important to maintain rigid standards of dating and not be taken in by the odd record or 'fisherman's tale'. The growth rings in the bones, shells and scales of some reptiles and fish leave an indelible imprint of the passage of time as a result of uneven seasonal growth at higher latitudes, like tree trunks. The maximum lifespans of fish vary enormously according to the environment. Some fish grow fast and die early; others take their time. For instance, guppies live for five years and perch for twenty-five, whereas sturgeon and Pacific rockfishes can last for over a century.

Simple creatures vary just as much in length of life, and some of them put up impressive records. A group of sea anemones collected off the Arran coast in Scotland some time before 1862 were transferred through various owners over the years and ended up in a tank in the Zoology Department at Edinburgh University. They outlived the original collectors and remained vigorous until someone forgot to feed them during a holiday break during the Second World War.

An advantage of possessing a simple body plan is that damaged parts can be regenerated more easily from less specialized cells held in reserve. Tentacles and shells, where appropriate, and even mouths and guts may be replaced. This may be why giant clams can survive to 200 years and giant squids can grow to enormous sizes, though nobody knows how long they need for this. At the other end of the invertebrate size spectrum there are no mean records either. Tarantulas have lived for several decades in captivity, and some beetles can make it to nine years old. Even the humble earthworm can reach six, which is three times the span of the predatory shrew. Dietary preferences in nature carry little sway where survival potential is concerned.

Gerontologists like curiosities, and the longevity of the rat's tapeworm is a memorable one. If we assumed that the parasite matches its host's longevity we would be wrong – it is superior. Someone surgically transplanted a tapeworm from one rat to another as each host became old. The tapeworm was able to outlast several hosts, and survived for fourteen years. The author of the study was a parasitologist of the old school which never accepted that a study was complete unless tested personally. The rat tapeworm survived in his own gut for barely two months, which only goes to show that it was either a discriminating feeder or had not learned how to outwit a human immune system.

We have seen that generalizations about ageing in invertebrates are hazardous, and some remarkable stories have yet to be told. Most invertebrates are subject to the whims of weather and of season, so their lifespans are less rigidly timetabled than those of warm-blooded species. Life processes slow down in the cold, and with them growth and ageing. Some stages of the life history of insects are much more flexible than others. The first brood of the tortoiseshell butterfly reaches maturity and has died by midsummer, but the last will overwinter in a state of torpor as pupae or adults. A pliable life history helps to maximize reproductive success, and none is more extraordinary than that of some American cicadas. These are large grasshoppers which remain underground as sap-sucking nymphs for periods of up to fifteen years, until they emerge above ground as adults whose life is finished in a matter of a month. The countdown for ageing does not begin until their début, no matter how long they have waited. There are fewer, but less impressive, examples of such flexibility in the mammalian world. Some deer, seals and badgers produce embryos that remain dormant in the uterus for periods of up to a year, until the mother's physiology signals the propitious moment to implant. Time can stop still in the womb.

Record lifespans are held not by animals but by plants. Trees dwarf us as much in survival power as they do in sheer size. Some old pollard oaks and yews in the British countryside must have witnessed historic events in their time, and a few were already standing in the days when trees were still venerated. Early Christian missionaries may have deliberately planted churches among groves of ancient trees worshipped by pagans. The yew in the churchyard at Fortingall, Scotland, may have lasted that long, but it is not thousands of years old, as reputed. What is more certain is that the yew in the Revd Gilbert White's churchyard at Selborne, Hampshire, was about 1,400 years old when it was torn up by its roots in the Great Gale of January

1990. After futile attempts to restore the great twenty-six-foot bole, a cutting was planted by the eldest inhabitant of the village, ninety-one-year-old Miss Trudy Atkinson, as a symbol of hope that both tree and church would survive for another millennium. A sprouting pollard also inspired the author of the Book of Job in a rare blithe moment: 'For there is hope of a tree, if it be cut down, that it will sprout again, and that the tender branch thereof will not cease. Though the root thereof wax old in the earth, and the stock thereof die in the ground . . .'

Ancient trees still give a sense of awe. John Muir, the Scots-born architect of the American National Park system, was one of the first to recognize the importance of preserving the big trees in the western states. The giant redwoods or sequoias are the largest living things on dry ground. Some ascend to heights exceeding 300 feet, while others, not so tall, have boles of some thirty feet in diameter. Not surprisingly, they are among the world's oldest lving things, surviving 2,000 years or more. For Muir, their qualities of endurance were virtues to match their majestic appearance. The sequoias caused him to fall into reverie:

> [they are] so old, thousands of them still living had already counted their years by tens of centuries when Columbus set sail from Spain and were in the vigour of youth or middle age when the star led the Chaldean sages to the infant Saviour's cradle! As far as man is concerned they are the same yesterday, today and forever, emblems of permanence.

Most people agree that big trees give us a due sense of our own proportion.

These days, things are seldom permanent. Trees that have taken a millennium to grow and have resisted scores of forest fires can be felled by a chainsaw in thirty minutes and be quickly reduced to garden furniture and matchwood. As forests are cropped back further, we are witnessing the rapid extinction of some of the most venerable living things on earth. This matters because some of the oldest plants are often the most productive in seeds and have proved their genetic worth.

The giant redwoods may be great survivors, but they are not the longest-lived conifers. Another member of the family, the bristlecone pine of the Sierra Nevada mountains in California, stands only fifty feet tall, yet some of these slow-growing trees were already standing when Abraham left the ancient city of Ur. A few have been estimated to be more than 5,000 years old – and are still growing. What is more, they go on producing fertile seeds until the very end.

We have to descend from the mountains into the Sonoran Desert of the south-western states to find still more ancient plants. On the way, we see the giant saguaro cactus, which, standing nearly fifty feet tall in a 'hands-up' posture, symbolizes a bygone cowboy era. These cacti are impressive but, at a few hundred years old, are mere striplings compared with our less prepossessing quarry.

We might easily overlook the scrubby-looking creosote bush crouching low over the desert floor. As the centre dies, the outer parts sprout new growth, and very gradually a ring some twenty feet in diameter forms. If the vagaries of a desert climate don't destroy it, the creosote bush seems to be able to survive indefinitely – or, according to conservative estimates, for at least 10,000 years.

To say that this is one of the most ancient plants is, admittedly, to stretch the usual concept of the individual. Some creosote bushes may have taken root when the glaciers were retreating to more northerly latitudes after the last Ice Age, and at no time have the plants paused for the genetic refreshment of sexual reproduction. Apart from the possibility of a mutation affecting some of its cells, each plant remains genetically uniform over its long history and is therefore a clone.

Many plants have adopted this way of propagating themselves naturally, while others can do it if forced to. Some of the more dramatic examples can be found to this day in the John Muir Grove, some twenty miles north of San Francisco. New growth sprouting vegetatively from the base of giant redwoods is stunted because the leaf canopy provides heavy shade. But, when the main trunk dies and falls over, a ring of 'new' trees reaches upwards to compete for its place. This clonal succession of trees from the same stock can go on for thousands of years. They are, one and all, chips off the old block, and this is as close as living things can get to immortality. Horticulturists take advantage of cloning when they take cuttings to avoid the subversive effects of pollination on genetic purity. Records show that some apple trees and grape vines have been propagated continuously by grafting for over 800 years. Vegetative propagation comes naturally to some cultivated plants, such as the banana, which cannot reproduce sexually at all.

But you don't have to be a vegetable to reproduce vegetatively. The *Hydra* kept in a tank in the school lab can bud again and again from the old 'root stock'. Corals are members of the same group, and a reef may form from a single colonizing polyp and reach hundreds of years of age. Single-celled animals and plants also reproduce in this way, although some have learned the advantages of sexual liaison with a partner.

Years ago, an argument raged over the question of whether protozoa could be immortal. A tiny slipper-shaped ciliate, nicknamed *Paramecium* 'Methuselah', was said to have divided in culture thousands of times. For practical purposes it could be regarded as immortal. Later it was found that the creatures had surreptitiously indulged in sex, and the old argument was inflamed again. When they were restrained in the appropriate medium they slid into decline.

After more investigation it turns out that the celibate life, which spells genetic annihilation for higher animals, is not merely possible but normal for some microbes. Each cell splits into two identical individuals in which there is no distinction between mother and daughter. Under favourable conditions the process can go on without apparent limit. For these organisms, survival of the self and reproduction are one and the same thing. Our usual concepts of individual identity and successive generations break down in the world of asexual reproduction, and we can reach bizarre conclusions. Cells of a clone may separate from one another and spread great distances, so the 'body' can be said to exist in more than one continent at a time.

The question of whether bacteria age like higher organisms seeded another controversy. From time to time, bacteria have been found surviving in ancient human remains, in the guts of mammoths, and even in coal deposits. Unfortunately their true antiquity is often unclear because it is difficult to rule out the possibility of secondary contamination of samples, but there is no doubt that bacteria can live for very long periods – especially as spores. When they are placed under harsh conditons, they may lose the ability to divide, but this is more of a stress reaction than true senescence. As far as we can tell, the protoplasm of some cells can survive indefinitely.

• Evolution of Life History

The teeming variety of modes and lengths of life may seem baffling, but it is turning out to be a little more intelligible. Most species exhibit one of only three types of ageing. In certain cases – *Antechinus stuartii* is a good example – senescence is triggered immediately after a single reproductive burst. Although an unfamiliar story to us, this is almost the rule in whole groups of animals. Secondly, there is the type that we characterize by ageing slowly and having several breeding opportunities. These types differ more in degree than in kind, because the distinction is essentially a matter of how rapidly the decay sets in and whether reproductive effort is the main trigger. A third type is found among some of the largest and also the tiniest living things, though apparently absent in higher animals. The individual can live for an indefinitely long period, and age changes are imperceptible, if they occur at all. This pattern is at the extreme end of a natural spectrum in which almost every possible shade is represented by one species or another.

The conclusion that there may be no definite upper limit to the surviving power of protoplasm may strike some readers as odd. It is still widely assumed that deterioration is a 'law of nature', but living things have evolved to be wily, and some cells can elude the rules of decay. Moreover, we should look to the biology of cells rather than to external factors to discover why some organisms are more vulnerable than others. All animals and plants are exposed to the rain of cosmic radiation and chemical hazards, yet those sharing the same environment may vary enormously in longevity. If differences in vigour and lasting-power are inbuilt, ageing must have a genetic basis. And if genes are involved then there must be an evolutionary rationale behind the phenomena.

Insights into the origins of ageing are causing seismic shifts in biological understanding. No one has contributed more to shaking the old ideas to their foundations than Californian scientist Caleb Finch. As if the challenges of unravelling the age problem and trying to reverse its ill effects are not enough, he also finds time to play the fiddle as a revivalist of old-time Appalachian music. His monumental tome *Senescence, Longevity and the Genome* is a distillation of the vast amount of information accumulated over many years. As knowledge grows, it may be impossible for even the most energetic visionary to repeat such a daunting task. Finch concludes that longevity has evolved not just once but many times. Received wisdom used to be that 'ageing ... was a necessary corollary to sexual reproduction'. More recent revelations show that we must discard the idea that ageing entered the history of life like a bolt of lightning from heaven when sex was discovered by an ancestral cell. The evidence of comparative biology denies it, as do a few organisms that age yet do not have sex.

According to Finch, 'evolutionary changes [in short-lived creatures] ... could yield closely related species ... that have vastly longer lifespans and negligible senescence'. No species has a longevity which is fixed for all time, and it is possible that, under the pressure of natural selection, a ceiling could be removed altogether. If this is theoretically true of whole animals it must apply to their cellular constituents, which have as much variety in their life histories and longevities as the creatures themselves. In time, almost anything is

45

possible. The programme for a short life in a cell or loss of the cell's ability to reproduce itself does not tie the species for ever. Over many generations, programmes can be edited to shorten or lengthen lives, or cells may even free themselves from the coils of mortality altogether. This explains a conundrum. The ancient family of sharks and rays has to make do with eggs formed at an embryonic stage, because cells lose the ability to make new ones. When the more advanced bony fish and amphibians came along, the same cells learned how to renew themselves but, oddly enough, this trait disappeared again when birds and mammals came on the scene.

We cannot be sure that this was the evolutionary course of events, but such striking differences in a single cell type demonstrate how readily life processes can be moulded by evolution. We can imagine how the levers controlling a life history, whether they be genes or hormonal effects, could be pulled to stretch the lifespan a little further. This is not just idle speculation, because the maximum lifespan of many laboratory species can already be extended. An atmosphere of cautious optimism is afoot in the research community. But, no matter how exciting the search for better theories or how remarkable the experimental results, we are generally much more interested in the implications of gerontology for human destiny. Despite the upbeat mood of the scientists, attitudes to our own ageing have changed little and often remain rooted in prejudice, superstition and ignorance.

CHAPTER 3 # Old Father William

'You are old, Father William,' the young man said.

Lewis Carroll

• Prejudice and Perception

Everyone wants to have a long life, but no one wants to grow old. We live in an age in which youth is prized and equated with beauty. We may make a virtue of great age because we aspire to it, yet we fear the downward spiral in health and social status. Most people are pessimistic about ageing and regard it as a sort of biological treachery. Just as we have reached the so-called prime of life, having raised our kids and now free to enjoy the financial rewards that mid-life brings (if we are lucky), we catch a glimpse of Old Father Time waiting in the wings. And even if we are healthy and prosperous in our later years, we cannot escape the consequences of how others perceive ageing. Most people do not dread the years themselves but rather the toll they take on the individual. Ugliness and dependency are particularly feared. Shakespeare represented life as seven theatrical roles, and the seventh and last was 'second childishness, and mere oblivion,/Sans teeth, sans eyes, sans taste, sans everything'.

Many people are uncomfortable in the presence of the very old, while others, unconsciously or otherwise, patronize them. Germaine Greer calls fear of the old 'anophobia', and rails against the double stigma that older women suffer as they lose their sexual attractiveness. We worship youthful beauty and vitality and would like to pause indefinitely at some respectable and attractive age. According to Oscar Wilde's fictitious Lady Bracknell, 'London society is full of women of the very highest birth who have, of their own free choice, remained thirty-five for years. Lady Dumbleton ... has been thirty-five ever since she arrived at the age of forty, which was many years ago now.'

Every era has had its ideal age. In Britain it is probably younger today than it was a hundred years ago. But, in many parts of the world, old age is still venerated. In traditional communities, men aspire to be admitted into the esteemed body of the 'elders'. A long life was a sign of good and prudent living, and therefore of God's favour. Elders were respected for their wisdom, and were consulted on every important occasion. But now the torrent of technological change sets them at a disadvantage, and it is the young who are best equipped to succeed in a rapidly changing world.

Their past contributions soon forgotten, old people are nowadays all too often regarded as burdens on society. Only on reaching the arbitrary age of 100 can they hope to enjoy a late reversal of their diminishing status. These gerontocrats have survived the odds either by good luck or by caution, or by a combination of the two. But even this silver lining seems set to disappear as centenarians become more common. As a population, we are living longer, and the higher birth rates early this century are progressing through the age groups. There has been a six-fold increase in the number of centenarians over the past thirty years. It will still be a rare privilege for members of the baby-boomer generation to reach the grand old age of 100, but the distinction of receiving that royal telegram is bound to decline.

While elders can no longer take the respect of the young for granted, we still admire older 'characters' – the plucky old widow who still dives from the top board of the swimming-pool, and the boffin who refuses to retire from the lab. They give us hope that we might be as vigorous when our time comes. Above all, we love old people to have a good sense of humour. If we cannot accept with a laugh what we cannot change, we may not be able to come to terms with our mortality at all. Lewis Carroll, the Oxford mathematician who wrote *Alice's Adventures in Wonderland*, put it this way:

'You are old, Father William,' the young man said,
  'And your hair has become very white;
And yet you incessantly stand on your head –
  Do you think, at your age, it is right?'

'In my youth,' Father William replied to his son,
  'I feared it might injure the brain;
But, now that I'm perfectly sure I have none,
  Why, I do it again and again.'

Carroll was cleverly pointing out that the risk the 'old boy' was taking was statistically less significant than when he was young. This is simply because the number of prospective years of life are diminishing all the time. Abstaining from petty indulgences – smoking, alcohol and so on – for the sake of better health carries less weight when we get older because we have fewer years to gain. This is for mathematical, not biological, reasons because the tide of ageing eventually overtakes other risks. As the economist, John Maynard Keynes, put it, 'In the long run we are all dead.'

In contrast to the prevailing pessimism, some see virtue in ageing and encourage us to look forward to growing old. To reassure us, it is often said that 'There's many a good tune played on an old fiddle.' We are expected to give in to ageing with as much grace as possible, and individuals who refuse to conform to the stereotype of passive acceptance of their lot tend to be looked at askance. Ageist attitudes are widespread in society and influence the way old people look at themselves. The expectations of many British old people are abysmally low – a fact which should be a source of shame and concern to us all.

Some people look back to the ancient past as a golden age of prosperity and long life. It is true that circumstances took a downturn during the Middle Ages in Europe when towns were becoming overcrowded and plague was rampant, but even palaeohumans mostly died young. Fossil human remains are rare and difficult to interpret, but, as far as we can tell, the average person survived only to about twenty years of age. Life expectation is thought to have remained much the same over a long period of prehistory – from the quadruped australopithecines of several million years ago to the Neolithic farmers some 10,000 years ago. The few present-day tribes of hunter-gatherers do rather better than their ancestors, averaging fifty to sixty years. The increase is striking, and may show how far tribes have been affected by contact with the outside world.

The rugged lifestyle of past generations was not necessarily a good protection against disabling diseases. Tell-tale signs of arthritis and other degenerative diseases have been found in the bones of Neanderthals living more than 30,000 years ago in Shanidar cave in what is now Iraq. Historical records indicate that Ramses II, the pharaoh who pursued the Hebrews into the Red Sea, suffered from circulatory problems at the end of his life, just as people do today, despite (or perhaps because of) his regal lifestyle. Life in the past, even for the rich and powerful, was never an idyll of health and longevity.

This is probably the first century in which people in Britain have been able to count on living to see their grandchildren grow up. There were always some tough individuals who survived to a ripe old age, but these were the exceptions. For every 100 boys born a century ago, only fifty would live to forty-four or more years. Their sisters lasted but a year or two longer. Those who survived into their forties would be likely to have another twenty years or more: by successfully fighting off infectious diseases when young, they had acquired some immunity to future attack. Even so, only 1 in 4 babies would have survived to today's retirement age. Their great-grandchildren are now growing up in healthier circumstances and have a life expectation at birth of between seventy and eighty years. If ever there was a golden age of long life, we are enjoying it here and now.

People used to be regarded as 'old' long before they are nowadays. Until early this century, both quacks and genuine doctors would accept patients as 'young' as fifty for rejuvenation treatment. Characters in the novels of Jane Austen and George Eliot were considered elderly at this age. Bath Abbey stands not far from the homes of some of their fictional characters, and on its walls the names, ages and dates of interment of some of their real-life contemporaries are immortalized in stone tablets. They show a wide variation in the age at death, but the average lifespan is only fifty years. The lifespans of the poor, lying in unrecorded tombs, were undoubtedly less.

Many people died young – often too young to leave offspring. Childhood morality was high because epidemic diseases thrived in the unsanitary conditions of the day. Whooping cough, scarlet fever and diphtheria were the scourge of young families. Tuberculosis was the leading cause of death in adults. Poor diets aggravated the danger. There were no effective answers to these problems, and hope for the sick rested on good nursing and prayer. In the Middle Ages, morbid images struck on one side of coins reminded citizens that survival was a game of chance, as it still is in some parts of the world. During the Victorian era, health and life expectancy slowly improved, but it was not until the 1960s that British women had a fifty-fifty chance of achieving the biblical lifespan of three score years and ten. We can expect life expectancy to grow a little more – unless there is an environmental disaster or a new pandemic.

It is surprisingly difficult to be sure of the upper age limit for a species, especially a species in which most individuals meet death accidentally. This is particularly true of long-lived trees like redwoods and bristlecone pines because most die as saplings. Disease strikes the few survivors with more or less equal force at any age. We do not find the steady accumulation of disease and decay observed in mammals – consequently the longevity of the species is still unknown, and we cannot even say whether it has a fixed limit.

The famous Russian immunologist Elie Metchnikoff, who lived in Paris at the beginning of the century, had a deep interest in the ageing process, as did many other leading biologists of his day. He had the impression that the risks of dying were much the same in every year of life, and he suggested that the limit for the human lifespan was upwards of 200 years. This may seem as wildly optimistic as his theory that yoghurt staves off ageing. Nevertheless, his guess was not wholly irrational, given that chance infections accounted for most deaths in his day, and biblical records of patriarchal longevity. Statisticians soon pointed out his error because after a certain age it gets more and more difficult to survive another year.

Most of the gains in human life expectancy have come from the reduction of perinatal and infant deaths. No doubt the medical profession would have liked to have taken all the credit, but it received a sharp rebuttal from within its own ranks in the person of Thomas McKeown. This professor of public health at Birmingham had a jaundiced view of the heroic tradition in medicine. He gathered evidence showing that social changes were the main driving-force for improvements in life expectation. The late Victorians invested heavily in public works, and made strides to safeguard public water supplies and drainage. At the same time, rising living standards for the masses were helping people to enjoy a better diet and improved housing conditions. And, although the condom, coitus interruptus and abstinence were the only available means of contraception, family sizes were falling, allowing a larger share of income to fall to each family member.

Like many a crusader, McKeown exaggerated his case to drive his point home. The introduction of mass vaccination and new medicines had undoubtedly been beneficial too, though the virulence of many of the contagious diseases had unexpectedly begun to wane at the same time.

• Life Tables

No profession has a greater vested interest in the accurate prediction of human lifespan than that of insurance actuaries. According to some recent figures, life cover to the value of £100,000 will cost about £3 per week for a thirty-year-old man seeking protection for the next fifteen years. The premium is nearer £4 if he indulges in a dangerous sport or is a smoker. A non-smoking woman of the same age would pay less than £2, because she is expected to live longer. By the time he has reached fifty, the same man would have to pay £16 per week at today's rates (or £26 if a smoker) for his fifteen-year cover. By age seventy the premiums would be very high because there is a fair chance that the man would die before age eighty-five.

While some actuaries are employed to estimate the chances of dying before the insurance term runs out, others in government departments project the future size and age composition of the population. Both of them use so-called life tables to reach their goals – although death tables is an equally accurate expression.

A shortened example of a recent life table for the Scottish population is shown on page 54. It starts with a round figure of 100,000 males or females at birth and then predicts the numbers surviving year by year until they have all died. In many ways, life expectancy at birth, rather than at later ages, is the most interesting statistic because it is a good indicator of a nation's health. It is the age at which half of the original group of babies will still be alive, whether in good or ill health. The Scottish figures currently stand at about seventy for men and nearly seventy-seven for women. These are over 60 per cent higher than they were a century ago, and are still rising slowly.

This would be a cause for celebration had Scotland's place in the international league stood higher, or if improvement were more rapid. As it is, the nation's score is much the same as its position in the last World Cup. A nation's health is not pulled up by some inexorable law of historical progress, and there is always the possibility of slipping back. High life expectancy is dependent on rising prosperity and standards of living, but better health all round requires the sharing out of wealth. Even within the City of Edinburgh there are pockets of social deprivation where rates of coronary heart disease are six times higher than in other areas. The statistical correctness of life tables can conceal an enormous gulf across the social spectrum.

Scotland's figures lag slightly behind those for England and

A Life Table for Scotland (1988)

The numbers of survivors of a starting cohort of 100,000 and the life expectancy in years at different ages (by courtesy of the Registrar General for Scotland)

	Male		Female	
Age	Number	Expectancy	Number	Expectancy
0	100000	70.5	100000	76.7
1	99050	70.2	99320	76.2
2	98980	69.2	99280	75.3
3	98940	68.2	99250	74.3
4	98890	67.3	99230	73.3
5	98850	66.3	99210	72.3
10	98740	61.4	99140	67.4
15	98610	56.4	99070	62.4
20	98160	51.7	98940	57.5
25	97620	47.0	98790	52.6
30	97090	42.2	98490	47.7
35	96430	37.5	98270	42.8
40	95560	32.8	97740	38.1
45	94150	28.2	96910	33.4
50	91760	23.9	95470	28.8
55	87840	19.9	93270	24.4
60	81550	16.2	89430	20.4
65	72110	13.0	83260	16.7
70	59240	10.3	74430	13.4
75	44070	8.0	62750	10.4
80	28090	6.1	47750	7.9
85	14020	4.6	30790	5.9

Life expectation (in years) at different ages (by courtesy of the Registrar General for Scotland)

Year	Sex	At birth	At 15 years	At 45 years	At 65 years
1888	Male	43.9	43.9	22.6	10.8
1888	Female	46.3	45.6	24.6	11.9
1988	Male	70.5	56.4	28.2	13.0
1988	Female	76.7	62.4	33.4	16.7

Wales, which have themselves slipped from twelfth to seventeenth place in the world during the past twenty years. Japan's economic success has something to do with its place at the top of the league table. In contrast, life expectancy in a Nigerian village is just forty-three; nearly a quarter of all children die before their fifth birthday. Those who live in the Nigerian towns enjoy better incomes and living standards, and an average lifespan of fifty. Live expectancy overall is affected as much by social differences in wealth as by gross national product or other macroeconomic indicators. That is why the United States, with its enormous economic gulf between rich and poor, comes way down the list at number 15. Countries with the most equitable distributions of wealth, such as Iceland, Switzerland and Sweden, appear near the top of the league.

But ever rising standards of living will give diminishing returns as we get closer to our biological limits for survival. Over the century, an infant has gained about twenty-five years in life expectation, an adolescent fifteen years, a forty-five-year-old six and a sixty-five-year-old only two. The social and medical battles against infectious diseases have been relatively easy compared with the intractable problem of the ageing process itself. We shall have to wait for a radical biological intervention before the life statistics of already elderly people can be substantially improved, because if one disease, such as heart disease, does not trip us up, something else, like cancer or stroke, will.

• The Slope of Mortality

All life tables have a common underlying mathematical rationale which predicts that, after a certain age, it gets progressively more difficult to reach the next age group. The equation was devised early in the nineteenth century by an Edinburgh actuary, Benjamin Gompertz, and the graph produced from it is aptly called the 'force-of-mortality slope'. Biologists use the Gompertz equation because it provides a good fit to the rates of growth and ageing in animals and humans. It has become gerontology's equivalent of $E=mc^2$.

Gompertz made the important discovery that the probability of dying from natural causes doubles every eight years during adult life. What is even more interesting is that, as far as we know, this figure is constant for all the different racial groups and populations across the globe and has not changed at least since Victorian times when reliable statistics became available. This exponential equation is one of the universal characteristics of the human species. It is something we inherit and pass down to posterity, and the force-of-mortality slope shows that life gets more fragile as we grow older. Activities that were once safe – from running up stairs to performing gymnastics – become less so.

In personal terms, my chances of dying at age forty-six are twice what they were at thirty-eight. When, or if, I reach fifty-four they will have doubled again. This doubling goes on every eight years until an age when virtually no one remains alive. This is the theory, but were it strictly true the world record for longevity would be somewhat lower than it is. The genetics of a very small minority of people mock mathematical exactitude.

Measurement of ageing in terms of dying rather than by vitality may seem perverse and even misplaced considering the vigour remaining at even advanced ages. The problem is that researchers have yet to find a better gauge. Besides, mortality is the inverse of vitality – the gerontology equivalent of the negative of a photographic print. Death rates do at least have the unquestionable advantage that they are unambiguous, so I make no apology for using them.

The mortality slope has proved a very useful tool in biology for comparing the rates of senescence in different species, and can confirm whether or not an experimental treatment has actually slowed the ageing process. Small animals that race through their lives have much steeper gradients than those with longer spans. The slope for mice corresponds to a doubling of mortality every eighty days, and for fruit flies just eight days. We should be thankful for eight years. Sea birds, bats and reptiles have much shallower slopes and hence slower rates of ageing than similar-sized members of the rodent and rabbit families. The fable of the tortoise outpacing the hare never holds more true than in gerontology.

Since humans live longer than other mammals, we might expect our slope to be the most favourable. But, according to Caleb Finch and his colleagues in Los Angeles, we are not as privileged as we had thought. They found that the slopes for some long-lived species are similar to, if not better than, our own. This apparent contradiction highlights the danger of depending solely on longevity records for comparing rates of ageing. Bats and monkeys enjoy the same slow rate of ageing as we do – yet none of them has ever lived more than a third to a half as long as the maximum human lifespan. This is as true of the wild state as of 'ideal' conditions in captivity.

The maximum span of life is limited by the ageing slope because the gradient dictates that the chances of dying grow surer and surer. But living things frequently die from sheer accidents – a forest fire or a flood – or they are eaten from within by a parasite or from without by a predator. Some of these risks are age-dependent, but many affect young and old alike. The shorter longevity of bats and monkeys than their mortality slopes suggest is due to greater misfortune at all ages. If it ever becomes possible to reduce this constant force of mortality by further improvements in health, our primate cousins and others will join us at the top of the longevity league.

Graphs and life tables are not everyone's cup of tea, so an enterprising British statistician of an earlier generation commissioned an artist to represent the Gompertz equation pictorially. Karl Pearson named the painting *The Bridge of Life*, and it is a striking, if rather sombre, piece of work. People are represented crossing a bridge on which they face many hazards. At the start, a newborn baby risks being hit by a skeletal figure raining down the bones of his or her ancestors. This is a clever depiction of the toll of genetic diseases from infancy onwards. Growing children who are unafflicted stride across the bridge to meet new dangers as marksmen take up position to fire potshots at them. The weapons are all potentially lethal, but they get progressively more accurate further along the bridge. First there is a bow and arrow, next a Maxim gun (a water-cooled machine-gun), then a blunderbuss. Finally a Winchester rifle is aimed at the passer – a weapon which represented the ultimate in accuracy in Pearson's day. Even mortals who have been lucky enough to avoid being knocked out early on will be annihilated eventually, for the bridge disintegrates before it reaches the other side and all must fall off into the abyss. Evidently this is not a bridge on which one can turn back!

Pearson's message is cold and simple: life gets more hazardous with the passage of time. If matters were otherwise and we retained the low mortality risk of adolescence, we could expect to live for several centuries. The bridge would then have a much greater span, but it would still not reach the other side (wherever that might be). Even the redwoods and bristlecone pines, which don't age, are not immortal. Their risks of dying are very low but, because they are not zero, even these patriarchs will not last for ever.

Some people still quibble about the definition of ageing. This is not surprising, given how mysterious this process is. One of the enduring mistakes is to confuse ageing with the loss of growth, because our rate of growth slows after birth. The words of the French novelist Anatole France are in this vein: '*Nous étions déjà si vieux quand nous sommes nés*' – 'We were already old when we were born.' The idea that we begin to age from the day we are born is a popular one and, in a sense, self-evident because in our beginning is our end. From measurements of the rate of tissue growth, Charles Minot, a professor at Harvard early this century, reached the conclusion that, as the capacity for growth and wound repair declines, so ageing raises its ugly head. These days the Minot theory does not swim with the big fishes of gerontology, despite its perfect logic, because it fails to predict the build-up of degenerative diseases occurring late in life. Many changes are occurring in the body over the course of time, but they are not strictly senescence unless they are harmful. In biological parlance, ageing is always regarded as a maladaptive state. For that reason, the disappearance of nerve, muscle and egg cells in the foetus does not qualify because this is a preparation for the proper functioning of organs. The first of the cross-links that stiffen collagen fibres are in the same category.

What is very significant about the mortality slope is that we do not begin to climb the ageing gradient until after puberty. Of course, some children die, but children's risks of dying do not increase as they grow from infancy to adolescence. If anything, the reverse is true because of the greater vulnerability during the perinatal period. Puberty marks the end of a period of comparative safety before the start of a heavenward climb in the statistical probability of dying. Actuarially speaking, ageing is a fact of being adult, and to speak of children ageing is nonsense.

The Gompertzian mortality slope is the sum of all the causes of natural death in the adult population and, once it has begun, the pace of ageing quickens with time without jumping or pausing or slackening. This may seem counter-intuitive, considering the sudden changes we sometimes notice in people seen infrequently, which the French call 'un coup d'âge'. Some individuals may be climbing steeper slopes than others and 'older' at the same chronological age, but we cannot be sure until a marker is available for measuring the biological age of the individual.

The number of 'stages' in life has been debated endlessly because of a human desire to mark the rites of passage. Seven has been popular since it is a prime number and has many biblical precedents. The product of seven times seven was regarded as being of particular significance, and the occurrence of the menopause around forty-nine years of age seemed to confirm the superstition. But biology is no respecter of magic numbers and recognizes only two stages of life after birth – immaturity and adulthood. That being so, it gives no blessing to set retirement dates. Rites of passage fixed by age alone are arbitrary and ignore the possibility that people develop and deteriorate at different rates. Until recently, High Court judges and clergymen were appointed *ad vitam aut culpam*, and the academic scene is going into reverse in America where a fixed retirement age for professors has recently been abandoned. The politics of ageing are much more unstable than its biology.

The menopause is a candidate for a third stage of life, although its impact on the ageing slope is less than the other problems an older woman faces. This is not to say that the problems of menopause or reproduction are inconsequential – far from it. The sex organs are as much (if not more) subject to ageing as any other organ, and their hormones play a part in the survival advantage of being female.

• The Gender Gap

Despite the hazards of pregnancy and childbirth, women have always led their partners in the survival stakes. Gender is a better predictor of life expectation than either racial differences or social class, and is bettered only by age itself. One widespread misapprehension can be safely laid aside: males do not age faster than females. An astute eighteenth-century doctor was nearer the truth when he wrote that 'human life in males is more brittle than in females'. For some of the same reasons, males are more at risk of accidents at all ages, even before birth. Afterwards, their mortality slope and maximum age limit exactly match those of women. The UK record lifespan presently stands at 112 for a woman and 111 for a man. Until recently the world record for maximum lifespan was held by a Japanese man, Shigechiyo Izumi, who died in 1986 at the age of 120 years and 237 days, but in 1995 this was beaten by the sprightly Mme Jeanne Calment of Arles, who remembers selling pencils to van Gogh when he was staying in the neighbourhood over a century ago.

Only in the most poverty-stricken parts of the world and in the

North American Hutterite community (which forbids fertility control) do we find evidence that women have consistently died younger than their husbands in this century. As women have gained better health and a greater measure of control of their fertility, their lifespans have increased ahead of the men's. A hundred years ago, they could expect to live to fifty, which was two to three years longer than their menfolk. By the beginning of the Second World War, women's prospects had improved so much that the average reached sixty, and by then the men were lagging a full five years behind. Since that time, the gender gap has widened still more, although there are signs in some countries that men are slowly catching up.

There is a host of explanations for the relative differences in lifespan. Gender differences exist in diet and smoking habits, and males trail in adopting healthier lifestyles. Young men are more prone to accidental injury, homicide and suicide than young women. Men even seem to be at greater risk from acts of God! The US National Weather Bureau reported that sixty-seven males and only seven females died from lightning strikes in 1990. Whether this merely indicates that men spend more time on the golf course they did not say.

Men are more likely to die not just from accidents but also from heart attacks and cancer of the lung and bowel as well as many other diseases. Long-term studies in Framingham, Massachusetts, have shown that heart attacks are ten times more common in men than women between the ages thirty-five and sixty-five, though the differences narrow and disappear at later ages. Women are protected by their oestrogen, an advantage which largely disappears after the menopause.

Since heart disease is rarer in traditional farming and hunter-gatherer societies, it seems to be as much the lifestyle that men choose as their biology that sets them at risk. Nowhere is this conclusion better illustrated than by the almost equally long lives of men and women in the Seventh Day Adventist Church. Presumably, it is their prudent habits – including abstinence from tobacco, alcohol and coffee – that bless them with long life, rather than their eschatology!

The bigger the gender gap found elsewhere, the greater the opportunity for improvement.

Men clearly have greater physical strength than women, but they have less physiological endurance. Charles Darwin, a chronic hypochondriac, was well aware of the disadvantages of his gender, and drew the conclusion that a shorter life was 'a natural and constitutional peculiarity due to sex alone'. More recently, Alex Comfort confirmed that 'in most species that have been studied, the male is the shorter lived'. Over the years, a great deal of debate has been generated about the causes, and many question whether it is good for the species.

The most enduring theory holds that testosterone shortens the male lifespan because it is a 'dangerous hormone', and the antics of *Antechinus stuartii* would seem to bear this out. Yet this explanation fails to account for the unusual reversal of the gender gap in hamsters, nor the shorter male lifespans of many worms, crustaceans, insects and spiders, none of which use testosterone as a sex hormone.

Another theory assumes that the female advantage is due to the possession of two X-type chromosomes, the minute sausage-like structures which package the genes within the nucleus of each cell. Men have only one X plus a much smaller Y chromosome, which is responsible for maleness but carries few other genes. The female can call on alternative genes from either of the X chromosomes and has no need of the Y. Indubitably, the possession of only one set puts the male at greater risk, especially since the majority of genes on the X chromosome are required for essential housekeeping tasks in cells rather than purely for sexual development. The chances of a mutation affecting both copies of a gene in a female cell simultaneously are vanishingly small, but a male does not have a backup copy if a change occurs. Males are consequently more often victims of 'sex-linked' diseases, which include many common genetic disorders such as muscular dystrophy and defects in the haemoglobin of blood cells. But these are special cases, and the theory does not explain why males have a higher risk of many other diseases. Nor does it explain why male birds generally do not live any longer than females, for in these creatures the supposed advantage of a pair of chromosomes equivalent to the Xs in mammals is held by cock birds.

There is a popular view, admittedly based on a somewhat circular argument, that mortality differences have evolved to whittle away an excess of male births. In Britain, and it is much the same elsewhere, for every 100 girls born there are about 103 boys. By age thirty-five, or the mid-point of reproductive life, the numbers are on a par. By eighty there are twice as many women as men, and the chances of widowhood are even greater than statistics suggest because women have traditionally married older, higher-status males with little thought to the far future. Hence many women have had to face the prospect of their final years alone or in the company of other widows in homes for the elderly. A healthy, single male who survives may then, perhaps for the first time in his life, be able to be choosy as he weighs his prospects!

A more persuasive theory is that males are the more expendable of the two sexes. If they make a smaller contribution to the outcome of reproduction, the argument goes, the refining influence of evolutionary selection will be less stringent and the male will be physiologically less robust than his partner. This explanation may be valid, as we shall see later on, but it has to account for a variety of domestic arrangements. The male's contribution is often much more than just the act of mating, and many long-lived birds, like albatrosses and swans, are monogamous and share the parenting role. Sometimes the conventional roles are reversed for mysterious reasons. Female phalaropes fly south from Iceland leaving the males to brood the young, and male seahorses become 'pregnant' by carrying their brood. It will be interesting to discover whether these males are rewarded for their responsibilities with a longer lifespan.

• Disease and Disability

Medicine has been as guilty as other professions of patronizing and institutionalizing older people. Some geriatric patients may be incontinent and demented, but these indignities can also strike people as early as in their forties. Doctors are very good at sniffing out diseases, but have no remedy to offer for the underlying problem of ageing. Some regard ageing as the wearing down of the body by past injuries and diseases; others go so far as to argue that ageing should be regarded as just another disease. If that were the case, a young physician could be confident of passing an exam in at least one diagnosis – that we are all suffering from an incurable illness with a fatality rate of 100 per cent!

This pessimism is reflected in the almost complete absence of gerontology in undergraduate medical education. The medical discipline of geriatrics is correspondingly regarded as the Cinderella of medicine. In a sense, it is a false speciality because its patient group is defined more by chronological than biological criteria. Age is not a disease in itself, and the nature of patient care should not be determined by the birth date on a patient's record card. Interestingly, the veterinary profession seems to ignore the distinction of age, if the absence of textbooks on geriatric animal medicine is anything to go by. Yet much of veterinarians' time, like doctors', is spent attending to aged patients, which they deal with as a normal course. Perhaps human animals would benefit from this approach.

Age changes are not lethal in themselves, but they do lay the body open to infection, injury and malfunction. The diseases of ageing do not fit into a single, neat category. Some are universal, progressive and irreversible, and the hardening of arteries, wearing of joints and emphysema fall into this group. Others are more common later on, though not actually universal, and include cancer and high blood pressure. There are also illnesses and reactions that may occur at any age but have far more serious consequences in old age. Broken bones, pneumonia and influenza are the major examples in this group.

Old people may have built up an 'immunological wisdom' over the years from exposure to viruses or parasites, but this fails to protect them when the immune system weakens. For example, *Herpes zoster*, or shingles, causes acute neuralgia and is a scourge of the old. It is caused by a recrudescent form of a virus which will have lain dormant for decades since childhood, when it sparked the milder condition of chickenpox. Pneumonia is even more serious in an older person because what had laid him low as a young man now lays him out. It used to be regarded as 'the old man's friend' because it hastened a slow death, but it can now be treated so we can die of other things. The point is that people do not die of age *per se*, and the mortality slope represents the sum of all terminal diseases.

Since the law requires doctors to record the cause on every death certificate, we might assume that we have a good knowledge of what old people die of, but that is far from the case. Only rarely is the cause of death checked by an autopsy, and when an autopsy is performed the results often do not tally with the clinical diagnosis. Frequently, more than one disease is present, and it may be difficult to say which was the primary cause. When there is uncertainty, 'atherosclerosis' is likely to be recorded or, if there were respiratory problems in the final days, then 'pneumonia'. It is hardly surprising that some pathologists have called for a new category to be added to the certificate – 'senescence' – despite the fact that no one dies from the sheer weight of years.

Society does not tolerate such imprecision on a death certificate for a young person because the attitude of resignation is absent. We demand good explanations of premature deaths. Perhaps we need not worry too much about uncertainties in an old person, unless foul play is suspected, since the cause of 'natural' death is arbitrary in a sense. He or she is probably harbouring several diseases.

This could be illustrated with any number of real-life cases but, to give an arbitrary example, there was an old man of 102 who died with gangrene in his leg after a bout of influenza. An autopsy revealed the anticipated thrombosis in the leg, but many other problems came to light after a more thorough investigation. The great blood vessels had narrowed considerably, there was a tumour in his bowel, there were 'nodules' in his thyroid and he had an enlarged prostate gland. Any one of this motley collection might have proved fatal in time but, despite this burden having been accumulating for months or even years, he had reported feeling fine a few days before he died. That he claimed as much demonstrates how much expectations of 'feeling good' change as we grow old.

Disability is as much a sign of age as is unmistakable disease, and is often feared almost as much. The bent old man leaning on a stick, and the knobbly fingers of a woman disfigured by arthritis are the results of processes affecting almost every corner of the body and which may begin as early as age thirty. Deterioration of our senses affects the quality of life as much as, if not more than, immobility. The losses of sight, hearing and smell are not fatal conditions, but they certainly increase vulnerability to accidents and hence contribute to the mortality slope.

By middle age the human eye has lost so much of its power of accommodation that we need to wear spectacles for reading. In this condition of farsightedness, or presbyopia, the lens has grown larger and less elastic and can no longer 'squash' sufficiently to bend light rays to a sharp focus for close objects. Books and newspapers have to be held out at arm's length for the print to be read. The handicap is not strictly a pathological change; it occurs in healthy eyes, and affects everyone sooner or later. It is partly caused by the continued onion-like growth of the lens, and to this extent it is a biological 'design fault' and as 'natural' as the menopause.

'Hardness of hearing' is another problem of old age – and an apt expression, because deafness is a much underestimated disability. As children we can hear sounds ranging from 20 to 20,000 Hz, although even this enormous waveband is narrow by comparison with that of some animals. Stiffening of the tiny bones or ossicles that transmit vibrations from the eardrum combined with a loss of hair cells in the water-filled inner ear (cochlea) is responsible for the loss of sensitivity to high-pitched sounds before low ones. Like many age changes, this is imperceptible at first, unless you are trying to listen to bats calling in the countryside. But, as the hearing level deteriorates to the point where it becomes a problem in conversation, a sense of profound isolation can develop. Unfortunately, younger people are often less than sympathetic, and when grandad refuses to acknowledge his deafness the disability can become a family joke.

Hearing loss may not be quite as inevitable as we assume. Auditory studies of an isolated tribe of Sudanese pastoralists, the Mabaan, show that they lose only a quarter as much of their sensitivity at all frequencies as Westerners. Since they rarely encounter loud sounds, there is the intriguing possibility that our noisy environment contributes to the faster rate of hearing loss. Perhaps there is only so much 'noise' that we can stand, and we become steadily more hard of hearing after reaching our quota. If this were so, it would be a powerful argument for campaigning for noise abatement. The explanation is unlikely to be quite so clear-cut, however, because the Mabaan people are free of many other problems plaguing Westerners, such as arterial disease and hypertension, which go hand in hand with deafness.

Smell is a much underrated sense, and its loss is often regarded as of little consequence except to the connoisseur. Is it not remarkable, then, that our noses are sensitive to ten thousand different odourants, and that the gene family responsible for our olfactory finesse is one of the largest? This may be an evolutionary carry-over from the time when it was a matter of survival to be able to distinguish between what is good to eat and what is poisonous, or to detect the whiff of a predator or follow an animal trail. However good the nose we inherited, its sharp sense is blunted by age. A Philadelphia study showed that 50 per cent of people have lost their sense of smell altogether by seventy years old – men earlier than women, and smokers long before others. We ought to conserve whatever sense of smell remains, if not for aesthetic reasons then for safety. Noses have provided advance warning of leaking gas on many an occasion that has saved a life.

Ageing is not, therefore, just a matter of dangerous diseases raising their ugly heads. Among insects, worms and molluscs we find evidence of ageing, but never any signs of cancer or the major diseases encountered in warm-blooded creatures. Ageing may bring one disability or another, but not necessarily disease: age differences are more often a matter of a degree of change in physiology or structure, though these may lead to unhealthy effects. We cannot be sure whether palaeohumans lived long enough to be affected by this, but the dimming of senses gradually cuts individuals off from their environment and makes them more vulnerable. In no respect can ageing be regarded as beneficial, and in biological parlance it definitely is 'maladaptive'.

While we may not be able to stop our biological clocks, some of the timetables can be rescheduled by our own actions. The Director of the New England Research Institute, Alan Jette, recently declared, 'We don't believe that disability is an inherent part of the ageing process, solely determined by biological losses or restrictions. Rather it is influenced by many factors (physical, cognitive and social), some of which can be changed.' Many of the changes attributed to ageing are not really caused by it at all. Many others would not emerge until later if we were more careful with our health and fitness. Studies pioneered by Nathan Shock in Baltimore forty years ago prove the point and helped to explain the increasing variability between the constitutions of people of older age. In what has become the most famous long-term study of Americans, he recruited community-living men and women of all ages for regular testing of physiological and psychological well-being. The study showed that muscular power declined almost imperceptibly until middle age, except by the standards of athletic trials or the physiology laboratory. Further weakening was almost halted by a programme of regular exercise. Stretching of muscles and nervous activity helped to maintain the size of individual muscle fibres, although their numbers were not increased. Most of the decline in lung capacity was also prevented by aerobic exercise, but a low volume taken in at each breath was still a predictor of early death. The most encouraging finding was that even unfit sixty- to seventy-year-olds considerably improved their breathing capacity and reduced their blood cholesterol levels by an appropriate fitness programme. We do not know how far this principle can be extended to other aspects of physiology. No doubt, some would like to believe that practice would maintain sexual and intellectual vigour too, but exercise cannot postpone all types of disability. For example, exercising the eyes to postpone presbyopia is wishful thinking because the problem is more a matter of programmed growth of the lens rather than muscle weakness.

Many of the changes commonly regarded as 'pure ageing' are nothing of the sort. It is sometimes said that 'we are as old as our arteries', but even the clogging of blood vessels is not as inevitable as is supposed. Laboratory rats and rabbits are extremely resistant to atherosclerosis, even when fed a cholesterol-rich diet, and it is more a disease of Westerners than of our species as a whole. Indeed, there is plenty of encouraging evidence that heart disease is declining in the USA and some European countries (though sadly little in Scotland). Cutting down on dietary fats, giving up smoking, and taking more exercise no doubt help health, though healthier lifestyles may not explain all. The seeds of heart disease are thought to be sown when we are young, perhaps even before birth, and are only fertilized by smoking and a bad diet.

Some forty years ago, Hardin Jones, a medical physicist at Berkeley, California, suggested that a person's biological age is programmed by disease experience early in life. He found that improvements in life expectancy were mirroring the steady decline in infant mortality that had occurred over the past century. Jones compared the mortality slopes over several generations in Sweden, because statistics have been recorded longer there than almost anywhere else. To his surprise, he found that they all ran parallel to one another, despite the much improved living conditions of later generations, which implies that people were still ageing at the same rate. What differed was that the slopes for more recent generations did not begin an upward climb until later ages. This means that people today are biologically younger for a given age than in earlier generations.

It seems that the ageing process, once begun, follows a strict time schedule which is unaltered by the circumstances of life. People are climbing the slope at the same rate all around the world. Jones estimated that at a given chronological age the generation born in the 1940s is five to ten years biologically younger than that born a century earlier and is therefore less vulnerable to the diseases and disabilities of old age. Experiences early in life have a greater impact than being a rugged survivor of a hostile environment. While a healthy infancy does not slow the ageing clock, it may reset the time at which the lifespan begins to tick away.

Unfortunately, Jones's theory is not easily tested, because people living in poor and unhealthy conditions when they are young are likely to remain so for the rest of their lives. His explanation also flies in the face of evidence that some serious illnesses of later life, such as breast cancer, are more common in wealthier communities. It therefore became neglected by researchers and has only recently been resurrected in a new form as a result of studies by English epidemiologists.

In the counties of Hertfordshire and Lancashire, records of the weights of newborn babies have been preserved from earlier in the century. David Barker and his colleagues at the Medical Research Council Epidemiology Unit in Southampton consulted medical histories to see whether people's birth weights bore any relationship to their health sixty-five years later. They found that those weighing less than three kilograms at birth had ten times as much heart disease, stroke, high blood pressure and diabetes as those who were more than 4.5 kilograms. This difference persisted even after taking smoking, alcohol and social conditions into account. Jones's prediction that favourable conditions during childhood carry lifelong benefits is therefore good for the environment of the womb too, as conditions there affect birth weight. It is ironic that it has taken so long to rediscover the importance of the early programming of health when so much evidence already pointed to this in animal nutrition. Indeed, animals too have been beneficiaries of improvements in husbandry throughout the century.

How much further progress in human health and lifespan will go depends on economics and politics. In trying to stave off the diseases of old age, health promoters and medical researchers are dealing only with secondary conditions. The primary cause of vulnerability is the ageing process itself, and that seems to be genetically 'hard-wired'. Were it possible to make the ageing slope shallower, the diseases of ageing would emerge later on and centenarians might be able to play a good game of tennis or even run marathons for charity. This is not entirely a flight of fancy. It is possible to alter the mortality slope in rats and mice – to slow the ageing process itself – by dietary means, and to postpone the onset of disease. This may not be a successful strategy for humans, for reasons I shall give later, so, for the present, we can only hope to age as graciously and healthily as possible.

• The Enigma of Age

Newborn babies look much alike to all but their adoring parents, but we become more and more different from one another as we grow older. Individuals develop at different rates. Girls reach puberty before boys, and some girls much earlier than others. Although these differences do not usually amount to more than four or five years, menopause can occur at any time between forty and sixty years of age, and sometimes earlier still. People who were like peas in a pod as children may look ten or twenty years apart by their seventies. And it is not just a matter of appearances: some seventy-year-olds seem to have the vitality and constitution of fifty-year-olds, while others might be described as 'seventy going on ninety'. It is not always easy to explain why people of the same chronological age have different biological ages. Genetics has something to do with it. The lifespans of identical twins, like those of highly inbred animals, are closer to one another than are those of unrelated individuals. Even so, substantial differences remain. Each person has a unique history of lifestyle factors, including housing, diet, reproduction and occupation, all of which can affect health and survival.

Tests are increasingly available for genetic diseases, but the biological crystal ball is very cloudy when we come to ageing. Gerontologists dream of a 'biomarker' which gauges biological age and predicts lifespan more precisely than calendar age. Just as growth rings in fish bones and tree stumps give a fair estimate of the number and quality of the growing seasons, a biomarker would give an impression of how far along the force-of-mortality slope an individual had travelled.

The most desirable place to find a biomarker is on the surface of the body, because it could then be easily monitored. Fingernail growth can be measured by filing a groove near the cuticle and measuring the distance travelled up the nail over the following months. An American physician measured his nails continuously over a period of thirty-five years of adult life. The nails grew at a rate of 0.1 mm per day at first, but progressively slowed down with age. Hair is made of the same protein and becomes less abundant and greyer with age, and on some heads more than others. Unfortunately, neither of these biomarkers gives a much better indication of biological age than the calendar. They are too far removed from the underlying cause of ageing to be much use, and they are far from being universal. In fact the greying of hair varies greatly between human races, and so might nail growth for all we know.

Hormone levels and immune responses, blood pressure and the capacity of the lungs have all been considered as biomarkers at one time or another. So have 'age pigment' in tissues and the non-enzymatic addition of sugars to proteins ('glycation') which is a feature of diabetes. Many of them change with age, and some have an impressive record in the diagnosis of disease, but none of them gives a true measure of the underlying ageing process. This is because gerontologists demand a lot of a good biomarker. It must be something that is general and that can be measured repeatedly without harming the subject, and it must measure the basic ageing process rather than the effects of disease. Finally, it should be accessible at all ages and in different species. But the search for an ideal biomarker is turning out to be another disappointing Grail quest.

Some may say that it is just as well that the biomarker trail has been so inconclusive. Were a biomarker available, employers and insurance companies might use its information against us. But the lack of a good biomarker is an obstacle to progress in science. In its absence, we cannot tell precisely where a subject is on the ageing curve, nor assess the effects of treatments aimed at extending life. We can tell if ageing has slowed only by waiting to see how long members of the group survive, which, for human beings, is a long-winded affair.

Ageing remains something of an enigma. We see evidence of it all around us – loss of fruiting power, sapping of energy, disability and disease. The process is general if not universal, intrinsic yet affected by the environment, inexorable yet proceeding at different rates in various organs, individuals and species. Researchers have cautiously tackled the problems of disability and disease individually, on the principle adumbrated by Arthur Koestler that science is the art of the soluble. It has always been much easier to tackle the secondary effects of ageing rather than its root cause. In much the same way, we can understand how to use a wordprocessor while remaining blissfully ignorant of the wizardry of the computer software and hardware behind it.

Edward Elgar never revealed the meaning of the *Enigma* theme in his elegaic musical vignettes of the lives and personalities of his family and friends. 'Its dark saying must be left unguessed', he wrote. Whether the theme behind it is 'mortality', as some think, is beside the point: the experience for the hearer does not depend on knowing exactly what the composer had in mind. The enigma of ageing is that it is expressed in each one of us but its underlying nature remains a mystery.

CHAPTER 4

Programmed Senescence

Genes may be direct determinants or may set indirect constraints on the lifespan.

C. E. Finch

• Fires of Life

The energetic Victorian designer and socialist William Morris expired in 1896 at the age of sixty-five. When asked about the cause of death, his doctor reported simply that he had 'died of being William Morris'. Like many doctors, both then and now, he thought ageing was the result of wear and tear plus disease, and that Morris would have lasted longer if he had taken a more laid-back attitude to life.

There is something intuitively appealing about the idea that those who choose to live in the fast lane must pay the price. It harmonizes with our sense of natural justice and encourages faint hopes that biological destiny is not beyond our control. If each individual were given a fixed quantity of 'vitality' – like a financial endowment – he or she could decide how and when to spend or invest it.

At the beginning of the century, these notions underpinned one of the most important theories of ageing. The 'rate-of-living' theory was an ambitious attempt to solve the big question of why animals have fixed lifespans. According to its chief advocates, Max Rubner in Germany and Raymond Pearl in America, animals are born with a limited ability to make energy. As they near the end of their quota, they burn out and die off. And the faster they live, the sooner their candle begins to flicker and fade.

Energy is at the root of biochemistry. It is needed for everything we do – from kicking a football to composing my next sentence. We obtain our energy by eating fats, carbohydrates and proteins, and in that order of abundance in the Western diet. After digestion in the intestines, the smaller molecules like glucose can be taken into cells. After further breakdown, the products enter into the hundreds of tiny power stations called mitochondria within the cells, where oxidation reactions finally produce water and carbon dioxide and lots of chemical energy in the form of ATP (adenosine triphosphate). The process of oxidation is very efficient, because each molecule of glucose produces thirty-eight molecules of ATP and all of the available energy has been released when the breakdown process is complete. Some organisms, like brewers' yeast, have adopted the process of fermentation in the absence of oxygen. This is only 5 per cent as efficient because the sugar is only broken down as far as alcohol; still, efficiency isn't everything!

The basal metabolic rate – or BMR – is the minimum amount of energy needed just to keep ourselves alive – to keep the heart beating, the kidneys filtering, the brain sparking, and so on. In a resting human body it represents a consumption of about 200 millilitres of oxygen per minute. In terms of power output, this is roughly equivalent to an eighty-watt domestic lightbulb. Put another way, for every twelve people at your party you can economize by turning down the heating by the equivalent of one kilowatt – until the dancing starts. During exercise, the metabolic rate can rise ten to twenty times above the BMR, depending on a person's age and fitness, and much more heat is generated in the process.

The BMR is a baseline that can be established for almost every animal by measuring either oxygen consumption or the energy being lost as heat. It is a gauge of the 'rate of living' of a species, if ever there was one. Obviously, a large animal needs more energy to keep its enormous bulk alive than a small one. This is why an elephant consumes a vastly greater amount of food than a mouse. But what is more remarkable is that the mouse looms large when we compare the energy released per gram of body weight. Calorie for gram, the mouse consumes energy twenty times as fast as the elephant. It is as though the furnaces of life in small creatures burn much brighter and hotter.

What is true for some of the smallest and largest animals also holds for most of those in between. There is, in fact, an inverse relationship between the adult size of the species and the energy produced per gram of weight. We can read 'cell' for 'gram of weight', because animals differ greatly in the number of their cells but not in their cell sizes. So convincing is the relationship when plotted on a graph that it became known as 'Kleiber's rule', after the American physiologist who discovered this in the 1940s. It seemed to be the key to proving the rate-of-living theory, yet it opened the door to a great deal of controversy which continues even to this day.

The downward slope of BMRs from small to large species implies that mice and their kindred are much less efficient users of energy than are larger species. One of the main reasons why mice have to stoke up their metabolic fires is to generate heat simply to keep themselves warm because small bodies with a large surface area for weight chill very quickly. Big animals use energy more parsimoniously without compromising their ability to maintain all the vital activities of the body, and still have some spare capacity for extra bursts.

The heart of a browsing pachyderm beats with a ponderous thud every two seconds, or thirty times a minute. A mouse's heart ticks at 300 times a minute. The first can live to seventy, whereas the second is unlikely to last more than three years. In round figures, both animals have a maximum of 1–2 billion heartbeats in a lifetime. And the heart is not the only organ which seems to have a fixed performance quota. Elephants breathe more slowly than mice, yet both take in roughly the same number of breaths in a lifetime – about 200 million. Even at rest, mice live at a fast pace like super-stressed executives burning the candle at both ends. Yet this is their natural lifestyle, and the typical mouse has normal levels of stress hormones. They are, in fact, well adapted to their highly-strung existence and would soon die if their metabolism was artificially damped down.

Whatever the size or longevity of animals, capacities converge on fixed limits. What is true of the pumps and bellows of the body applies to the BMR too. Rubner calculated that on average during a lifetime 200 kilocalories of energy are consumed for every gram of body weight. He reckoned that this figure was much the same for all animals, but in humans the figure is closer to 800.

Mammals and birds have much the same BMR throughout their lives, because they have a biological thermostat to ensure that they keep warm whatever the weather. If their body temperature falls below the norm, they quickly lose consciousness and will die unless they belong to a species that is specially adapted to torpor or hibernation and so are capable of spontaneously rewarming themselves with an inbuilt 'electric blanket' of brown fat. For so-called cold-blooded animals, such as reptiles, amphibians and fishes, the pace of life is heavily influenced by the ambient temperature. When cold, they are sluggish because their metabolism is running slowly. But when they warm up in the sunshine, their biochemical fires flare up and their body functions run in fast-forward mode. Their lives are natural experiments in the rate of living.

Creatures living in warmer climes eat more, grow faster, mature earlier and are in greater haste to complete their lives than those in colder parts of the world. Or so it would seem. Some of the longest-living fish are probably in the icy polar seas, or at great depths where it is equally cold. For practical reasons, few fish have been studied in much detail, though the wall-eye, a popular American sport fish, is an exception. Its life is compressed or stretched out depending on the latitude and climate it is living in. In the southern United States it survives just two to three years, compared with ten to twenty-five years in the cold Canadian lakes. The entire life history of southern fish is concentrated into a short span, and before going prematurely old they achieve the same spawning productivity as their longer-lived northern cousins. Whether translocation of northerners to the south, or vice versa, would reverse their fortunes is a moot point. It has been assumed that the differences between stocks are environmental rather than genetic. If that is true, it helps to clinch the proposition that the rate of living is responsible for the rate of ageing.

This theory is seductive because it appeals to our wish that nature is, at root, simple and intelligible. But while there must be reasons for everything we observe in the living world, nature is far from simple. Given the glorious variety and complexity of biology, a theory which claims that ageing is rigidly predestined by a biochemical quota system fails to satisfy.

The rate-of-living theory has itself become senescent as more and more flaws in it have come to light. The first is a theoretical difficulty of explaining *why* there should be a fixed quota of energy in the first place. Why, when living things have been able to overcome the challenges of colonizing almost every conceivable habitat on earth, should the evolution of lifespan have been stopped dead by the energy budget? This difficulty is compounded by the knowledge that some organisms and cells can apparently live for hundreds or thousands of years. As we saw earlier, there are no hard and fast limits to life.

Bats have a tendency to defy simple explanations, and this is as true of the rate-of-living theory as it was of the body-weight rule. They have a high BMR, so they should be much shorter-lived than they actually are, but their ability to hibernate during the winter months seemed to explain away their long lives. By letting their temperature fall to that of the roost in a cave or roof, they allow their metabolism to shut down during winter food scarcity. But do slumbering bats dream of stretching out their lives like the Canadian wall-eyes while the rats and mice on the ground below scuttle headlong into oblivion? The idea seemed plausible enough until someone pointed out that tropical bats do not hibernate and yet live as long as the rest.

Bats are not the only deviants either. Kleiber's rule was drawn from observations of domestic mammals which have a body temperature of around 37°. What of others? Creatures with warmer bodies should live shorter lives, and those with lower temperature settings should be longer-lived. In reality, these predictions are turned upside down.

Marsupials have a slightly lower body temperature than 'standard' mammals and therefore a lower BMR, but many of them lead brief lives. The Australian antechinus may be too much of an oddball to qualify as an example, but even the Virginia opossum survives only three years. At the other end of the spectrum, birds are warmer-blooded than mammals and should have more compressed lives, but in fact they are much longer-lived than mammals of the same size.

Even experimental studies cannot be taken at face value. The British geneticist John Maynard Smith found that when the temperature of fruit flies is raised they die sooner, as the rate-of-living theory predicts. But their life expectancy returns to its former level if the flies are returned to the cold, as if they had never been in the warm or had to 'pay back' a metabolic debt. Warming up increases the general risks of accidents rather than accelerating ageing.

Flatworms, like the liver fluke, are simple segmented creatures which regenerate into new worms after being chopped into pieces. If they had a fixed energy quota, the parts would carry the mortalizing effects of the parent's history down to the next 'generation' and would have a shorter life. In fact their lifespan is no different. Likewise, our own reproductive cells do not pass the full toll of metabolic time down to our children, otherwise their lifespan would be shorter than ours.

One of the most striking discoveries of gerontology is that low-calorie diets prolong a healthy life in mice and rats. Simply switching the animals from a cafeteria-style of eating *ad libitum* to fasting on alternate days makes the ageing gradient shallower and increases longevity by an impressive 30 per cent. This is not an isolated phenomenon, as dietary restriction works in nematode worms, flies and probably many other animals too. According to the rate-of-living theory, we would expect to find that the diet had lowered the BMR, yet studies show that the BMR is surprisingly unchanged.

What, if anything, can we conclude from these conflicting facts? Although there may be something in the theory, the rate of metabolism is not a sufficient explanation for length of life. Nor is there much evidence to suggest that hyperkinetic members of a species live shorter lives than their fellows. William Morris, to name one, actually lived to a good age for a Victorian. But science has the disconcerting habit of turning the wheel of history. Just when it seemed safe to lay the rate-of-living theory to rest it has risen again, phoenix-like, from its ashes. However, the new theory is not simply a reincarnation of the idea that biochemistry sets an immutable limit, but a radically new creature.

• Free Radicals

A human foetus growing in the womb lives in an environment relatively low in oxygen. From its first breath, the emerging baby has to cope with potentially harmful concentrations of oxygen in the air. We see all around us evidence of how reactive oxygen is – fuels burn, metals corrode and fats turn rancid. A similar challenge faced early life forms when oxygen first began to appear in the earth's atmosphere.

Primitive bacteria-like organisms generated energy from sulphurous and other compounds, just as those in geysers and swamps still do. Some produced oxygen as a by-product of their metabolism. They flourished, since there was little competition, and the concentrations of oxygen gradually rose – very slowly at first, then a little more quickly. Quantities of this gas began to appear in the air until it approached the 20 per cent level we have today. This was not good news for other organisms, because their fats are vulnerable to oxidation. These organisms had to make brave attempts to adapt to survive in this new environment. One solution was to use the oxygen biochemically by combining it with carbon and hydrogen atoms to make less toxic substances such as carbon dioxide and water. This not only helped them to cope with the oxygen but, as a by-product, produced energy which could then be used for growth and reproduction.

At some stage in this saga, some of these oxygen-using bacteria infected more naïve cells, perhaps as uninvited guests taking advantage of protection or food stores from the host. For their side of the bargain, the visitors mopped up the oxygen in the host cell and continued generating energy which could be shared. So beneficial was this arrangement that it has stuck ever since. In every cell of every organism, from yeast to human beings, the cytoplasm – living substance of the cell which surrounds the nucleus – is loaded with these modified bacteria which became the mitochondria. Like the Vikings in Britain, the cellular invaders gradually settled into a harmonious existence with the natives and eventually reached the point where they could not return to a free-wheeling life-style even if they had wanted to. The mitochondria remain wedded to their hosts, where they serve as the power stations meeting most of the energy requirements of cells. This historic union was a key event in the evolution of plant and animal cells as we know them today.

The story that cells harbour symbiotic bacteria seemed hard to swallow when it was first mooted a century ago. It is impossible to be certain of what happened 2 billion years back, but the theory that the ancestors of mitochondria were free agents has now assumed almost the status of dogma. What were once uninvited guests have become some of the most important parts of the cell, helping it to generate nearly twenty times as much energy as it otherwise would be able to from the same amount of carbohydrate.

This may look like a perfect arrangement, but there is a snag to cashing in on oxidative metabolism. Electrons leak from the processes in the mitochondria and can become attached to atoms, making unstable and highly reactive chemical entities called 'free radicals' which can start harmful chain reactions ending up with damaged molecules. It is rather like the game of tig in a children's playground. The child designated 'it' must pass on the stigma by touching another player, and the game comes to an end only when the slowest child is 'tigged', because he cannot catch anyone else.

This is a crude analogy to what happens in cells where the loose electron can end up in various parts of the cell's fabric and machinery, or even on the chromosomes which carry the genes in the nucleus. It has been estimated that the average human cell receives an 'oxidative hit' every few seconds. This is the price paid for generating energy to keep alive. On top of this, ionizing radiation and chemical compounds such as pesticides and chemotherapeutic drugs add to the body's burden of free radicals. While this is bad news for the individual, free radicals do have some virtues. White blood cells fire them in bursts to kill invading bacteria, and the mutations caused by free radicals may have served to speed up the rate of evolution.

Even though mitochondria can no longer survive on their own, they still have some control over their destiny and can divide independently of the rest of the cell. They possess chromosome-like rings that have genes carrying the codes to produce a mere thirteen proteins. These are involved in energy production, but unfortunately they are much more susceptible to damage than the genes lying in the nucleus. For a start, mitochondrial genes are much closer to the source of free radicals and, unlike the nucleus, they lack the histone proteins which protect the genetic material from being exposed to damage. Most remarkably of all, unlike nuclear genes, mitochondrial genes do not have an efficient means of correcting mutations. And, being purely vegetative propagators, mitochondria cannot even use sexual reproduction to reinvigorate themselves. The sum of these disadvantages is that mitochondria accumulate mutations sixteen times faster than the nucleus. The odd mutation matters little because there are many other mitochondria to compensate for it but, in time, the numbers of mutant mitochondria build up to potentially harmful levels and reduce the ability of cells to generate energy. We begin to puff during heavy exercise long before the age when our arteries narrow or our lungs are weak, and our damaged mitochondria probably have something to do with it. If only mitochondrial transplants were available!

Free radicals are suspected of aggravating a number of diseases, and sometimes triggering them. Cancer, arthritis and cataracts are just a few of the degenerative problems being laid at their door. Cells types that consume most oxygen are likely to feel the effects of free radicals before other cells. The brain is only 2 per cent of body weight but it is responsible for 20 per cent of all the oxygen consumed – and for many of the problems of ageing. Heart and skeletal muscles are also major users of oxygen – and they account for the early decline in peak athletic performance. Relics of free-radical action can be seen in these tissues even with the naked eye. End-products of the oxidation of fats and proteins accumulate as yellow-brown pigment called lipofuscin or age pigment. Since neither brain nor muscle cells eliminate it, the pigment steadily builds up. Its colour is one of the better biomarkers of ageing, though possibly harmless in itself.

Free-radical effects are likely to be worse in small, active, short-lived animals than in bigger, more sluggish and long-lived ones. A mouse's lifetime risk of cancer is much the same as a human's, even though we live thirty times longer and have 3,000 times as many cells. Assuming that cancer starts with a single aberrant cell, the average mouse cell has a risk of cancer about 100,000 times greater than one of ours. This is exactly what we might predict, since the BMR per gram and the numbers and activity of mitochondria are higher. A more rapid rate of breakdown and replacement of proteins in the cells of such small animals may be the way they try to cope with cumulative damage. Even so, the explanation for the higher risk associated with being small is unlikely to be quite as simple as that. After all, birds and bats have very high rates of energy expenditure, and presumably lots of free radicals, yet are long-lived. In fact, cells are not completely at the mercy of free radicals and, during the course of evolution, they have acquired smart genes that enable them to mop up radicals and convert them to harmless products.

Genes are segments of coded information stretched out in linear arrays along enormously long DNA molecules in the chromosomes. The code was cracked many years ago by Francis Crick, James Watson and Sydney Brenner. The big task today is to read the message in the 70,000 or so genes in each human cell. This is biology's moon-shot programme, and is known as the Human

Genome Project. Yet it has to be said that the genetic code in the DNA has turned out to be relatively simple compared with the highly sophisticated processes going on downstream. The unravelling of gene action is the great challenge for twenty-first-century biology, and the phenomena of ageing must ultimately be explained at these levels.

The genes are the agents of inheritance. They are the top of the information pyramid in the cells – the senior managers of the company, so to speak. From their offices in the nucleus (plus a few in the mitochondria), they send down instructions in code via inter-mediaries (messenger-RNA molecules) to shop-floor workers in the cell's cytoplasm. Some genes have a more administrative role within the nucleus and, by sending memos to other managers, they control the outflow of instructions.

Down in the cytoplasm, proteins and fats are manufactured and deployed. It is the protein composition of a cell which, more than anything else, is responsible for the cell's character – whether it turns out to be an egg, sperm, brain or liver cell. All cells carry the same genes, but not all are switched on. Prudent administration ensures appropriate levels of production of the numerous proteins and other molecules for each cell. Not all of the DNA code is active at once, otherwise chaos would reign. A typical cell contains some 10,000 different types of protein, and nerve cells contain many more, each with its own job to do. Some proteins are the struts and walls of the cell's fabric, some act as gates in the membrane, and others as hormonal messengers. Still more are enzymes for speeding up biochemical reactions.

Each enzyme is involved in a specific chemical reaction. One of them, superoxide dismutase, or SOD for short, converts the free radical called superoxide into oxygen gas and hydrogen peroxide. SOD is abundant in the mitochondria where it is most needed. Superoxide is not the most reactive or harmful radical and it decays spontaneously. A bigger menace lies in the combination of superoxide with hydrogen peroxide to form the highly reactive hydroxyl radical, which is the main agent of oxidative damage. So SOD alone is not sufficient to protect against free-radical damage. For another thing, hydrogen peroxide is itself dangerously reactive. That is why a gene coding for yet another enzyme is present. Catalase (or CAT) grabs hydrogen peroxide and rapidly converts it to oxygen and water which can be usefully deployed in the cell.

If SOD and CAT are important defenders of longevity, we might expect to find more of them in longer-lived species, and this is indeed so. Amounts of these enzymes also vary between cell types in the same body. Such differences help to explain why resistance to free-radical damage and disease varies so much between species and organs. Human cells have some of the highest concentrations of SOD and CAT, though even these fall short of the ideal. In theory, we should enjoy better health and longer lives with more of these enzymes. But there would be little benefit in having more SOD without a corresponding amount of CAT. This is because the extra hydrogen peroxide generated would be converted to the mischievous hydroxyl radical.

We can now test this prediction in the laboratory by gene-transfer experiments – though not on humans yet. Transferring novel genes or knocking out existing ones from laboratory animals is now a routine way of investigating their role. The tiny fruit fly or *Drosophila* (quaintly meaning 'dew-lover' in Greek) is the favourite subject of geneticists because it is easy to 'culture' in large numbers in the laboratory and numerous mutants have been recorded. A research group in Dallas recently transferred extra copies of SOD and CAT genes into fruit flies with the aim of producing more of these enzymes and prolonging the lifespan. There was no benefit from adding the SOD genes alone, but when both genes were transferred the flies lived 30 per cent longer than the normal span of ten weeks. They were also stronger and healthier. In another laboratory, mutant flies have turned up that totally lack any SOD. They developed normally through the larval stages, but lasted only about ten days as adults. They were also much more sensitive to the weed-killer paraquat which produces free radicals.

These results highlight the importance of free-radical protection;

but, as often happens, one question answered leads to lots of new ones – the paymasters of research must sometimes despair at the expanding course of science. One question is this: If the genes for SOD and CAT are so health-giving – or 'eugenic', to use a word now out of favour – why do fruit flies have less than the optimum? Another is: Why should humans have so much more of these genes than other animals? We shall not tarry over these puzzles here. For the moment, it is important to note that no single gene or family of genes has been shown to be an 'elixir of life'. Nor do we expect to discover one. Lifespans can sometimes be extended, but only to a limited degree. Evidently, there are many genes affecting the lifespan, some positively and others negatively.

As far as the positive ones are concerned, biology appears to have adopted a 'belt and braces' approach. By that we mean that the body is over-engineered when it really counts, such as at birth and in resistance to disease. The more we learn, the more we find that there are backup processes in case the main mechanism fails. Protection against free radicals partly depends on the diet. This is a rather risky strategy because it leaves protection to chance, according to the abundance and quality of food. On the other hand, it allows privileged and prudent individuals to adjust the odds on their chances of long and healthy lives.

Laboratory researchers have found that antioxidants can extend the lifespan of flies and rodents. Mice lived a third longer than usual and were healthier than normal, with fewer tumours and less age pigment deposited in the brain. Detractors will say that the benefits simply point to the inadequacy of the standard diet of laboratory animals. It was also significant that the *maximum* lifespan for the strain did not change. An enhanced diet was simply allowing more of the mice to reap more of the time which is allotted to them by their genes.

There is a triad of antioxidant vitamins in the human diet. The name 'vitamin' is a misnomer, because, although vitamins are certainly vital, they are a chemically diverse group and not 'amines' after all. The signs of deficiency are all too familiar in malnourished peoples and are specific for each vitamin. Vitamin A is to night-blindness as B is to beri-beri, C to scurvy, D to rickets. What disease, then, does vitamin E prevent?

Vitamin E is particularly abundant in wheat cereals and has antioxidant properties. It mops up radicals before they damage vital parts of cells and is particularly effective in the protection of cell membranes. The most dramatic sign of E deficiency in rats is the build-up of substances which look suspiciously like age pigment in the muscles and uterus. This association with the reproductive organs gave vitamin E the reputation of being a fertility vitamin, but it is now acquiring celebrity status as the 'anti-ageing' vitamin, even though actual cases of acute deficiency are rather rare.

Vitamin C has also become a fashionable dietary supplement on the strength of its antioxidant actions. It has been credited with the power to protect against everything from the common cold to cancer when taken in sufficiently large amounts – far more than is needed to prevent scurvy. Linus Pauling, the Stanford chemist and twice winner of a Nobel Prize, was its principal advocate and took several grams every day until he died in 1994 at the grand old age of ninety-three.

To C and E we add a third antioxidant, vitamin A (available as beta-carotene in green plant matter). Manufacturers do just that, and the product combining them goes under the gimmicky acronym ACE. Beta-carotene is reputed to be a beneficial agent too, though a recent study of 30,000 people in Finland taking supplements for several years was unable to confirm any significant benefit. Antioxidants are undoubtedly important for protecting cells, but the biology of human disease and ageing is more complex than we like to think, and we should pause before buying anything claimed to be a panacea. It is surprising how long the megavitamin fad is persisting with no fully convincing proof of benefit, and since most vitamins are excreted in the urine, we can only safely say that it produces the most expensive urine in the world

Vitamin pills are sometimes necessary, but they can trivialize nutrition and are a poor substitute for a balanced diet with plenty of fresh fruit and vegetables. Diets can explain a good deal of the variation in some of the major diseases across the world, and much can be learned from comparing them. But we have to look to genetics to explain why the upper limit of the human lifespan is so constant across the globe.

• Chips off the Old Block?

A previous generation of gerontologists became preoccupied with reports of unexpectedly high numbers of male centenarians in isolated communities in Soviet Georgia and the Andes. The village people claimed that a local yoghurt and clear air were responsible for their privileged existence, but was it the environment or the genes? One of those who investigated was Zhores Medvedev, a Russian expatriate living in London. His biggest difficulty was to verify the ages of the old men, because there were no official records of birth dates. The claims began to look suspicious when the age distribution of the population was studied. If ten-year age bands from birth to 100 are piled on top of one another in normal communities, there should be a neat pyramid of numbers unless epidemic, migration or war has decimated a generation. But in the Georgian community there were far more very old males than females, and certainly more than there should have been in relation to the numbers in the age bands below.

Science had almost been hoodwinked, because cases of exceptional long life interest us all. The most celebrated hoax was the 'longest living Englishman', Thomas Parr, who died in 1635 at the alleged age of 152 and is buried among the good and great in Westminster Abbey. Parr was old, but not that old, and certainly no fool. He duped wealthy patrons into moving him to London, where he was exhibited like an exotic animal. He enjoyed a very agreeable life in the capital, wining and dining with his new friends while keeping his secret – if indeed he ever knew his date of birth.

Many explanations were proffered for Parr's long life. Some wondered whether his modest habits and roots in the countryside had given him an advantage. According to one view, a simple diet and a bucolic lifestyle had kept him well preserved, and his ruin was to be introduced to the polluted air and tempting fleshpots of metropolitan life. At his death, public curiosity was aroused because, according to ancient wisdom, healthy genital organs which have neither been used immorally or immoderately are good omens for a long life. William Harvey, then physician to King Charles I, was called on to perform the post-mortem examination, and a lengthy report was published afterwards.

> The organs of generation were healthy, the penis neither retracted nor extenuated, nor the scrotum filled with any serious infiltration, as happens so commonly among the decrepit; the testes, too, were sound and large; so that it seemed not improbable that the common report was true, viz. that he did public penance under a conviction for incontinence, after he had passed his hundred years; and his wife, whom he had married as a widow in his hundred-and-twentieth year did not deny that he had intercourse with her after the manner of other husbands with their wives, nor until twelve years back had he ceased to embrace her frequently. The cause of death seemed fairly referable to a sudden change in the non-naturals, the chief being connected with the change of air ... And then for one hitherto used to live on food unvaried in kind, and very simple in its nature, to be set at a table loaded with variety of viands, tempted not only to eat more than wont, but to partake of strong drink, it must needs fall out that the functions of all the natural organs would become deranged ... no wonder that the soul, little content with such a prison, took its flight.

Experience has made gerontologists wary of claims of exceptional longevity. As far as we know, there is no race or isolated community that is much more privileged than any other in this respect, given a similar standard of diet, housing and health care. This does not deny the importance of genetics for the individual lifespan, which helps to explain some human variations. It was the records of nineteenth-century clergymen and their families that first hinted that we can inherit a potentially long life along with worldly goods. Just as the height of our parents is a predictor of our own, so are their lifespans, if rather less so. If they lived to ripe old ages, we stand a good chance of following suit, and a good set of genes is the most precious endowment to pass down to our heirs. The world's longest-living woman, Jeanne Calment, got off to a good start since her parents lasted until they were eighty-six and ninety-three years old. Nature's experiments occasionally grant us revealing insights into the importance of the genetics of age. When an early human embryo splits, the identical twins live, on average, to within three years of each other, whereas non-identical twins growing up together in the same home differ by six years in lifespan.

The strength of the genetic influence has been studied in 7,000 American families. Where the parents had died at not less than eighty-one years, the subjects lived on average six years longer than when parents had died at sixty or less. A correlation between successive generations could be due as much to similar economic and social circumstances as to the sharing of genes, but in that study the genetic factors appeared to dominate. The Edinburgh-born inventor of the telephone, Alexander Graham Bell, had dabbled in this question, and speculated that lifespan was inherited only through our fathers. In the American survey, however, it was maternal age that showed the stronger correlation. Whether this was a spurious result is hard to say, though it is interesting to ponder the possible role of those mitochondrial genes which are passed down on our mother's side.

Whatever the correlation with genes, the lifespans of our parents and grandmothers provide only a rough guide to our prospects. For one thing, the generation gap in living conditions and medical care is greater than it used to be, and, for another, the packs of genes in our parents' egg and sperm were reshuffled before we were conceived. We are not simply chips off the old block like cuttings from trees. Whether we like the way we have turned out or not, we cannot change our genetic spots – and it will be some time, if ever, before gene therapy can remove all the blemishes.

Laboratory animals offer better opportunities for testing the genetic question. We can control their diet and environment throughout their lives, and modify the size of the gene pool by inbreeding. After forcing brother and sister mice into incestuous relationships for at least twenty generations, the offspring are more or less genetically uniform. Yet the lifespans of the members of an inbred strain still vary, even though they are more closely bunched than the original stock. It has been calculated that the lifespan is about 25 per cent determined by genetics – which leaves 75 per cent to lifestyle and environment.

As each strain becomes more and more inbred, the lifespans of different strains may drift apart, like pedigree dogs. This is because short-lived ones are more susceptible to fatal diseases which have an earlier onset, such as mammary or pituitary tumours and kidney disease in rodents. Long-lived strains have fewer genetic flaws and may have genes that increase resistance to the agents of disease. The same is likely to be true of humans as well. Families which boast of good genetic stock and record lifespans usually have a low frequency of heart disease.

Inbreeding may produce desirable traits for pedigree-fanciers and researchers but it encourages hidden genetic faults to surface. Some genes are known as 'dominant', because one copy is enough for their effects to be felt. If the gene is a harmful one, it could lead to disease or death as soon as it is turned on. On the other hand, two copies of a 'recessive' gene need to be present for it to have an effect – one on each member of the pairs of identical chromosomes (other than the sex chromosomes).

I learned this lesson as a schoolboy naturalist with an interest in badgers. Imagine my amazement to see an albino badger emerge ghost-like out of a dark wood on the outskirts of London. It was the only anomaly in the litter of three and was born to normal parents. 'Snowball' later mated with a normal sow and, to my disappointment, produced only normal offspring. The recessive gene had merely gone underground, however, and another albino turned up as a road victim some time later – which mystified the community because no one imagined a badger without stripes.

The albino gene is a harmless mutation in humans, provided that those affected avoid much exposure to bright sunlight. Most mutations are likely to be harmful because during the course of evolution the healthier genes have been selected and the faulty ones have been weeded out. Even so, each of us carries a few harmful genes. Most of us are not aware of them because of the dominating effect of a normal gene on the opposite chromosome, and only about 1 per cent of children are born with unmistakable genetic disease. But, if we marry a partner who carries the same harmful gene, there is a chance that our children will not only inherit the genes but develop the disease. The cystic-fibrosis gene is carried by 1 in 20 of the population and so there is a 20×20 probability of both partners being carriers. And, by the rules of Mendelian inheritance, 1 in 4 of their babies will carry both mutant genes – or 1 in 1,600 in the population, making this the most serious inherited genetic disorder.

Recessive genes tend to become unmasked in communities in which family marriages are encouraged, but the problem is all the more obvious for breeders of pedigree animals. Breeding stocks have to be ruthlessly culled to weed out individuals with harmful genes. Even so, the loss of genetic variety tends to reduce longevity and fertility. This decline in vigour can be reversed by outbreeding, and when members of different breeds of dogs or strains of mice are mated, the hybrid offspring are healthier, more fertile and live longer than either parent. Had there been only one or a few genes for long life, recovery of normal longevity would have been sporadic at best. On this evidence there are many genes affecting the lifespan, though we can pinpoint few of them at the moment.

• Blighted Genes

We know of far more genes which hasten death than ones that prolong life. Fresh mutations crop up all the time at a low frequency and the majority of these changes are undesirable. Errors sometimes occur spontaneously during cell division or as a result of exposure to harmful substances or radiation. Occasional mistakes are inevitable, and it is a greater wonder that the process of copying thousands of genes every time a cell divides is not more error-prone. Even when something does go wrong in the nucleus, there is a proof-reading mechanism for checking for mistakes and repairing the DNA which is the only molecule in our cells that can be repaired. But a few errors still get through the net.

The sporadic mutation in an ordinary body cell is of little consequence unless it affects the machinery for controlling growth and encourages cancer. Mutations that occur in a 'germ' cell – an egg or a sperm – are a different matter because their effects are passed down to the offspring to affect every cell in the body. Some are so serious that the embryo dies at such an early stage that the mother does not even know that she was pregnant. Others become apparent much later, unless they remain hidden as single-copy recessive genes.

Some genes have very specific effects. The cystic-fibrosis gene affects the clearance of mucus in the lungs, and the gene for sickle-cell anaemia alters haemoglobin in the blood cells, to name two of the more common ones. Others code for proteins that are present in many cell types and have a range of effects. The distinctive set of signs and symptoms caused by these so-called 'pleiotropic' genes is known as a syndrome, and progeria is one such syndrome with a dramatic outcome for its unfortunate victims.

Imagine a child who by the age of ten is already turning grey and bald and has wrinkled skin. By the teens, the heart and other internal organs are deteriorating fast, though the brain and IQ are mercifully unaffected. He or, less often, she, will not survive beyond twenty with the Hutchinson-Gilford syndrome, whereas those with the later-onset type, Werner's syndrome, last until fifty or sixty years of age, when they develop similar signs and die from heart disease. Since both syndromes are caused by a single, dominant mutation, one copy of the gene is enough for the full-blown disease. Fortunately, these premature-ageing syndromes are extremely rare.

Accelerated ageing in humans is not so much the compression of life history as a truncation of the adult phase of life. Were the condition a true parallel of the fast-forward lifestyles of our pets, puberty would have been correspondingly earlier and the characteristics would be identical to those of normal ageing; but that is not quite the case. George Martin of the University of Washington in Seattle has shown that progeroid syndromes mimic only about half of the normal characteristics of ageing, and those afflicted rarely suffer from diabetes or serious memory loss.

A few doctors achieve immortality by having a new disease named after them, though this is something of a dubious tribute. As a young man in the 1860s, George Huntington accompanied his father on the rounds of his family practice in Long Island, New York. One day they came upon 'mother and daughter, both tall, almost cadaverous; both bowing, twisting and grimacing'. When he took up a medical career later, this remembered experience led Huntington to study the inherited condition that became known as Huntington's disease. About 3,000 people are affected in Great Britain, and 100,000 more worldwide. One of the better-known sufferers, American folksinger Woody Guthrie, was incapacitated for the last fifteen years of his short life. Symptoms of premature ageing of the nervous system appear between thirty-five and forty-five years of age and rapidly prove fatal. Patients develop diabetes, brittle bones and memory loss, and exhibit the jerky movements that gave the disease its other name, 'chorea', from the Greek for 'dance'. So the gene responsible is a pleiotropic one too. The gene was identified after a long search, giving hope of early diagnosis and perhaps treatment one day. It has a curious repetitive motif – the more repeats are inherited, the earlier the disease sets in.

Alzheimer's disease needs little introduction because it is all too common. Between 30 and 50 per cent of the population are reckoned to be affected by eighty-five years old, or 2 million people in the USA alone, and everyone is at risk – from former presidents down. The tragedy is that its devastating effects on memory, intellect, personality and control of bodily functions eventually reduce the person to helplessness and round-the-clock care. The roots of the disease seem to lie in the tangles of nerve fibres and 'plaques' of amyloid which is a normal protein in the brain but is produced to excess in sufferers.

Alzheimer's disease is not inherited as a mutant gene, which denies a popular assumption that age changes are always a result of an underproduction of something or of the miscoding for a protein. Since most hormones and enzymes are as active from an old body as a young one, the genes have presumably been preserved unblemished by the years. Some genes become more active and some less with age, and many simply carry on as before. So there is no universal pattern, and changes in gene action in old age are more subtle and less dramatic than during the development of an embryo. Nevertheless, there are some changes that we can all see.

By age forty there is both increased and decreased activity of the keratin gene responsible for making hair in different parts of the body, especially in men. Longer, thicker hairs sprout from eyebrows, the nose and other surfaces of the body, while hairs on the scalp become scarcer and scarcer. Some men of Middle Eastern origin grow conspicuous plumes from the margin of their ears after thirty years of age. The so-called *hairy pinna* gene is rather unusual, for we know of few genes that have a late onset of action, and this is the more interesting for being associated with masculinity. Changes in the activity of other cells alter the thickness, suppleness and pigmentation of the skin. And degenerative changes in the eye affect the crystallin proteins of the lens and lead to cataracts.

None of these examples abets one of the old chestnuts of gerontology which is the assumption that mutations simply accumulate with age. This 'somatic-mutation' theory puts the phenomenon of senescence entirely down to chance. Through being bathed in background radiation and a sea of potentially harmful chemicals in everything from our diet to the air we breathe, we cannot escape threats to the integrity of our genetic apparatus. But, despite much research effort, remarkably little evidence has been obtained of the 'somatic-mutation' effect, except as a cause of sporadic cancer. Perhaps this should not surprise us, because the theory requires both copies of the gene to mutate, which is statistically improbable. If the theory were true, fruit flies with three sets of genes would live longer than those with the normal complement of two, and gall wasps with two would live longer than those with just one. In fact none of these lifespans bears any relation to the number of sets of genes in the insects.

There is little doubt that mistakes are made more frequently when chromosomes pair and separate during cell division. As any Scottish lad or lass knows, it is easy to get pulled away from a partner when dancing Strip-the-Willow and end up in the wrong row. When the equivalent happens in a cell, the error is just as difficult or clumsy to rectify. One of the two new cells will carry off an extra chromosome with its thousands of genes at the expense of the other cell, and both may suffer in consequence.

The normal complement of chromosomes in a human cell is forty-six, but the numbers of cells with forty-seven or forty-five chromosomes creep up slowly as we get older. This is a particularly serious problem in the germ cell because a chromosome imbalance will be inherited by every cell of the embryo. When an extra copy of chromosome number 21 is present, the baby will suffer from Down's syndrome which is far more common in the babies of older mothers. Besides the handicaps that are all too well known, almost all the patients will have Alzheimer's disease by age fifty, probably because chromosome 21 carries the amyloid gene. With a frequency of 1 in 700 deliveries, Down's syndrome is the major cause of progeria.

• Cellular Immortality

Some cells become so committed to a special role in the body that they lose the ability to multiply and so to replace themselves. For instance, it would be physically difficult for a sciatic nerve cell to divide since its slender fibre stretches for half a metre down the leg. Likewise, it is impossible for a red blood cell to produce progeny, because it lacks nucleus. As we shall see in Chapter 9, the egg cell cannot multiply until after it is fertilized to become an embryo – a fact which makes menopause inevitable. The loss of a significant number of cells spells trouble for the future, and this is likely to have more widespread and serious repercussions if they are nerve cells, even for animals with a simple brain. Fruit flies carrying the mutations *drop-dead* and *dunce* have fewer nerve cells and die prematurely. *Dunce* flies may not be quite as dim as their name implies, because they compensate for the same disadvantage by mating more frequently than normal.

Human brains are so large that the loss of a few cells goes unnoticed and is in fact natural. It is not easy to count the numbers of cells in an organ which contains about a thousand billion (10^{12}). Sampling methods have not always taken account of shrinkage as the brain slowly dries out with age. Improved methods now show that we lose cells in our cerebral hemispheres, cerebellum and hippocampus, but not in all parts of the brain. The oft-quoted estimate of 100,000 brain cells lost every day is nonsense. The pattern of brain-cell loss also differs between species, and there is no cell type or location in which attrition always occurs. Perhaps this should give cause for optimism that a way might be found one day to avert the decline, but for the moment neurologists are grappling with the question of why some people are more vulnerable to memory loss and disability than others. Irrespective of genetic diseases, some people have larger endowments of cells at birth, which later on could provide the advantage of a buffer against ageing and postpone the onset of disability and memory loss. A few post-mortem cases have shown that some people had Alzheimer-type changes in the brain without suffering from the handicap of dementia. They evidently had the advantages of a larger reserve of nerve cells to cope with the changes.

Most nerve cells are made to last a lifetime, but cells in the blood, skin, intestines and anywhere exposed to physical or chemical danger have a short life and are replaced frequently by stem cells which are the equivalents of the growth zone or cambium in plant stems. Each stem cell divides into two asymmetric daughter cells such that one of the new ones replaces the specialist that has been lost while its sibling remains the same as before. This strategy ensures that stem cells survive for as long as they are needed for replenishing the working cells lost by the natural processes of wear and tear. Stem cells both in skin and in bone marrow, to name only two, have not worn out even at the end of life, and they can still provide serviceable grafts for young individuals. But, if they can outlast their owner, are they potentially immortal?

Alexis Carrel, a French expatriate working at the Rockefeller Institute in New York in the 1920s and 1930s, believed they were. He obtained fibroblasts (fibre cells) from chick embryos and cultured them in Petri dishes with a nutrient medium prepared from chick-embryo extracts. Once the base of the dish was full, he split the cultures into two and allowed the cells to resume growing until they had filled the dishes again, when they were split once more. His technicians repeated this process for three decades, by which time the cells had divided thousands of times more than could have happened in a chicken. Normally cautious, Carrel said, 'It may be considered certain, therefore, that fibroblasts will proliferate indefinitely and the fibroblasts *in vitro* were no longer subjected to the influence of time as they are when living within the organism.' This gave rise to the belief that cells do not have an intrinsic age programme but deteriorate only because of secondary influences from the experiences of living, such as diet, hormones and external agents. Only in 1960 did Carrel's error become apparent. Evidently, fresh cells had been slipping though the sieve used to prepare the culture medium, making the long labour a farce and leading gerontology astray.

Leonard Hayflick, at that time a cell biologist at the Wistar Institute in Philadelphia, set the record straight, and he, as much as anyone, can be called the father of the cell biology of ageing. He carefully repeated Carrel's experiments using fibroblasts from human embryos and found that they divided for only a year in culture, or about fifty times. This was a definite upper limit which was unaffected by attempts to improve the culture environment. Even though the numbers of divisions exceeded those expected in the lifetime of a human body, the 'Hayflick limit' was a biological brick wall of some sigificance. Fibroblasts obtained from adults and children only managed about ten or twenty divisions, according to age, whereas those from patients with progeria divided even fewer times. The 'limit' for a newborn animal depended on the maximum lifespan of the species: in the giant tortoise 150 divisions were possible, whereas mouse fibroblasts could barely manage ten. Hayflick had firmly established that cells have some kind of intrinsic programme, even if its full significance for ageing is still debated.

Each cell type has its own inbuilt biological clock which is set according to the cell's *raison d'être*. A strict ration of cell divisions runs out early for the brain, heart and eggs, but the stem cells of the bone marrow, skin and sperm divide far more frequently to meet the needs of the body. Long survival or huge productivity is not necessarily an appropriate goal for every cell. If it serves the interests of helping the body to survive and produce offspring, it may be better for some cells to cease dividing or even to commit suicide. Sometimes the reason is clear, as when a red blood cell lacks a nucleus, but what is true of individual cells can apply equally to whole organs. No organ ages faster than the placenta, for there is no point investing in something that is doomed after nine months in the womb.

One of the ways in which cells count time is by snipping off the caps or telomeres at the ends of chromosomes bit by bit. Loss of telomeres is inconsequential at first because they don't code for proteins, but when chromosomes are eroded by many divisions the genes are exposed to harm and the vitality of the cell is affected. Tumour cells and the stem cells that make sperm possess a special enzyme, telomerase, which puts the caps back on chromosomes and helps to fend off the mortalizing effects of growth.

When the bonds of the 'Hayflick limit' have been loosened, cells can multiply fast and ignore the social norms. The antisocial properties of a cancer are its own downfall if it kills the body, but if it is removed to a culture dish it can divide more freely – and almost indefinitely. The HeLa cell line has been cultivated since the 1950s, when it was obtained from a cancer patient (Helen Lake) who died long ago. The genetic change responsible for the immortality of the cancer cell is not a dominant trait, because fusing this cell with a normal one produces a mortal product. When a conflict arises in a cell, health and obedience rule over disease and chaos.

The potential damage if growth runs out of control may be one explanation for the existence of a Hayflick limit in cells. Natural selection may have favoured the evolution of a mechanism for restricting growth, which could swing into action when required to halt a cancer in its tracks after a certain number of cell divisions. Regrettably, this is an imperfect mechanism, as it often fails to save the body from the growth and spread of malignant cells.

We know little about the nature and number of the genes that set the quota of cell divisions for each cell type. Certainly there is more than one, and if that is the case for an individual cell it is all the more true that the survival of whole animals is not determined by a single gene. If that were the case, an 'immortal' mutant would have turned up by now. According to Caleb Finch, 'There is no evidence for a single gene or cluster of genes that uniquely determines the duration of the adult phase in any species.' Anyone waiting for the Human Genome Project to come up with a simple answer should not hold their breath. We may be little wiser about the biology of ageing once we can read all the genes because the greater complexity lies beyond the DNA code, at the level of how the proteins behave within cells and how cells talk to one another by hormonal and other signals.

The longevities of even closely related species can be quite different, depending on which genes have been selected for action. Were it possible to rewind life history like a videotape, we might find that it was possible to replay it with a somewhat different course and outcome. The world of social insects illustrates this particularly well. The length of life of castes of bees is enormously variable, even though they all possess identical sets of genes. Female workers live for six weeks in summer, or rather longer in winter, until they have completed some 500 flying miles. A queen living in the hive lays eggs for six or more years, but, once the sperm stored since her nuptial flight is exhausted, the workers commit regicide. The reason for the longevity gap lies in the diet in infancy. Any ordinary grub fed on Royal Jelly could also grow into a princess, but this regal diet would not help a worker to live longer if she stole it when fully grown.

The properties of the jelly are fascinating, but even more wonderful is the flexibility of the genetic programme that makes individuals so different in form, behaviour and longevity according to the needs of the hive. The greater challenge for research is not the discovery of new diets or hormones to prolong life but to delve into the question of how these programmes work and what interventions into the ageing process are possible.

Gerontologists cannot agree on how many genes are involved in ageing. Estimates vary from a few score in the programmed lifespans of annual plants and animals like antechinuses and some insects, to hundreds or thousands in humans. Not all of the genes are life-promoting like SOD though, and recent studies give credence to the old idea of 'death genes'.

• Death Genes

Cell death has had a hand in shaping us from when we were in our mother's womb. Far more cells were formed in our brains, muscles, ovaries and elsewhere than were needed for the working life ahead. Even our hands started off like clumsy paddles, and cells had to die before the digits could form. All these changes were due to a programme of cell death, and without it we would have remained as formless blobs of tissue.

Cells do not make their fateful decision at random but have a suicide pact under strict social control. Martin Raff in London believes that death is the default programme of every cell. They would all die but for the hormones and signals from neighbouring cells which restrain them from switching on genes to make enzymes that chop DNA into useless fragments and kill them. So convinced is he, that he has offered a reward of £1,000 to anyone who can disprove his theory. If he is right, suicide genes are dangerous baggage – like carrying a wad of Semtex in your pocket – because, long after doing their job in shaping the body, they can still act. Why court disaster by taking such a chance?

During the course of diagnostic work as an Edinburgh patholo-gist, Andrew Wyllie has studied thousands of tumour specimens under the microscope. Dead cells are not unusual at the centre of tumours, but one day he noticed some that had unaccountably died, despite being well nourished and apparently clear of immune cells. Wyllie suspected that a genetic programme lay behind this apparent suicide of cancer cells. The process was given the name 'apoptosis' by a professor of Greek, meaning the fall of autumn leaves which is programmed by a seasonal change in plant hormones.

Death genes are, by and large, for our good, because it is better to carry ammunition for plucking out rogue cells rather than run the risk of ruining the whole body. When a cell is invaded by viruses, it is prudent to dispose of it by switching on death genes if this avoids the infection spreading. The same rationale applies to cells that become tumorous. One of the most important guardians of cells is a gene called $p53$ by its discoverer, David Lane of Dundee. It is like a genetic policeman which becomes active only when there is trouble brewing. If the DNA is damaged or mutates, which is often the case in cancer cells and after radiation, $p53$ switches on, either to help repair the damage or to kill the cell. When the activity of $p53$ was knocked out in mice by gene-targeting technology, the animals were far more resistant to radiation than normal but they all died shortly after puberty because cancerous cells arose spontaneously. Unfortunately, even our cells are not engineered to perfection, and $p53$ often mutates and is then helpless to protect us against uncontrolled spreading. This often happens in tumours of the bowel, breast and lung. If ways can be devised to rectify the death programme by gene therapy, tumours might be despatched more effectively and without the dreadful side-effects of chemotherapy and radiotherapy.

This paints a rosy picture for apoptosis but is not the whole of the story, as other mortalizing genes have been found with different effects in other species. One rather paradoxical gene which speeds up senescence has been found by Tom Johnson, a geneticist at the University of Colorado. Mutants of the nematode worm called *C. elegans* age at only half the normal rate and consequently live twice as long. He named the gene *age-1*, in expectation that other 'age' genes would eventually be found – as in fact they have been. Most mutations are harmful, or neutral at best, and so this one is remarkable for extending life, implying that the normal *age-1* gene must have been responsible for keeping the lifespan in check.

This is the first 'gerontogene' to be identified and, though the worms are only very distantly related to humans, we do well to heed their genetics because time and again genes involved at crucial stages in life-history development have been found to have cousins in higher animals. Genes which proved to be valuable in the remote evolution-ary past continue to serve posterity to this day. Many of the genes of mouse and man are similar, and some are shared with invertebrate animals. The words of Friedrich Nietzsche in *Thus Spoke Zarathustra* are fulfilled in biology: 'You have made your way from worm to man, and much in you is still worm.' What this means we shall have to wait and see, but the discovery opens new avenues for tracking down ageing genes and throws up new questions.

The truncation of life by a native gene, on the one hand, and the failure of genes to provide full protection against free radicals and other noxious substances, on the other, seem to shake our faith in the optimistic theory that evolutionary selection optimizes the powers of survival and fertility. What at first appears odd turns out to be more rational on closer inspection. The mutant worms that were living longer were only a fifth as fertile as their normal counterparts. It seems that fertility triumphs over longevity when they are set against one another. This remarkable conclusion has provided a clue for deciphering the riddle of why ageing exists, and has become a cornerstone of modern biological theory.

CHAPTER 5　**The Great Trade-Off**

Pluralitas non est ponenda sine necessitate – plurality should not be assumed unnecessarily.

William of Occam

• The Decline of Natural Selection

Darwin was too preoccupied with other matters to bother about the origin of ageing, but it troubled the co-author of the famous 1858 paper which launched the theory of evolution. Metaphysical questions were of great interest to Alfred Russel Wallace, who had even dabbled in spiritualism from time to time. He pondered why something as obviously undesirable as ageing should have evolved in so many creatures. Could it be biologically good for the species if it is bad for the individual? Ageing seemed to be the joker in the pack: it didn't play by the rules of the evolutionary game. Individuals with the longest lifespans should come out on top because they would leave more offspring to carry forward their longevity genes. Natural selection should encourage species to drift towards longer lives.

The idea of inexorable progress appealed to Wallace's socialist sympathies but, in this particular case, ever lengthening lifespans could result in diminishing returns and eventually spell disaster for the species. If old individuals no longer gave way to the young by obligingly dying off, there would be more social tension as the habitat became overcrowded and food supplies were exhausted. The young would be at a competitive disadvantage in finding the best feeding and nesting places and in winning mates compared with their wiser elders. The old would ruin the species!

Wallace believed that ageing must have an evolutionary rationale, and in the late 1860s he penned some thoughts to August Weismann, Professor of Zoology at Freiburg and one of Prussia's leading biologists:

> when one or more individuals have provided a sufficient number of successors they themselves, as consumers of nourishment in a constantly increasing degree, are an injury to those successors. Natural selection therefore weeds them out, and in many cases favours such races as die almost immediately after they have left successors.

In other words, Wallace suspected that evolution favoured races of animals and plants in which the old are sacrificed for the sake of the young. He knew from field studies that such altruistic behaviour was common in nature. Many insects are destined to die after a short breeding period. Some cannot even feed as adults because their jaws do not develop. The Australian antechinus would have bolstered Wallace's hunch, but its extraordinary life lay undiscovered for another century.

Wallace thought that senescence was just as much a characteristic of a species as, say, the antlers of a deer or the stripes of a badger. Each species had a definite upper limit to life at a given stage in its evolutionary history. But this was not set for ever; it could be in the interests of the species to truncate the lifespan if this increased the success of the population as a whole. These ideas added shreds of comfort to the otherwise glum facts of ageing. The elderly bowed out to allow a younger and more vigorous generation to thrive.

Weismann had been thinking along similar lines. He agreed that ageing existed because the body was 'designed' with built-in obsolescence. The disabilities and diseases of old age were purposeful safeguards which helped the species as a whole to compete in the struggle for existence. 'Worn-out individuals are not only valueless to the species, but they are even harmful, for they take the place of those which are sound.' This was a teleological argument but it had a strong intuitive appeal.

The notion that a characteristic evolves because it is 'good for the species' still sways popular thinking. Darwin himself never held that view, but it is still used to rationalize apparent acts of altruism among animals. Lapwings put themselves at risk by feigning a broken wing to draw a passer-by or a marauding fox away from their nests. And bees sting honey-robbers even though they eviscerate themselves in the process. An individual might be sacrificed, like a pawn in a game of chess, for the sake of the whole side. The more successful the tactic, the more altruistic the chessmen would become. Each unselfish act would give the side a chance to play again in the game of survival.

Modern biologists are cynical about some of these rather senti-mental interpretations of nature. According to the Oxford zoologist Richard Dawkins acts of apparent altruism are a sham and the underlying motive is always selfish. These acts evolved because, in the evolutionary way of things, it pays individuals to look after themselves and those who are genetically related. If cooperative behaviour helps a clan to survive and breed, the more these traits will spread in the population assuming, of course, that the behaviour is heritable.

These are hard conclusions to swallow, and an often bitter battle has been fought over them. On one side are those who argue that natural selection favours behaviour that is good for the group: on the other are those who believe that the individual is the supreme unit of selection. In this academic struggle for supremacy the Dawkinites have generally gained the upper hand. Evolution is driven by the selfish ambition of individuals to pass on their genes most successfully, whatever the personal cost. Self-sacrifice is not so much a noble act as a gambit to achieve genetic advantage. The political implications of this conclusion may be unwelcome to many people, but we must accept the biological evidence as we find it.

Weismann's arguments about geriatric biocide were flawed because they assumed what they set out to prove. He claimed that ageing evolved because animals get 'worn-out', but he failed to explain why they deteriorate in the first place. We have already seen examples of species that can live for hundreds or even thousands of years without signs of decay. Their construction and repair mechanisms must be nearly perfect to stave off decay processes for so long. Why isn't every living thing constructed likewise?

To be fair to Weismann, he was aware of short-comings in his argument and set about correcting them, though he was handicapped by the hazy notions of inheritance which prevailed in his day. Later in life he came to doubt that senescence was either purposeful or advantageous for the species. He imagined that, if individuals lived long enough, natural selection would cease to maintain quality assurance over the various cell and organ functions, allowing defects to creep in. If these defects were heritable, they would be passed on to the next generation rather than being lost. He thought ageing was rather like the useless eyes of a blind cave fish – a lingering vestige.

Weismann laid some important foundations for future theoretical work, but his lasting contribution was to point out that ageing is not immutable. This countered those who were pontificating that the phenomenon was divinely instituted and beyond the reach of science. Unfortunately, gerontology turned into a cul-de-sac at the start of the twentieth century – as we shall see in the following chapters. Wildly optimistic hopes about reversing senility led to a fad for rejuvenation therapy. Clinics sprang up everywhere, giving hope to old men longing to reverse the ravages of time. Research into ageing which had commanded the attention of some of the best scientific brains of the day now fell into disrepute. Gerontology was no longer a safe and respectable subject on which to launch a scientific career.

It was not until the 1950s, more than forty years after Weismann's death, that the subject began to be rehabilitated. One of those responsible was the zoologist Peter Medawar, though his contribution to gerontology was more theoretical than experimental. He set about unravelling this unsolved riddle of biology in an intellectual *tour de force* worthy of a Greek philosopher.

Medawar accepted the logic that ageing is an evolved characteristic and not simply determined by the laws of physics. He pointed out more clearly than anybody before that evolutionary selection pressures lose their keen edge as animals get older. In other words, the main force for improving the survival power of the body falters with age. There is nothing particularly mysterious about this idea – it is simply a matter of statistics because, in terms of population structure, the older the age group, the smaller its size.

Taking the example of the garden robin once again, the chance of surviving from year to year is only fifty-fifty. It follows that for every 1,000 birds aged one to two years old there will only be about sixteen older than seven, so most of the reproductive effort in the population is made by younger individuals. The vast majority of parents are young. This must be true of all animals and plants, irrespective of whether or not the fertility of individuals declines with age. This rule would also apply to potentially immortal species, because even a perfect body will die accidentally sooner or later. Only in our generation do we find that older individuals are becoming more common than younger ones, but that is a special case and another story.

Since most babies are born to young mothers and fathers, these parents have most impact on the future course of evolution. Some of them will be sufficiently vigorous or lucky to reproduce for longer than others, but it is merit as a young parent that counts most of all. These individuals carry forward genes that favour good health and fertility in future generations of young parents. By sheer weight of numbers, their descendants overwhelmingly influence the future evolutionary development of the species. As the headwaters supply only a trickle to a great river compared with the volume of all the sources downstream, so the impact of older individuals on evolutionary change is slim. Any influence they had would be swamped by the majority, even if they had superlative genetic qualities.

Here is an illustration of Medawar's logic. Let us imagine that a genetic novelty turns up as a result of a chance mutation in an individual. Its single effect is to improve resistance to disease in young animals. The offspring of this parent will have an advantage compared to their peers and are more likely to be successful in producing babies. These, in turn, will pass on the gene and its advantage to their offspring which will become all the more numerous. In this way the 'good' gene multiplies and spreads rapidly through the population as success breeds more success.

Now let us assume that the genetic novelty cannot exert its beneficial effects until late in life. Since there will be no advantage in having the gene when young, carriers will not survive any better. And the few that last long enough to enjoy the benefits of a late-acting gene will produce too few late babies to have much impact on the gene pool of the next generation. Natural selection is, therefore, sapped of its strength when it comes to encouraging good genes that have a delayed action.

Medawar's theory of evolution favouring beneficial genes that act early in life is a neat explanation of why we are at our most vigorous when young. Old age undoubtedly brings some major advantages – experience for finding the best places to eat and shelter, and immunological wisdom for throwing off infections. But these count for less in evolutionary currency than fitness when young.

So much for good genes. Most mutations, however, are 'bad' because animals are already genetically well adapted to their environments after millions of years of evolutionary selection. Sporadic mutations which crop up in eggs and sperms will never be passed on if they prove fatal before the individual reaches adulthood. Many examples exist – from Hutchinson-Gilford progeria to the tragic 'bubble-boy' born with the SCID (Severe Combined Immuno Deficiency) mutation that left him without an immune system.

If the 'bad' gene is not expressed until later, its reproductive disadvantage depends on when it begins to affect the chances of mating and raising babies. Huntington's disease does not affect patients until past the age of thirty, so this menace may be passed down to children and does not depend on fresh mutations cropping up all the time. Genes that delay their action until much later are theoretically even more persistent. The later they are expressed, the less likelihood that they will be weeded out by natural selection over the course of time.

So, what about bad genes which act only after the age at which the species normally survives in the wild – or after the menopause in humans? There can be no reproductive penalty for possessing such a gene if it takes effect after the family size has been completed. Natural selection fails to oppose it, and so it can gain a footing in the population and become part of the normal genome. By the same token, natural selection does not actively encourage good genes that do not operate until late ages. Thus may the mysterious phenomenon of ageing, which philosophers have pondered for centuries, be explained on the basis of straightforward arithmetic.

Nineteenth-century biologists had speculated that senescence evolved in the interest of the species, but it appears to have crept on to life's stage by default. Medawar thought that genes carrying unfavourable effects have drifted into the later scenes of life, bringing the play to an abrupt end. This is very different to the somatic-mutation theory which holds that each of us accumulates genetic faults over the course of our lifespan. Grasping the evolutionary theory of ageing requires us to imagine genes, favourable or other-wise, spreading across the population from generation to generation according to their effects on breeding success. The process does not have a goal, nor does it ever reach a final state, because there is always the possibility of a change of circumstances selecting this or that gene. But, according to Medawar, we end up with what he called a 'genetic dustbin' of unfavourable effects late in life and, because natural selection fails to oppose them, the species is stuck with the genes responsible.

Accordingly, the effects of good genes acting at the beginning of the lifespan could be quite independent of bad ones acting at the other end. Excellent health and outstanding physical stamina in adolescence are not necessarily good omens for a vigorous old age. Nor are the prospects of long life inevitably dismal for the sickly youth. Such thoughts bring quiet satisfaction to those of us who notice that our more athletic classmates are now sporting a bulging waistline in middle age. A tortoise may at last overtake a hare!

Medawar had neatly explained why we are most vigorous when young and why late-acting genes are tolerated in the genome. But his theory failed to address the question of time-scale, or when it is getting 'late' in the lifespan. Why is two years late for a mouse and not for a human being? And why do some animals age gradually while others burn out rapidly in a big bang? Was the evolutionary theory of ageing to founder on these rocks?

Shortly before Christmas 1957, George Williams, then at the University of Michigan, published a theoretical paper in the *Journal of Evolution* that tackled the shortcomings in Medawar's theory. He suggested that some of the key genes in senescence have both good and bad effects at different ends of the lifespan. As we have seen, genes having more than one effect are called 'pleiotropic', and many examples exist in clinical syndromes. What was original about Williams's contribution was the idea that these effects may be expressed at different times of life. Whether the gene is, on balance, more good than bad depends on how long an individual might last.

One of the most familiar pleiotropic genes produces sickle-cell anaemia. This disease is widespread in Africa and the Arabian peninsula and occurs when the haemoglobin gene miscodes just one of the amino acids in this vital protein. The condition is dangerous because the blood cells change from a disc to a sickle shape, which makes them liable to block the tiny capillary vessels. Those who are unfortunate enough to carry two copies of the gene die in childhood.

People who carry only one copy of the abnormal gene are much luckier because they are more resistant in childhood to tertian malaria and its fatal complication, cerebral malaria. A harmful gene has persisted and spread through populations in areas of endemic malaria because carriers have a survival, and therefore a reproductive, advantage. Where malaria is absent, so is the gene, because natural selection opposes it. For example, when malaria was endemic among the oasis people of Saudi Arabia, a quarter of the population had the sickle-cell trait, whereas the Bedouin of the same region have never had a serious malaria problem and rarely carry the sickle-cell gene. The sickle-cell gene is not an isolated example. There is a family of pleiotropic genes responsible for the so-called lipid-storage diseases. Despite the name, they have little to do with obesity: they are associated with enzyme abnormalities which cause fats, or lipids, to be deposited inappropriately in brain and other cells rather than being processed by normal metabolism. Tay-Sach's is the most serious of this family of diseases and is usually fatal in infancy. Most of these enzyme mutations and their disease effects are rare except among Ashkenazi Jews. Since they are caused by independent mutations, why should lightning strike these people so often? The favoured explanation is that carriers have a greater resistance to tuberculosis and bubonic plague. This is of little value today, but may have improved survival in the European ghettos of the Middle Ages.

Evolution is guilty of ageism, because genes that are favourable in the young are preferred. Williams predicted that 'natural selection may be said to be biased in favour of youth over old age whenever a conflict of interest arises'. Genes persist in the population when any undesirable effects are outweighed by a reproductive advantage. In other words, a trade-off operates across the length of the lifespan between successful reproduction at one end versus disease and disability at the other. Even a small benefit in youth can counterbalance a serious disadvantage that emerges only in old age. This genetic tension has been called antagonistic pleiotropy. One of the attractions of this theory is that it accounts for the different lengths of life in animals. Longevity depends on the balance of the trade-offs between reproduction and survival – and it was this balancing act which led to the evolution of ageing.

Williams did not have any genetic or experimental proof, so he presented a simple illustration of his theory. Imagine a gene, he said, that encourages more calcium to be deposited in bones at young ages. This gene would strengthen the skeleton and probably improve the prospect of successful breeding. Yet, if the same gene continued to act throughout life, it might prove harmful in the end. Calcification of other parts of the body, such as the arteries and kidneys, would eventually have dire effects on the circulation and general health. To my knowledge, no one has discovered such a gene – though it is plausible enough.

A great deal of effort and ingenuity has gone into testing the genetic theories proposed by Medawar and Williams. As so often happens in science, the theorists turned their ploughs to new furrows, leaving others to examine the pickings. It has proved to be difficult to look inside Medawar's 'genetic dustbin', and such experimental evidence as exists for late-acting mutations is untidy. If pleiotropic genes are largely responsible for the ills of human ageing, we should find examples among the genes which affect immunity and suscepti-bility to cancer from hormonal effects. This search is still under way, but general evidence for their existence is turning up and will be described in another chapter. The theory of antagonistic pleiotropy is turning out to be an undeniable triumph.

• Fruitful Flies

Mike Rose boasts like a proud grandfather about his amazing fruit flies. Working at the University of California in Irvine, he has produced the Methuselahs of the bug world. The tiny fruit fly is an ideal subject for juggling the genes of senescence because it has a short generation interval and can be 'cultured' in large numbers. Genetic changes can therefore sweep through generations of flies very quickly when biologists overrule natural selection in the labora-tory by picking the traits that interest them.

If trade-offs exist between reproduction and ageing, as Williams had predicted, flies that are bred from old parents should live longer because they carry genes favouring longevity. If only old flies are allowed to reproduce, their genes will tend to become fixed in the population whereas those genes responsible for fertility and vigour early in life will be suppressed. Rose and his colleagues divided their stock of outbred flies into two groups which were kept under identical conditions but bred separately. One group served as the 'control', as it was allowed to breed *ad libitum* like normal flies. As expected, the lifespan and fecundity of this group was stable from generation to generation. The second group was bred only from eggs that were laid towards the end of reproductive life. This arrangement was repeated for fifteen generations in their first set of experiments, although the results were becoming apparent long before the end. After a few generations, flies bred from older mothers were living and breeding longer. The researchers were able to collect eggs slightly later each time round, so extending the generation gap. But those living longer paid a price in reduced fertility and produced fewer eggs than either the controls or their ancestors.

It appears that the life history of these flies had been telescoped. The flies had not changed in either size or appearance and were eating as much as controls, yet they were tougher. They were more resistant to starvation, desiccation and alcohol, and they could fly longer. After a few generations, the ageing slope had become sufficiently shallow that the maximum lifespan had increased by some 30 per cent, and there was no sign of a limit being reached by continuing the breeding programme.

Rose's experiments satisfied Williams's predictions. By artificially selecting late breeders, he had reversed the tendency of natural selection to favour the young rather than their elders. The trade-off of advantages was tipped towards longer survival at the cost of poorer fertility. For practical reasons, it was easier to select from older mothers rather than fathers, but offspring of both sexes benefited equally, so the advantages were not limited to genes involved with the ovaries or those on the sex chromosomes.

These experiments are among the most dramatic and elegant in gerontology. They have dispelled any doubts that longevity is heritable, and give impetus to efforts to track down the genes responsible. The life history of a species is not as immutable as we had once assumed.

Fascinating though they are, these results have no immediate practical implications for ourselves. The doubling of life expectancy in this century is due to improved living conditions and better protection against the ailments of childhood. In no way does it parallel the inherited changes in Rose's fruit flies. Were our ancestors to be reborn now, they too could expect to live some seventy or eighty years like ourselves. Were our children to be transported back to the Victorian era, or to parts of the world where comparable conditions still exist, they would suffer a reversal of fortunes. They could expect to live, on average, for no more than fifty years. The demographic shift in human lifespan has not been built into our genes and is consequently insecure. Rose's fruit flies, on the other hand, can rest assured that they possess a genetic privilege that is theirs for good. The change is quite different from the longer lives of animals that are kept cool or given a low-calorie diet. These cannot pass the benefits down to their offspring because such effects are due to impermanent physiological changes rather than to genetic novelty.

The discovery of a means of extending the lifespan carries much more scientific significance than identifying mechanisms that shorten it. There are many ways of truncating life that do not necessarily accelerate the intrinsic ageing process. But something fundamental has been touched when longevity is prolonged, and we are getting a little warmer in the search for the causes of senescence.

Some people may question the value of studying artificially created variants, on the grounds that they bear little, if any, relation to the real world of nature. This is a fair comment about laboratory experiments, but not a serious criticism on this occasion because trade-offs have been found among wild fruit flies too. On Hawaii there is a species which has a natural variant with an abnormal abdomen, designated '*aa*', which has a shorter lifespan than normal. This disadvantage is offset by its ability to produce more juvenile hormone early on, and hence more eggs at younger ages. The drought-resistance of these variants is no better than that of normal flies but, by breeding earlier, more of them are productive in arid years. In wet years they are at a competitive disadvantage and their fortunes go into reverse.

A group of American gerontologists planned to breed a Methuselah mouse using Rose's strategy to clinch the pleiotropy theory for mammals and open opportunities to track down genes responsible for human ageing. There are far more genes in common between mouse and man than differ between them. At a cost of $10 million over a decade, the project would admittedly have been expensive for biology, but peanuts compared with 'Big Science' in physics. A recent bid for funding was turned down because the authorities chose to support a number of smaller projects rather than the one big one. This is a pity, though the evidence of trade-offs is now so well established that identifying a mammal in which a trade-off occurs would be the icing on the cake.

Antagonistic pleiotropy has become a cornerstone of gerontology, but it takes more than one stone to make a wall. We should beware of falling into the temptation of latching on to a single attractive theory and forgetting the fact that the majority of genes are favourable for life at all ages. With pleiotropy, however, you only need a few genes to account for many of the phenomena of senescence as well as its timing and, more intriguingly, these genes often have roles in reproduction.

• Disposable Soma

One of Weismann's most enduring evolutionary theories was that ageing emerged only when a species had reached a certain degree of complexity. In the simplest creatures, there is little or no division of labour between the parts of the body, and most cells have the complete repertoire of functions. They absorb food, excrete waste, move the body from place to place, sense its surroundings, and reproduce – and all at the same time if necessary. More complex animals have cells set aside for these special tasks – glands, kidneys, muscles and nerves, and so on. Each cell type has its own unique protein composition as a result of switching on a particular combination of genes. Weismann thought that once the degree of specialization had passed a certain point, reproductive ability was lost, and this is sometimes true.

117

He called the parts excluded from reproduction the 'soma', to distinguish them from the eggs and sperm, or germ cells. The soma is like a ship which is subject to rust and engine failure, whereas the germ cells are the lifeboats, carrying the precious cargo of genes to the safety of another vessel. The eggs and sperm are the threads of life connecting one generation with another, and Weismann would have agreed with Samuel Butler's famous dictum that 'a hen is only an egg's way of making another egg'.

This dichotomy of body parts presented a dilemma. If the somatic cells were just the mortal carriers of uncorrupted germ cells, how could both types of cell emerge from the same fertilized egg? Weismann found that, in some species, a special patch of cytoplasm in the egg, or 'germplasm', was reserved for making germ cells, while the rest was destined for somatic development. From generation to generation, the somatic and germ cell lineages were kept separate, and never did the twain meet. Germplasm had made only germ cells from time immemorial. This theory came to be known, rather grandly, as 'the doctrine of immortal germplasm', and is about as close as biology has come to Calvinistic predestination.

We now know that the fate of different patches of cytoplasm in the eggs of mammals, birds and many other animals is not preordained in this way but is more a matter of chance. The cytoplasm of the egg is a cocktail, and a decision to share it out between germ cells and somatic cells is delayed until after fertilization when many cells have been formed. The existence of germplasm as a discrete entity passing through the generations is clearly ruled out in plants too because their fruiting bodies sprout directly from somatic cells in their stems.

Much of Weismann's speculative theory was inspired by wondering how babies are born without the burden of ageing that so obviously affects their parents' bodies. This is still something of a mystery. We now know that both eggs and sperm are vulnerable to age changes, yet their genes are able to run a perfect life programme from scratch again.

Despite the flaws that have come to light, Weismann's ideas

have been given a new lease of life by a theoretical biologist, Tom Kirkwood, who is now at the University of Manchester. He proposes that the maximum lifespan of a species depends on the outcome of a competition between maintenance of somatic cells versus production of germ cells. The principle of Occam's razor – postulating only the bare essentials – seems to hold in biology as in economics and politics.

Kirkwood's argument begins with the undeniable fact that an individual's resources are finite. He or she can consume only a limited amount of food and can invest only so much in the care and repair of the body fabric. A balance has had to be struck between self-maintenance and reproduction.

Living things are caught on the horns of a dilemma. Should they invest in a Rolls-Royce body if they will then never be able to afford a replacement? Perhaps they should opt for a cheaper car which can be disposed of and replaced? Choosing a Rolls-Royce soma would risk putting all the eggs into one basket because even a perfect body would succumb to an accident one day. The soma is therefore disposable to a greater or lesser extent, and reproduction is always necessary. On the other hand, an all-out effort in reproduction may not be the best strategy either. You don't have to choose between a Rolls or a Lada but can select an intermediate model, and it may pay to reproduce at less than the maximum possible rate if this improves fertility or survival.

Pleiotropic genes are responsible for apportioning energy, materials and repair work between these competing demands. They have many agents for doing this work, but the sex hormones are among the more important ones because they control the fertility switches and the distribution of resources between the reproductive system and other parts of the body.

Reproduction, as every parent knows, is not a light undertaking. No aspect is entirely without some personal risk, and the costs can be considerable. Making babies can place heavy demands on energy and materials. The gonads, or 'roe', of some fish species can weigh as much as 25 per cent of body weight at spawning, and a clutch of birds' eggs represents a heavy investment too. Human eggs and sperm are minute by comparison, but maintaining fertility and making a successful product is at least as expensive in mammals. At full term, a woman will have put on an extra twelve kilograms, or 25 per cent of her weight. In the wild, the extra costs of nutrition for pregnancy and lactation can even jeopardize survival. On the Scottish Isle of Rhum, red deer store more fat in the summer if they are without calves – and survive the harsh winters better.

Sex hormones seal the fate of the male antechinus and other such species: the price of sexual maturity and the ability to procreate is death. Even the possession of reproductive organs – male or female – is potentially dangerous, because their cargo of cells has immense capacity for growth and malignant changes. Castrates often live longer, and tend to be the fatter cats. Chastity even prolongs the lives of flies of both genders. Reproduction counts for more than personal survival for, when starved, flies break down their flight muscle to maintain egg production, even though the muscle cannot regenerate when feeding resumes. In women, a loss of weight to below forty-five kilograms shuts down the hormonal system and causes periods to dry up, thereby avoiding the huge demands of pregnancy and increasing the chances of surviving famine. But once weight is put back on again the system springs back to life and fertility returns.

Trade-offs between longevity and reproduction help to explain why some species live much longer than others. The balance of advantages is influenced by the circumstances of life – the ecological niche in which a species finds itself. In this way a diversity of environments can account for the variety we find in life histories. Species that live in risky environments would be well advised to invest heavily – and soon – in reproduction, even if this threatens their very existence. When the food supply fluctuates wildly, or where predators and parasites are abundant, those that are more fecund early on will be the winners in the struggle for genetic survival. This is the strategy adopted by the mouse and its cousins.

The TV cartoon *Tom and Jerry* illustrates the case well. The hyperactive little rodent lives in hazardous circumstances and is always on the lookout for an opportunity to take advantage of the situation. His feline adversary, Tom, tries to live a quiet life and exerts himself only when absolutely necessary. Were this an adult cartoon story, we would surely see the contrasting life strategies reflected in their sexual habits.

The mouse has no time to lose in the formalities of courtship. This is also true of antechinuses, salmon and a whole host of small invertebrate animals. They reach maturity quickly and make an all-out effort to reproduce while they have the chance because the likelihood of surviving for long is slim. They produce many offspring, to which they devote little parental care. These opportunists of the animal kingdom are perfectly adapted to living under pressurized conditions. Such life histories have been given the name 'r-strategy' by the father of sociobiology, Harvard biologist Edward O. Wilson.

Cats, primates and other animals at the top of the food chain live in more predictable circumstances. They can afford to take time to grow larger and brainier because their chances of survival are better. To achieve this, they have to exert strict discipline over the allocation of resources to reproduction, but they need to produce only a few babies to continue the genetic line, provided they care for them. Had our primate ancestors lived under riskier circumstances, our exceptionally late puberty, big brain and longevity would never have evolved as they have. Our type of life history is called the 'K-strategy', and characterizes all long-lived animals.

Species do not always fall clearly into one camp or the other, and a continuum exists between the extremes of r and K. Humans pride themselves on being the archetypal K type – but we have some surprising bedfellows. Besides the rest of the primate family and cats and dogs, the K club includes bats, some marsupials, and the weird naked mole rats living under the African veldt.

There are some surprising implications of categorizing species in this way. For a start, humans appear to have more in common with bats than with mice and rats, though the latter have been the chief subjects for biomedical research. This fact should make us cautious about extrapolating from mouse to man, but is unlikely to make the rodents redundant. The dramatic extension of the lifespan in rodents by calorie restriction is possibly another peculiarity of r strategists, as they may have needed to telescope longevity during periodic cycles of feast and famine. For this reason, low-calorie diets may not be life-enhancing for K-type humans. We should continue to enjoy good food without fearing that we are denying ourselves something better, unless we learn otherwise!

In animals, the competing demands of reproduction and somatic maintenance seem to eliminate the possibility of the evolution of a Malthusian demon which reproduces so fast and competes so effectively that it overruns its environment. Still, there are a few sly characters around that are prodigious breeders and still get a free lunch. Some parasites only have to worm their way into a host and evade detection by its immune system to stay on as non-paying tenants. Once secure, they have minimal housekeeping needs and can afford to be both superfecund and long-lived.

Whether trade-offs exist in long-lived plants, as in animals, is less clear. Some venerable trees produce huge harvests of acorns and mast, although their seeds may not store as well as some others. Plants that have no fixed upper limit to survival propagate vegetatively and so cannot have a distinction between somatic and germ cells – which neatly avoids any question of whether trade-offs exist.

The idea that senescence has evolved like any other biological characteristic is not new but has only recently taken hold. At one time it was disregarded simply because few animals were seen to become senescent under natural conditions. But they do not have to become senile for ageing to happen, and there is even evidence now that some animals age in the wild state. This is not because naturalists have brought back stories of decrepit wild creatures from remote jungles – examples have come to light almost on our own back doorstep.

Ringing studies have shown that both great tits in an Oxford wood and collared flycatchers in Sweden age under natural conditions. These birds are not ageing visibly: only their breeding performance declines. The reproductive system is as subject to ageing as any other bodily system – and in humans it is even more so.

Other examples show how important the environment can be in moulding the evolution of ageing. A former lion-tamer for the Hollywood studios and lately professor at Harvard and the University of Idaho, Steve Austad, is a specialist in this field – and especially on the Virginia opossum. This is a North American marsupial and most commonly encountered as a possum pancake on the highways of the southern states. Austad reasoned that a lower environmental risk should encourage successive generations of animals to move closer to the *K* strategy, because they could afford to take more time to make reproductive decisions. He guessed that favourable circumstances might be found in an island population.

Sapelo Island is a Georgia state wildlife refuge and has impressive stands of tall pines and gnarled oaks covered in Spanish moss. It is five miles offshore – too far for opossums and their enemies to swim. The opossums there were separated from their continental cousins about 5,000 years ago, when the island formed. Their descendants are luckier than others because they do not have to contend with any natural predators nor that most voracious one, the automobile. The animals have grown accustomed to security and wander about or doze lazily in the sun while their relatives on the mainland only emerge cautiously from their dens after dark.

Austad caught some animals from both populations and fitted radiocollars so he could study their life histories. The islanders aged more slowly, just as he expected – surviving at least a year longer. Collagen in their tails was tested for tensile strength and was found to be biologically younger than its chronological age would suggest. What is more, the opossums gave birth to litters of five instead of the normal seven, and, most unusually, many of them managed to last long enough to litter a second year. The pressure to reproduce quickly – with all its costs – was slackened in the island population, just as it is in birds that nest in oceanic islands and are exceptionally long-lived for the same reason.

Life on a desert island may be the dream of some city-dwellers but it has not yet resulted in lifespan extension in humans, nor is that likely to happen. Humans have a very long intergenerational interval and no population has been isolated long enough for differences to emerge. Record lifespans have been claimed for communities living in remote parts of the Andes, the Caucasus and the Himalayas, but none of them has withstood close inspection. The only consistent difference within the human population, as in most other species, is between the sexes.

The gender gap too can be explained by differing lifestyle pressures during evolution. Males generally lead riskier lives than their mates, and may have to fight rivals and defend a breeding territory. This implies that they are slightly less K-selected than their females because it is in their best genetic interests to father offspring with minimum delay. Females cannot breed at the same rate. Their role begins only when they have been impregnated and it makes sense for them to space their reproductive effort. They are better advised to lead more prudent lives and keep themselves in good condition. The human female is arguably one of the most K-selected of all earth's creatures. This view presents a somewhat different picture to the original caricature of our primate ancestry, which has the human male proudly striding out in front of his wife, followed by a motley collection of apes, monkeys and other animals.

Gerontology has at last come through its erratic youth and grown into a mature science. The melting-pot of half-baked ideas has been replaced by a solid evolutionary theory and an explanation of why the pace of ageing is not the same in all creatures. The evidence from nature and laboratory experiments is so elegant and consistent that we can be swept along with Rose's optimism. He has said that 'the general problem of the cause of senescence can be considered as completely solved as any comparable problem in biology'. How is it, then, that many biologists in other fields of study are only dimly aware of this achievement, if at all? And why has such a big discovery not been greeted with worldwide press coverage and Nobel Prizes? Perhaps it will take a more dramatic example than the humble fruit fly to bring the message home.

This tiny creature has shown that the timetable and full span of life are not necessarily fixed for ever, and there is no reason to suspect that the human animal is any different in this respect. But any extension of longevity by giving evolution a helping hand, as Mike Rose did with his flies, would hardly be perceptible in our species even after many generations. A much more radical attack on the process of ageing will be needed if a significant gain is to be enjoyed in the future. Over the centuries, there has been no shortage of elixirs and operations reputed to promote a healthy and long life, nor of quacks and cranks claiming to be able to rejuvenate the body. Just occasionally, however, an offbeat experiment produces a scientific sea change, and there is no better example of this than Professor Charles-Édouard Brown-Séquard's vain attempts to rejuvenate himself.

Part Two

The Fruits of Time

CHAPTER 6

Brown-Séquard's Elixir

[We should] prize the fruitful error, full of seeds bursting
with their own corrections

Vilfredo Pareto, on Kepler

• Sexual Pessimism

The idea that the preservation of health and the procreation of
offspring are competing demands is an appealing one, with some
horticultural precedents. Threatening the existence of unproductive
trees by half-ringing their bark, like using a tourniquet to stop the
flow of blood in a limb, is an old trick used by gardeners to spur them
into fruiting. Similarly, when a cauliflower's growth is curbed by dry
weather it prematurely 'curds'. It is a wise plant that switches from a
vegetative mode to invest in a genetic future when its organic
existence is jeopardized. Contrariwise, a deflorated annual plant
conserves its resources and can survive for a second year.

Rapid ageing of the Australian antechinus after mating appears
less extraordinary when viewed in this light. Rather than being a
quirk of nature, this species should be regarded as an extreme example
of when it is more prudent to invest in reproduction than to strive for
survival and a long life. The balance point varies between species, but
the evolutionary trade-off principle applies to us all.

None of these examples should seem strange, given our cultural
history. Both pulpit and surgery used to proclaim that sexual activity
is a rather hazardous affair and better avoided except when essential
for perpetuating the family tree. The Victorians took this dogma to

129

extremes by sternly censoring sexual overindulgence and 'wastage of seed', which they regarded as causes of weakness, infertility and even insanity. Their arguments were more moral than biological, and shored up the theology of sexual moderation taught by the early Church Fathers who passionately condemned sexual excesses, even within marriage. St Jerome pronounced that 'he who loves his wife to excess commits a mortal sin', and Pope John Paul II has said as much.

Christianity is not the only world religion that has warned against the abuse of sexual powers. The ancient Hindu document the *Mani Nag* held that seminal fluid is life-maintaining as well as life-generating. The active principles in semen were thought to be strictly limited, every drop being made at the cost of forty drops of blood (or in some versions 100 times 100). Gandhi too held celibacy within marriage to be a virtue, and the yoga philosophy originally taught that chaste thoughts, words and actions enable the generative powers, or 'Ojas', to be used for physical and spiritual stamina instead.

The Chinese Taoists were less pessimistic about sex and believed that copulation stemmed the growth of the prostate gland and was a gift to be enjoyed. But they agreed that sexual practices, just like diet, exercise and breathing, should be under strict control. Devotees were taught how to engage in sexual stimulation without wasting the life-giving semen (*ching*), and this involved a bizarre form of *coitus interruptus*. Normal ejaculation was prevented by contracting pelvic muscles, taking a deep breath and grinding the teeth. When this failed, semen was forced to return to the body by pressing a finger against the base of the penis at the moment of climax, hoping it would be diverted to the spinal column to rejuvenate the brain! Little did they know that the semen was soon voided after temporary displacement to the bladder.

These exotic exercises and their underlying philosophies are pertinent because they influenced the ideas of pioneering scientists at the end of the nineteenth century. Researchers were often led up blind alleys by excessive adherence to pet theories, but their faith in the ultimate conquest of senility and the suspicion that sex hormones were a key to winding back biological time drove them on. Most of their remedies were naïve and bound to backfire; nevertheless, these fits and starts eventually led to the discovery of the sex hormones, which has brought immense benefits in the form of treatment of infertility, safe and effective contraception, and the prevention of disease.

It is in this shady area between science and mythology that our story continues. I have reconstructed from written records a lecture which set the ball rolling a century ago. Admittedly, I have indulged my imagination here and there to fill in unrecorded details, but I believe that the gist of my account reflects the underlying attitudes and aspirations of the time.

• Paris, 1 June 1889

Despite the warmth of the afternoon, the wood-panelled lecture theatre of the École Pratique was packed with students and doctors for the weekly meeting of the Société de Biologie. A sudden hush descended as the chairman stood to announce the speaker.

'I call upon Monsieur Brown-Séquard to deliver his paper entitled "Some effects produced in man by subcutaneous injections of a liquid extract of fresh guinea-pig and dog testicles".'

The professor rose at the chairman's words. For a man of his years he was remarkably sprightly as he mounted the steps, and, in a dark frock-coat, he presented an impressive and dignified figure. On reaching the lectern, he lifted his grey head to peer at his audience, most of whom he recognized. At the back of the room he spotted his principal assistants, d'Arsonval and Henocque, sitting up attentively. This could be a pivotal day for them too. D'Arsonval's studies of muscle heat production were well regarded and, if today's paper ushered in a new chapter in medical science, he might one day succeed to Brown-Séquard's chair at the Collège de France.

The professor cleared his throat and began:

'Distinguished members, I expect the title of my paper puzzles you and may even provoke mirth. But today I shall report a discovery of some gravity: one that is of greater importance than any I have yet delivered. I refer to no less a problem than human ageing.

'For many years I have been investigating whether glands secrete invigorating substances into the bloodstream, which carries them to every corner of the body. The seeds of this idea were sown back in '56, when I discovered that guinea-pigs died even faster after removing their adrenal glands than their kidneys. Not long before, the English physician Thomas Addison found that some of his patients died soon after their adrenal glands became diseased. The explanation for the disproportionately large effect of these small glands might be that they are secreting a tonic that is essential for life and cleansing the blood.

'Originally we thought that glands only released fluids on to the surface of the body, like saliva and sweat, or into cavities, like the digestive juices. We now know that they can also secrete substances directly into the bloodstream. My research on the adrenal glands and that of my predecessor, Claude Bernard, on the liver were the first hints of a general phenomenon. I now suspect that every gland is involved in internal secretion and helps to promote good health. But there is one pair of glands, Messieurs, that is more important in this respect than any other.

'We all know that removal of the testicles has a profound effect on man and beast. But castration goes far beyond quenching sexual desire and potency and shrinking the male member. Muscles and other organs that are not directly involved in reproductive processes are also affected in one way or another. Consider the vocal cords, for instance. They lengthen during puberty when the testicles are growing and cause the voice to "break". No such change occurs in eunuchs, and they consequently do not lose their alto voice. They are also much more compliant and milder in nature than normal men.

'Bearing in mind the strength given to the body by the testicles, let us not forget the dangers of masturbation. Most physicans agree that this perversion of the natural sex instinct causes actual physical and intellectual harm. Emission of seminal fluid weakens the constitution and may even lead to mental illness, the more so when it is excessive. This is particularly true in adolescent boys, when the spermatic glands have yet to acquire full power, and at advanced ages when that power is declining. It is said that young men who remain strictly celibate have enhanced physical and mental powers by virtue of the vitality of their nervous system. I therefore draw the conclusion that the testicles are the source of a natural tonic that pours out to reach all corners of the body, but which can be lost in the semen.

'This brings me to the subject of old age. At the age of seventy-two I can speak with some authority on the matter. Despite centuries of speculative theorizing by philosophers and doctors, we seem to have made no progress towards understanding its causes. The whole subject is still shrouded in a fog of ignorance and superstition. But I think I can now shed a little light on it.

'The problems of old age have more than one cause. First, there is a series of changes causing the various parts of the body to lose the vigour of youth. These changes are natural, unavoidable and probably irreversible. Second, the waning powers of the spermatic glands make matters worse by accelerating the deterioration of physical and mental strength. But, if the natural tonic they produce is replaced, it should be possible to slow the pace of ageing and reinvigorate the nerves.

'I have mulled over these ideas for twenty years since I first aired them in a series of lectures here in Paris. In 1875, while visiting Louis Agassiz at his summer home near Boston, I had the opportunity to carry out a few experiments to test my theory. I engrafted young guinea-pig tissue into a dozen old male dogs and obtained one positive result. The following years were so preoccupied with travel and lecturing that I had little time to follow up this encouraging start.

'Only recently did I find an opportunity to put my pet theory to the test again. I ground up the testes of young animals with a pestle and mortar to make a watery extract for injection into old animals. They soon became healthier, sleeker and more vigorous. There were no side-effects. What had worked in animals should be equally effective in humans, and so I planned a self-experiment.

'Dr d'Arsonval and I prepared an extract in water from the testicles of a two-year-old dog and young guinea-pigs. The juice was mixed with semen and blood from the testicular veins and diluted three or four times with distilled water. The result was a cloudy red liquor. On 15 May I began to inject myself daily with one millilitre of the fluid under the skin of either my left arm or leg. Filtration of the extract clarified it and reduced the inflammation and soreness at injection sites. Before I go into details about my findings, I shall explain my condition so that you can properly judge the effects.

'Throughout my early and middle years I had a robust constitution and an enormous appetite for work. Research, lectures and patient care absorbed sixteen or more hours of each day, which I started at about 3 a.m. This healthy state began to change about ten years ago. I used to run up and down stairs, but now have to move cautiously and steady myself on difficult staircases. Worse still, I had to sit down after only half an hour of laboratory work. Even after writing at my desk for only three or four hours I would have to rest because of exhaustion. On reaching home by carriage at six o'clock I was so tired that I had to retire to bed immediately after a quick supper. Even so, I would waken in the early hours unrefreshed by sleep.

'After just eight injections I felt much better, and more like my old self or a man half my years. I have regained the strength I used to have and can carry out experiments continuously for several hours without needing to sit or rest. For some years I had been unable to do any serious mental work in the evenings, but on 23 May, after three and a half hours of continuous laboratory work, I felt so alert and energetic that after dinner I was able to write for nearly two hours on a difficult subject. You can imagine how the return of my old energy has lifted my spirits.

'The benefits are not only mental. I had lost the ability to hold much water in my bladder, and the flow of urine was little more than a trickle. When I measured the jet in the *pissoir* again after the injections, I found that its length had increased by one-third!

'Constipation is even more of a misery. The muscles of the

bowel, like those of the bladder, are controlled by nerves in the spinal cord, and as nervous activity declines so does muscular strength. After a few days of treatment, however, the power and regularity of my bowel has improved more than any other function and I no longer need laxatives. The tonic evidently improved all aspects of my spinal functions.

'For scientists like ourselves, an improved feeling of well-being is not enough to prove that a real organic change has taken place – we need objective facts and figures. I have therefore used a dynamo-meter to provide an accurate measure of my forearm strength. Before my experimental trial, the average weight I managed to move was about 34.5 kilograms, but afterwards I lifted 41 kilograms. This is the weight I used to be able to lift when I lived in London twenty-six years ago. This result implies that treatment was improving my muscles as well as my nerves.

'I don't ask you to accept my claims uncritically. In your place, I would be among the first to question whether the good results were due to auto-suggestion rather than an organic change. I cannot yet be absolutely certain, but the good outcome was so unexpected that I doubt this interpretation. Confirmation is urgently needed by inde-pendent researchers. I challenge members of the Society to test for themselves whether testicular fluid possesses rejuvenating powers.'

The professor shuffled his papers into an untidy pile and turned his head to signal that he had finished. In barely fifteen minutes, he had made the most startling claim in his long and distinguished career. The chairman addressed Brown-Séquard with a few courteous words and invited questions from the floor. A forest of arms strained forward. Brown-Séquard was heartened to see an old friend rise to his feet.

'My dear Brown-Séquard, I wish to compliment you on your paper – one of the most significant in the history of the Society and, who knows, for medical science generally. I would like to offer myself as a guinea-pig for testing your theory but have to admit that I am a coward before the hypodermic needle. Do you think the organ extracts will be effective if taken by mouth?'

The professor smiled as he replied. 'It all depends on whether the digestive juices in the stomach and intestines destroy the active substances and if absorption into the bloodstream can occur. Oral administration is very important because it would improve the acceptability of treatment, and many people regard the needle as an instrument of torture. We have yet to test for oral activity, but perhaps you will try.'

Another questioner was interested more in the composition of the extracts than in their route of administration. 'I am surprised you did not emphasize the significance of finding that a testicular tonic from one species acts on another. If organs from dogs and rodents work in humans, the larger ones of farm animals could be used for production on a commercial scale.'

'Thank you for that astute observation. Perhaps we should not be surprised if the beneficial substances turn out to be universal in higher species. According to Darwin's theory, we expect each species to have evolved a constitution that promotes its best health. There would be very strong pressures to avoid losing a tonic during evolution, for this might risk extinction of the species in the struggle for existence.'

The professor was at last beginning to relax in this supportive company. Then one young man at the back of the hall caught the chairman's attention.

'Monsieur Brown-Séquard has suggested that the properties of the body can be transferred to a third party by injecting organ extracts. Surely he should have mutilated giant tortoises rather than furry animals. After all, they are known to live for more than a century, and the patient would not be running the risk of acquiring excessive body hair.'

The Frankenstein story had left a deep impression on public consciousness, and the image of an elderly professor transforming into a hairy ape was both mocking and alarming. There were giggles from the vicinity of the questioner, but Brown-Séquard found great difficulty in descending from his plane of scientific seriousness. He was not gifted in the art of repartee, which might have defused these ribald remarks. Sensing his confusion, the chairman quickly passed on to the next question.

'Does the professor agree that rejuvenation therapy should force the College to abandon its policy of unlimited tenure of senior professors?' An unmistakable ripple of laughter passed through the hall, and the professor's few muttered works of reply were barely audible.

Brown-Séquard must have been thankful to retreat to his seat when the chairman precipitately drew the session to a close and called for the next speaker. He probably heard little of what was said as he mulled over the mixed reception of his message. Had his peers assimilated the implications of his discovery of substances '*essentiels à vie*'? Had he ended the centuries-long search for the cause and cure of ageing that day? And would his discovery fix his reputation like a star in the firmament of French science, beside Pasteur and Bernard?

When he left the Society's meeting-room at the end of the session, newspaper reporters were already scurrying to their offices to prepare their stories. The society had introduced a press table at its meetings so that important discoveries could be quickly brought to public notice rather than being spread by hearsay. The journalists were delighted to have a far more sensational scoop than anything they had ever trawled before from these erudite meetings. Few, if any, of them would have guessed that they had witnessed that day the birth of a new science of hormone research which would later be called endocrinology. Paradoxically, it was founded on a mistaken belief in sexual pessimism – but this error proved to be a fruitful one. Their reports succeeded in raising public curiosity as well as fuelling fears about where advances in medical science might lead. They ushered in a period of intense press interest in rejuvenation therapy that would last for decades.

• Flow Tide for Organotherapy

The year 1889 was an auspicious one in French cultural history. The Eiffel Tower had been opened. It was the tallest structure yet built, and was hailed as the engineering wonder of the world. Paris was the artistic capital of Europe and the cradle of many a gifted painter, and down in Saint-Rémy a Dutchman was adding olive groves to his *œuvre*. Paris could also claim to be the medical centre of the world. Some of the best students from both sides of the Atlantic flocked to rub shoulders with the likes of physiologists Claude Bernard and François Magendie, and Louis Pasteur. Brown-Séquard was among these stars, and his amazing claim to have rejuvenated himself brought his fame to a wider public.

Most doctors first read about the remarkable effects of testicular extracts in their newspapers. The modern medical profession is a cautious one, and sensational stories will find few sympathizers. Only when Brown-Séquard's paper had been published in the official journal of the Société de Biologie could its true value be weighed. Some medical practitioners were, at best, sceptical about this reputedly seminal paper and feared it might bring the profession into disrepute. Their scientific colleagues in physiology openly scoffed at the spectacle of a grey, bent old man administering himself an elixir of life. Besides, the treatment seemed to be a recycling of an old and discredited idea that youthful vitality could be transferred from one individual to another. Infectious diseases still took a heavy toll on babies and children, and it was felt that prime attention should be given to the epidemic diseases that strike people down in the bloom of youth rather than trying to preserve the old and frail.

But by the autumn of 1889 Brown-Séquard had received hundred of letters congratulating him on his success and requesting samples of his organ extracts. Patients were clamouring for the miracle cure they had read about in the newspapers. By the following year, 1,200 physicians were administering his elixir to patients, and the organotherapy tide was beginning to flow strongly. Many believed that this was the dawn of a revolution for curing the intractable ailments of old age. For them, the reputation of Brown-Séquard and the Collège de France were sufficient guarantors of good faith and authority. A few were no doubt counting the pecuniary benefits for their private medical practices. Reservations about the value of organotherapy were massaged away by the knowledge that virtually all revolutionary developments are resisted at first. The new science of sex-organ extracts was pregnant with possibilities.

One of the first doctors to test testicular extracts was a Parisian physician, Dr Variot. He did not feel the call to self-experimentation but selected 'old' men – aged fifty-four, fifty-six and sixty-eight – for organotherapy. Two others of a similar age were recruited to serve as the control group and received injections of pure water. Variot's experiments were ethical enough by the standards of his day. He was not required to seek approval from ethics committees, for they did not yet exist; nor did he need to inform his subjects that they were about to become human guinea-pigs. They were simply told they were receiving 'fortifying' injections.

If Brown-Séquard felt any irritation with Variot's methods and the unseemly haste to be first to test his theory, it must have vanished when he heard the results of the trial, which were reported to a packed meeting of the Société on 5 July. Those receiving testicular extracts felt and looked much better. The treatment had rejuvenated the old men! The subjects' ignorance of whether they were receiving organ extract or water seemed to rule out the possibility that the improvements were due to a placebo effect.

In comparison with the time and labour needed to make any significant scientific advance today, the speed with which organo-therapy was tested and published is breathtaking. Clinical trials were soon being carried out in many countries, from Russia to America. Brown-Séquard and his assistants were kept busy answering corre-spondence and entertaining inquisitive visitors eager for the latest news. Among its other achievements, Paris seemed set to become a scientific Lourdes. Despite the drain upon his time, the professor welcomed these enquiries because his claims would be accepted by instinctively suspicious scientists only after they had been confirmed in the best research institutes and hospitals around the world.

Biologists and medical men were not alone in joining the bandwagon – chemists climbed on board as well. Quite reasonably, they thought that it should be possible to purify the active ingredient in 'Brown-Séquard's Elixir'. Pure preparations would be much more acceptable to patients than crude semen, and freer from the risk of contamination and side-effects. If the active ingredient turned out to be simple, or to resemble a substance that was already available, then the way was open to synthesis on an industrial scale. The organotherapy business would be revolutionized, and it would become an economic proposition to offer treatment to every man who needed it.

By the summer of 1891, Alexander von Poehl of St Petersburg reported the isolation of a relatively simple substance called spermine from seminal fluid. In fact spermine was not new to science – it had been discovered as long ago as 1677 by the Dutch microscopist Antoni van Leeuwenhoek, who had noticed that crystals form in semen when it is left to stand. He mentioned this finding in the same letter to the Royal Society of London in which he reported his momentous discovery of sperm. We now know that spermine phosphate is present in human semen at a concentration of about two grams per litre, which is very much higher than in other body fluids or in animals. As spermine appeared to be a physiological tonic, it became a prime candidate for the Brown-Séquard effect.

Von Poehl tested spermine on patients and started supplying it to other doctors. Numerous clinical conditions – from syphilis to senility – were reported to have been remarkably improved. This was the first substance claimed to have hormone-like properties to be produced commercially. But while shipments of the precious cargo were still in transit from the chemists to customers in distant parts of the globe, laboratory workers were investigating its biological actions. It undoubtedly affected the circulation and critical organs, but they could not confirm any revivifying effects. The frothy enthusiasm for spermine therapy dried up.

Despite this turn of events, demand for organ extracts continued to flourish in many parts of the world. In America, the stamp of Brown-Séquard's name on the elixir carried some authority: he was remembered from the times when he worked in Virginia, in New York and at Harvard University. Approval of the new treatment was often granted on the slenderest of evidence. Double-blind clinical trials and statistics were not required in those days as seals of approval: one or two impressive results were sufficient for some doctors to reach for their pens and go into print. Newspapers quoted one exuberant practitioner: 'The paralysed walked, the lame threw aside canes and crutches, the deaf and the blind regained their senses.'

Not everyone was taken in by such hyperbole, but the elixir was gradually becoming more acceptable, even fashionable. In an optimistic social climate, even panaceas for the problems of ageing may appear plausible. Many illnesses that had been regarded as incurable, including cancer, were said to be yielding to this wonderful elixir; only epilepsy was stubbornly resistant. So seriously were these results being taken that moralists preached fiery sermons against hubris, condemning attempts to reverse old age as Providence had set the natural span of human life at three score years and ten. Worse still, the treatment caused offence because of its sexual undertones and raised fears of it kindling lasciviousness.

Sir Arthur Conan Doyle, himself an Edinburgh medical graduate, played upon public anxieties and gullibility in one of his stories, 'The Creeping Man'. An elderly professor felt he needed extra energy to woo a beautiful young woman. He misjudged the dose and overdid the monkey-testicle extract. It not only boosted his lust but transformed him into a savage ape. Fortunately for the woman, Sherlock Holmes came to the rescue – accompanied by a large dog (a traditional enemy of monkeys in Indian legend). This idea of scientists opening a Pandora's box has a familiar ring, though they are in fact far more conservative than many people want to believe.

Advertisers say that any publicity is good publicity. The promise of rejuvenation has always been irresistible, and people are prepared to pay dearly for even a faint hope. I would like to think that the pursuit of wealth has not been a prime ambition of most members of the medical profession in Great Britain, although attitudes are not always so high-minded. The profit motive was anathema to Brown-Séquard, and reports of unprofessional conduct made him lament that 'In the United States especially, and often without knowing what I did or the most elementary rules regarding subcutaneous injections of animal materials, several physicians – or rather the medicasters and charlatans – have exploited the ardent desires of a great number of individuals and have made them run the greatest risks, if they have not done worse.'

Brown-Séquard attempted to get a legal injunction to prohibit the marketing of testicular extracts in Europe and America. He was concerned that his discovery should benefit as many people as possible, and that the quality of the fluid should be stringently tested. These efforts proved to be futile because the patent rights of inventors are void once details of products have been published. His only recourse was to try to swamp the market with samples provided gratis to any physician who wanted them. Each sample was labelled with the address 'Laboratoire de Médecine du Collège de France' to ensure that the authentic product could be distinguished from unauthorized brands being sold under a variety of names. Brown-Séquard paid for the manufacture, advertising and postage out of his own pocket. He might have been a wealthier man had he taken the opportunity of lucrative private practice, and his generosity had to halt when the costs passed the 10,000 franc mark (roughly equivalent to 200,000 francs today).

The response of the British medical establishment was chary, which must have surprised and saddened him. He regarded himself as British, having held honours and clinical appointments in the UK, and a memorial plaque on the wall of the National Hospital in London records that he was a founder. The editor of the *British Medical Journal* bitterly complained about the new fad across the Channel: 'We find medical men writing of these ideas and of the cures achieved in the most sanguine strain, and often upon no better evidence than quacks produce for their cures.' This attitude was all too transparent in the title of an article written by an anonymous reviewer: 'The Pentacle of Rejuvenescence' – the pentacle being a five-pointed star with symbolic importance in magic.

The stiff rectitude of the British was based on moral as much as scientific objections. Antivivisectionists, who were already a powerful lobby in Victorian times, were outraged that animals should be exploited in an organ trade, even though slaughterhouse waste would provide the supply. Other critics were horrified to hear that patients might be tainted with animal products, especially seminal fluid. Brown-Séquard naïvely made matters worse for himself by suggesting that these products could be avoided by exciting the sex organs short of the climax of ejaculation to produce the same healthy effect. His detractors read this as encouraging the elderly to masturbate.

Despite official coolness, organotherapy was sufficiently attractive for a number of British doctors to test extracts of animal testes on their patients – with mixed results. At the Harveian Society meeting in London in 1890, a Dr Waterhouse reported a favourable response in some of his neurological patients. On the other hand, doctors at the Bridgwater Infirmary in Somerset and at the National Hospital were unconvinced, and warned that treatment might do more harm than good.

Four years after Brown-Séquard's announcement, untold hundreds or thousands of people worldwide had been injected with testicular extracts. Public attention was so intense that the editor of the *BMJ* began to fear that he had been too cautious and had overlooked an important development. More and more doctors were warming to the idea that some diseases may be due to chemical deficiency states. Indubitably, the diet provides for basic needs, but other substances have to be made within the body. It stood to reason that if something crucial were lacking, replacement should restore the body to full health. The editor wrote, 'It is now some years since Brown-Séquard announced the wonderful effects which followed the subcutaneous injection of testicular extracts as exemplified in his own person, and though many jeered at him as the discoverer of perpetual youth, the notion has steadily gained ground that there is, after all, something in it.' The British medical establishment felt bound to signal a change of heart because doctors at home were having striking success with extracts from another organ.

In 1891 a Newcastle doctor published the results of a novel treatment of a woman suffering from myxoedema – an underactive thyroid gland. After receiving injections of sheep thyroid, her hair started to regrow, her pulse quickened and she felt her old energy return. In fact she survived another twenty-eight years in comparatively good health. George Murray's paper was held in triumph, and his discovery soon led to the manufacture of thyroid pills to treat myxoedema. He was lucky in choosing the one organ in the body which stores large amounts of its hormone, and that the thyroid hormone, thyroxine, is active when taken by mouth. Murray had probably met Brown-Séquard during a visit to Paris in 1889–90, yet he made no mention of the older man's pioneering work in organotherapy. Perhaps he wished to distance himself from someone who was regarded as a maverick back home, or he simply did not want to share the credit for a discovery.

By this time, Brown-Séquard had become the foremost advocate of the 'theory of internal secretion', which we now call endocrinology. In suspecting that potent chemicals (later called hormones) exist in most organs, he was well ahead of his time. In March 1891, he wrote to his assistant from his winter retreat in Nice: 'all the glands of external secretion are at the same time glands of internal secretion, like the testicles. The kidneys, the salivary gland and the pancreas are not solely eliminatory organs. They are, like the thyroid, the spleen, etc., organs giving to the blood important principles, either in a direct manner or by resorption after external secretion.'

The nascent science of endocrinology was gathering pace elsewhere too – sometimes driven by avowed sceptics of the goings-on in Paris. In 1894 a Harrogate doctor, George Oliver, paid an unscheduled visit to Edward Schäfer, then Professor of Physiology at University College London. Oliver was seeking advice on how to interpret an experiment he had done on his son. The busy professor tried to excuse himself politely, but his importunate visitor was content to wait until he had completed the animal surgery he was engaged in.

Oliver then produced from his waistcoat pocket a phial containing an extract of adrenal gland which he had tested on his son. Schäfer reluctantly agreed to inject the fluid into an anaesthetized animal's vein, whereupon he was amazed to see the column of water in the blood-pressure recorder rise almost to the limit.

This was how another hormone, adrenalin (later called epinephrine in America), erupted on to the scientific scene without warning. Within seven years, John Abel at Johns Hopkins University in Baltimore had worked out its chemical formula and had synthesized it in pure form. The ease with which its potency could be tested at every step by blood-pressure measurements did much to hasten progress.

This development encouraged scientists to test other glands which were suspected of harbouring hormones. Hopes were high that dwarfism could be treated with pituitary-gland extracts and diabetes with extracts from the pancreas. The principles were correct but the technology was crude, and years of labour had to be invested before rewards were reaped.

The effects of growth hormone and insulin were at least easy to measure: given enough of the appropriate hormone, dwarf children grow normally and diabetics can control their blood-sugar levels. Judging the alleviation of ageing symptoms after testicular extracts was another matter because there was no objective way of measuring biological age. Old age does not suddenly precipitate overnight but comes on slowly, and most of the changes are rather vague. There could be no real agreement on whether treatment had put the clock back, and the physician could only rely on an experienced eye.

Ironically, Brown-Séquard's own health deteriorated rapidly after his celebrated lecture. He had never claimed that testicular extracts would produce a Faustian rejuvenation, but he had hoped to stave off the worst problems of old age. He kept up the injections, despite pain from the primitive hypodermic needles and becoming covered in sores. His faith in the injections remained firm until he died in 1894 at the age of seventy-seven.

• An Old Man's Folly

Brown-Séquard would have been saddened to see how far testicular extracts had fallen from favour by the late 1890s. The elixir was reputedly ineffective whether given by injection or by mouth. A rumour began to circulate that it was actually harmful. Experience of disappointing results was probably greater than published records suggested, because negative findings are always more difficult to publish than positive ones. And the professor's reputation had been so high that some doctors may have been tempted to doubt their own results.

Advertisements for Brown-Séquard's Elixir began to disappear from the new editions of drug catalogues, and fewer prescriptions were written. Sceptics glowed with satisfaction as their wait-and-see strategy was vindicated. His early triumphs forgotten, Brown-Séquard came to be regarded as a tragic symbol of the futility of trying to defy the inevitable.

The moral of this story is that old men should retire while their reputations are still intact. Brown-Séquard had a brilliant career behind him and his scientific instincts had proven reliable over the adrenal glands. Even more famous was his work showing that sensory nerves cross over in the spinal cord, which has implications for diagnosing the site of spinal damage. Yet he stumbled over the sex glands as a cure for ageing. Was it his assumptions or his observations that had let him down?

For a start, he had ignored the conventional wisdom of scientific detachment, which is a safeguard against overweening pride in pet theories. He was by all accounts a modest man, but pride is the great temptation for scientists and inventors. He wanted one last great achievement, but became so emotionally involved in the project that he dropped his critical guard. On this occasion he would have been wiser to have followed the advice of his former rival, Claude Bernard, to 'leave theories outside the laboratory as you would your coat'.

Brown-Séquard would have considered himself to be an independent thinker, but, like most of us, he was a hostage to his culture.

He accepted contemporary assumptions that led him to shore up specious ideas about the debilitating effects of sexual activity and the loss of semen. The Victorian fallacy that ejaculation depletes energy reserves was a gift for those who wanted to condemn sexual indulgence. Post-copulatory lassitude was taken as a sign of energy depletion, but we now know that the calorific costs of sexual excitement and emission are not high. Chemical analysis shows that the quantities of energy, nutrients and other constituents lost in a typical ejaculate of three millilitres are trivial compared with body reserves and daily intake – roughly comparable to losing the same volume of blood.

To be fair, Brown-Séquard did not regard the special 'nutritive substances' from the testes as so many calories or so much protein, fat and sugar. He held that there were other substances which were unique to the testes (though he did allow that there may be a little in the ovaries too). Their proper destination was the bloodstream and the far reaches of the body. They should be spent in the semen only when absolutely necessary.

These were original – perhaps revolutionary – ideas, and they had a germ of truth in them. Had he been bold enough to pursue the effects of substances from the testes on the ornaments of virility, such as the beard, he would have been on safer ground. Unfortunately, he had a compulsive fascination with the baffling problems of ageing, and he confused the weakness of eunuchs with the feebleness of old age. His fundamental error was to assume that ageing is a kind of slow castration, which is true only in a narrow sense.

With the advantage of hindsight, he was searching for testosterone, but it would take forty more years for others to purify and identify this hormone. We now also know that his watery testicular extracts must have been hormonally inactive, because sex hormones do not dissolve in water. And, even if testosterone had been present, the immediate benefits he experienced after taking the extracts are implausible because the 'anabolic', or muscle-building, effects of testosterone take time to act. It seems, then, that his observations as well as his assumptions had let him down.

His observations had proved unreliable on other occasions, leading him to jump to hasty conclusions. Self-experimentation, although commendable on ethical grounds, can easily lead the unwary researcher astray. At forty-five he was already fascinated by the age changes occurring in his own body. His beard was still black, but sprinkled with white hairs near the temples and ears. He recorded waking one morning to find white hairs on the front where none had been before. After removing five from one side and seven from the other, he found more on each side two days later and they were white from root to tip. After repeating the experiment, he drew the conclusion that long white hairs can appear in a single night! As we shall see in Chapter 10, this cannot be.

Rejuvenation of his body was a far more sensational claim on which to risk his reputation. If there was nothing in it, how can we account for his improved sense of well-being? My hunch is that he had dismissed the placebo effect too lightly, and that the relief he felt was not from ageing but from a depressive illness of which he was unaware.

Brown-Séquard admitted that he had a poor appetite, was constipated, slept badly and rose unrefreshed. He complained of little mental or physical energy. These are common problems in people of advancing age, but they also sound suspiciously like clinical depression, which is much more responsive to placebos than senile decline. A study for the British Medical Research Council in 1965 found that more than a third of depressed patients had relief from symptoms after placebo treatment. Organotherapy may have benefited many patients for the same reasons, particularly if their doctors had convinced them of its powers.

A century after the events, it is impossible to verify some of the stories about Brown-Séquard, but some do support my hunch. It was hinted that he had tried to commit suicide in middle age during a period of obsessive overwork. Depression and suicidal feelings are not uncommon when under stress. He had also whispered to friends that he had *fait une visite à Mme Brown-Séquard* on the very morning of his famous lecture. He was affirming, in as discreet a manner as a gentleman could, that he was enjoying sexual intercourse again. This achievement at the age of seventy-two does seem to rule out any organic disorder, which is more often the cause of impotence. Since loss of libido is a hallmark of depression – and reversible – his admission of an improvement in this area suggests a lifting of the veil of mental illness.

Brown-Séquard may have made a *faux pas* by declaring his rejuvenation, but he was not the last great victim of self-deception. However, by making immense claims, he had raised the stakes dangerously high and had exposed himself to critical attention with its risk of bringing ridicule upon himself and his enterprise. We regularly witness 'scientific breakthroughs' which do not live up to their promise, yet the vast majority of cases are published by honest researchers in good faith. The recent fiasco over cold fusion for producing cheap energy is a salutary warning of the pitfalls of presenting preliminary findings. And if the pioneering fringes of physics are so uncertain, how much more so are the frontiers of gerontology?

The theory that Brown-Séquard had developed was rooted in the fallacy of sexual pessimism, but it produced fertile offshoots nevertheless. Chemists continued the search for hormones in the sex organs – and in just about every other gland. Physiologists investigated how hormones are released into the bloodstream and how they affect body chemistry. But progress was slow, and some doctors who had shared enthusiasm for the testicular elixir still dreamt about the possibility of rejuvenation. While orthodox science was content to plod the long march, a few entrepreneurs stubbornly hoped for an easy way to beat the blight of ageing.

CHAPTER 7

The Gland Grafters

We are as old as our glands.

Eugen Steinach

• New Glands for Old

At the start of the twentieth century the prospects for organ trans-plantation were brighter than ever before. Striking improvements in aseptic surgery enabled more patients to survive abdominal oper-ations. In 1912 the Nobel Committee gave its blessing to the promising new field by awarding the prize for physiology and medicine to Alexis Carrel at the Rockefeller Institute of New York. Together with the Chicago physiologist Charles Guthrie, he had perfected a method for joining the blood vessels of organ grafts to those of the host. In a technically brilliant series of experiments, they showed that the heart, kidneys and ovaries could be removed and safely returned to the same animal afterwards. But Carrel doubted whether it would ever be possible to graft organs from one individual to another, so he turned attention to growing cells outside the body, or *in vitro*. Despite his warnings, however, hopeful rejuvenators pressed on with sex-gland grafting, encouraged by some celebrated results from the past.

The Scottish surgeon John Hunter had grafted testes from cocks into hens, and ovaries into cocks, as early as the 1780s. The reason behind these bizarre experiments was a fascination with the tendency for females to become more masculine with age. He noted that this 'obtains to a certain degree in every class of animals. We find something similar taking place even in the human species.' He was also aware of the possibility of sex changing in the opposite direction, including the case of the famous cock pheasant in fifteenth-century Basel, which was solemnly tried for witchcraft after laying an egg. After the luckless creature had been burnt at the stake, three more 'cock's eggs' were discovered among the roasted remains.

After one of his experiments, Hunter recorded in his notebook, 'I have formerly transplanted the testicle of a cock into the abdomen of a hen, and they had sometimes taken root there, but not frequently, and then had never come to perfection.' Some of his more successful grafts were pickled, and can still be seen in the museum at the Royal College of Surgeons in London. He must have been puzzled at the mixed success, given that grafts from trees and shrubs take automatically, but the reasons for rejection were not discovered until much later.

The Göttingen biologist A. A. Berthold was not deterred and, by luck or good judgement, grafted excised cockerel testes back into their original owners in 1849. Blood vessels soon sprouted and nourished the organ as if welcoming back an old friend. The size and appearance of both comb and wattle were well maintained compared with those of capons, and the birds showed 'the customary attention to the hens'. Since any testicular nerves would have been severed during the operation, Berthold rightly inferred that the male organ must have exerted its effects on body shape and behaviour by releasing something into the bloodstream. The significance of his paper was out of proportion to its length of only four pages, for it was the first hint of the existence of testosterone. But, like the contemporary geneticist Gregor Mendel, Berthold did not live to enjoy recognition for a momentous discovery.

By the turn of the century, gland grafting was playing a major role in the infant science of endocrinology. Scientists had discovered that, unlike most other organs, hormone-secreting glands are often successfully grafted by simply implanting them into a tissue without hooking them up to the blood vessels. They even work in unnatural sites of the body. In a few days there is an ingrowth of new blood vessels which bring oxygen and nutrients to the glands and carry away hormones to act on distant parts of the body.

Eugen Steinach, Professor of Physiology in Vienna, was one of the pioneering grafters. Early in the new century he had discovered the glandular cells in the testicle that produce the male sex hormone, testosterone. He followed John Hunter's lead by testing the effects of testicles and ovaries grafted into castrated rats of the same and the opposite sex, and obtained the results he expected. Whether an animal appeared male or female depended on the sex of the organ rather than the original sex of the individual. He went on to conclude that homosexuality is caused by an abnormal hormone balance, which is still argued over to this day.

At this point he switched attention to grafting sex organs to rejuvenate animals on the assumption that, if the characteristics of gender can be altered, so can those of age. From his position at the head of a prestigious laboratory, Steinach inspired the notion that rejuvenation science was the natural sister of endocrinology, and equally respectable. Having satisfied himself that Brown-Séquard's elixir was inactive, he tried grafting young testicles into old rats in the hope that they would produce a more lasting effect. The results impressively vindicated his hunch. Formerly decrepit animals now easily defeated inexperienced rivals, rediscovered an interest in females and lived 25 per cent longer than usual.

It seemed that Brown-Séquard had been on the right track all along, even if his methods were flawed. Sex organs were the power-houses of the body, and hormone deficiency was the root of ageing. Any means of boosting hormone levels should therefore reinvigorate the whole body and preserve its vital functions. Carrel had recognized the potential ability of grafts to overcome the failure of specific organs, but Steinach grasped the enormous significance of transplanting the sex glands as a tonic for everyone.

But gland grafting was still far from reliable, and many a sceptical head was wagging. Would grafts last long enough to rejuvenate patients? Would they have to be given repeatedly, and, if so, would there be enough material to go round? Steinach was listening to these worries, and he came up with some reassuring news – young organs actually reinvigorated the failing testicles and ovaries of old animals. He claimed that the benefit continued even after the grafts had failed or been removed, so they needed to last only long enough to rekindle the native organs. These results quickened the gung-ho efforts being made at the same time by an enterprising breed of surgeons whom I shall call 'the rejuvenators'.

In 1916 in Chicago, Dr Frank Lydston dumbfounded a colleague by taking him aside to show a lump of tissue in his scrotum. He had stitched a slice of testis from another man beside his own pair. At fifty-four he had reached the summit of his career, but had felt less energetic until his self-experiment. Now, he claimed, 'I feel strengthened in my ... impressions of the value of sex gland implantation, notably in the matter of increasing physical efficiency and especially physiosexual efficiency'.

Within a few months, Lydston performed similar operations on patients whose own organs were abnormal or had been accidentally damaged. His first patient had needed to be castrated twelve years earlier following a crush injury while playing football. An organ procured from the autopsy of a teenage boy so improved the situation that the patient was said to need an ice pack to control the frequency of erections! Even if the graft had been a success, we now realize that testosterone is not required for penile tumescence, as the erections of infants testify. Still, the positive result was taken as a good omen at the time.

A wave of success often brings a tide of problems behind it. There was the problem of where to obtain suitable young donors, and men eager for treatment soon outnumbered them. Supplies were unpredictable, not to say seedy, because the main sources were accident victims and electrocuted prisoners. So precious were the organs that if they arrived on a weekend they were stored in the refrigerator until the following Monday morning. Few glandular cells will stand up to this sort of treatment, and testes deteriorate quickly after removal from the body, but Lydston still claimed remarkable cures.

The publicity greeting his announcements encouraged others to set up their own trials and clinics. One of Steinach's medical colleagues, Robert Lichtenstern, carried out an operation on a twenty-nine-year-old lance-corporal who had been wounded in the war three years earlier, in 1915. Gunshot had blasted off both testicles, and a 'spare' organ was procured from another soldier, who had been operated on for undescended organs. After stitching a slice to the abdominal muscle, the lance-corporal's beard regrew and his sex life improved, though he never fathered children.

The doctor in charge at San Quentin Prison in California, a Dr Stanley, was also an enthusiastic gland grafter. Prisoners have often been willing guinea-pigs in clinical trials as quite trivial inducements are attractive distractions from the tedium of prison routine. He also managed to persuade some of the other doctors and even a few women to become subjects for implanting testes from executed prisoners or, if suitable human material was not available, the organs of goats, rams, boars or deer. The tissues were ground to a pulp and injected through a wide-bore hypodermic needle into the belly muscle. He argued that hormone secretion was as effective at this site as in the scrotum, and that homogenization would encourage quicker ingrowth of blood vessels. Within a few weeks he recorded some striking recoveries from asthma, acne, rheumatism and senility. Even more dramatically, subjects were performing remarkably well on prison sports days.

As the 1920s dawned, gland grafting seemed to be a sure path to fame and fortune but for the shortage of human organs. The need to overcome this shortage became the stimulus for inventive genius.

• Steinach's Operation

Steinach hoped that he could avoid the need for grafting by boosting existing hormone production from old testes. During experiments on vasectomized rats he had noticed that the tubules in the testes where the sperm are made were degenerating. At the same time, the neighbouring Leydig cells responsible for testosterone secretion were enlarging and becoming more active. He drew the conclusion that back-pressure caused by tying the vas deferens had killed the developing sperm cells and created extra space for the hormone-producing cells to spread. Since there were fewer sperms to make demands on the hormone, more testosterone would be available to enter the bloodstream for invigorating the rest of the body. Could vasectomy, which was both simple and safe, achieve the same ends as gland grafting?

After a few weeks in his laboratory, Steinach had confirmed his hunch. Old rats that had been vasectomized looked younger and sleeker than before. They had renewed vitality and virility, just like grafted animals. He called the operation 'vaso-ligature', but it soon became popularly known as 'Steinach's operation'.

He persuaded Lichtenstern to test the operation on a patient. Only one tube was tied, leaving its opposite member as a backup for a future operation at a later date – for an additional fee. Word soon got around that the operation worked and could cure symptoms of 'male menopause'. There were said to be lasting improvements in blood pressure, tremor, vertigo and rheumatic pain, sight and hearing, and there was even regrowth of dark hair on bald pates. Some doctors praised the sexual benefits of the operation and claimed that testicles enlarged and sexual potency improved in undersexed men.

Steinach's reputation grew immensely as news of the revolutionary operation spread. His name became a byword for scientific wonders. It was said that even a cabbage could be Steinached! The press portrayed him as a kindly genius whose labours and wisdom would benefit everyone. Like other rejuvenators, he published popular books extolling his theories and methods. He cleverly adapted Sir William Ostler's felicitous dictum that 'a man is only as old as his arteries' to 'we are as old as our glands'. Every strength and weakness became attributed to hormones, just as genes are held responsible today. He also predicted, not entirely in jest, 'I think the day will come when vaso-ligature or some other process having a like effect, will be undertaken by the state for every man of fifty, just as every child is vaccinated for the prevention of smallpox today.' The lengthening queues of patients in clinics seemed, for a while, to confirm his dream.

Many patients were delighted with a greater sense of well-being after years of ineffective conventional treatment and quack remedies. Their enthusiasm contrasts starkly with today's negative attitude to sterilization by vasectomy, which is regarded by young men as sacrificial and definitely not therapeutic. No one is now heard to say that he feels reinvigorated by vasectomy and, if anything, men are anxious that tampering may have done them harm, despite the lack of much evidence. The power of suggestion is enormous in the realms of human sexual physiology and behaviour.

But what of the so-called weaker sex? With an eye to expanding business, the rejuvenators considered the problem of the ever-increasing numbers of older women in the population. Would they be helped by tying off the fallopian tube – the female equivalent of the vas deferens? The results were disappointing and doctors offered the quasi-scientific explanation that, because the tubes are not structurally connected to the sex gland (as in men), hormone secretion could not be stimulated. One wonders at the different responses between the sexes and why men were taken in more easily.

The attractions of practising rejuvenation therapy on the fringes of medicine earlier this century were that there were few controls and if one procedure failed there were always others to try in last-ditch attempts to help a patient. The 'Repetition Operation' involved cutting the tough coat around the testis to allow the tubules to extrude so that a few could be cut. This was like a crude biopsy, although the intentions were therapeutic rather than diagnostic and likely to do more harm than good. One of the more exotic suggestions was 'Autotransplantation' which required removing the testes to another part of the body, though I am unsure whether it was ever used. The only advantage I can see in this is that a less bruising site might be found!

Patients who did not relish surgery could be treated by 'diathermy'. The passage of up to one ampere of direct current from electrodes connected across the testicles would surely kick-start ailing glands. The pioneers of rejuvenation science certainly had creative imaginations and a remedy for every circumstance, but some treatments sound horrific to modern ears. 'Mildly stimulating doses' of X-rays and radium were used as an alternative to Steinach's operation, because they destroy developing sperm cells. The still mysterious properties of radiation added to the aura, but its dangers were not appreciated and safety regulations were non-existent. An American company used mail order to distribute apparatus containing radium designed to be worn in bed at night. This home rejuvenation kit was taking matters too far even for Steinach's transatlantic supporters. They rightly feared for public safety and were anxious that rejuvenation therapy should not be brought into disrepute because professional reputations and private fortunes were at stake.

The rejuvenators claimed they could achieve with a few deft strokes of the scalpel a complete overhaul of a man's physiology – whereas a cosmetic surgeon's handiwork goes only skin deep. A number of famous celebrities signed up for treatment, giving prestige and glamour to the reputation of clinics. For performers who felt past their prime and feared they would be written off by their fans, the possibility of rejuvenation was magnetically attractive, and even rumour of treatment spread by gossip columnists was welcome. Artists are often instinctively suspicious of science, but they too sat up and swallowed their doubts at the prospect of reversing Old Man Time. By 1934 W. B. Yeats, the Irish poet, then aged sixty-nine, had stopped writing poetry after losing his companion and mentor Lady Gregory.

He opted for a Steinach operation by the Harley Street sexologist Norman Haire and allegedly regained some of his strength and creativity.

Private patients often travelled great distances for treatment, which presented difficulties if the doctor wanted to gauge the clinical outcome. A captive population was needed for a proper long-term assessment of the benefits. A medical officer at an Indiana penitentiary tested the Steinach operation on his inmates and reported favourably:

> I have 465 cases that have afforded splendid opportunity for postoperative observation, and I have never seen any unfavourable symptom. There is no atrophy of the testicle, there is no cystic degeneration following but, on the contrary, the patient becomes of a more sunny disposition, brighter of intellect, ceases excess masturbation, and advises his fellows to submit to the operation for their own good.

Even the best treatments fail sometimes, and a failure cannot be concealed when the subject is a man of means. Albert Wilson was so rapturous about his successful operation – and sufficiently wealthy – that he hired the Albert Hall in London to deliver a lecture entitled, 'How I was Made Twenty Years Younger'. On the day before this engagement, he celebrated with a heavy drinking bout with his friends. As Haire later recalled:

> He was a man over seventy, who had been most successfully operated on by Steinach some time before, but too confident in his renewed vigour, he overtaxed his powers and died [the day before his lecture] from an attack of angina pectoris, a disease from which he had suffered for many years before the operation. He had been warned not to be prodigal of his new-found strength, but forgot that he was in his seventies and tried to live like a young man in the twenties. The result, of course, was disaster.

Some critics were so worried by the exaggerated claims being made that they condemned the entire enterprise. Morris Fishbein, the editor of a prestigious American medical journal, repeatedly thundered that all such attempts were worthless, if not dangerous. To encourage public revulsion, he pointed out that the hidden agenda was invariably a sexual rejuvenation. The rejuvenators were stung by this reproach. They scoffed at the editor's lack of professional experience in endocrinology, which was true enough, and accused him of sanctimonious attacks on the teachings of both Steinach and Freud. Steinach's reputation survived these skirmishes and the subsequent critical gaze of history, though he is remembered more as a great pioneer of hormone research than for his work on ageing.

• Goat-Gland Gospel

Just as the lucky strike by a gold-miner encourages a host of hopeful prospectors, so scientific and medical advances frequently attract charlatans and medical bootleggers to follow in their wake. One of the most colourful was 'Doc' John Romulus Brinkley. He emerged from the backwoods of North Carolina to become the leading practitioner of what became known as 'goat-gland science'. Although he had received only rudimentary training in an unorthodox medical school (yet claiming three degrees), he did not lack skill and certainly had plenty of native wit. From a small private clinic established in rural Kansas in 1917, he built an empire that attracted national attention and thousands of paying patients.

Many apocryphal tales have been told of Brinkley's launch into rejuvenation therapy but, whatever the truth, his choice of goat testicles demonstrated shrewd business acumen. The farming community respected the goat for toughness and resistance to disease. Readers of classical literature (admittedly few in those parts) were aware of the lusty reputation of chimeric fertility spirits with goats' legs and horns and stories about debauched Roman youths using goat and wolf glands to induce satyriasis. Brinkley hoped these supposed qualities, real or imaginary, would be recalled as allies in the fight against the loss of vitality.

Since the caprine testicle is relatively small, he grafted the whole organ into the human scrotum and anchored it near the spermatic cord. Those willing to pay a fee of around $750 were offered a 'four-phase operation'. After the grafting phase, the next step was a Steinach operation in which Brinkley injected mercurochrome into the cut ends of the vas deferens. This antiseptic would have coloured the patient's urine for several days, and doubtless reassured him that the treatment was having its magical effect. The third and fourth phases involved detaching a small artery and a nerve from the graft and hooking them on to the patient's own testis. Brinkley claimed that these manœuvres helped to nourish and energize the gland. In fact there is no firm evidence that nerves are necessary for hormone production, and it is doubtful whether additional blood vessels would have penetrated the tough organ capsule to the glandular tissues inside.

Shunned by the medical establishment, Brinkley was basically a businessman and kept his methods secret. Only rarely did he reveal his aims and means:

> the glands of a three weeks' old male goat are laid upon the non-functioning glands of a man ... After being properly connected these goat glands do actually feed, grow into, and become absorbed by the human glands, and the man is renewed in his physical and mental vigor ... For impotency, insanity, arteriosclerosis, paralysis agitans, prostate trouble, high blood pressure, skin diseases, diseases of organs of regeneration, and for prolonging life and rebuilding the human body, I know of nothing that will equal gland transplantation.

Encouraged by good reports from local clients, Brinkley began to advertise. He was one of the first people in the United States to grasp the commercial potential of radio broadcasting, and he built a powerful radio station with a range to the mid-Atlantic. He promoted country-and-western music and fundamentalist preaching, and gave a daily armchair chat on medical topics. By all accounts he was a mesmerizing speaker, and he attracted a devoted following across the social and economic spectrum of America. He realized that men are bashful about impotence, and so he went over their heads and appealed to wives to send their husbands to his clinic. He knew that women were not all icebergs.

Brinkley revelled in the publicity he was attracting. An article in the *New York Evening Journal* described his work as a blend of 'Old-Time Religion and New-Fangled Operations on a strange Medico-Gospel Farm'. Brinkley was featured carrying a child who was supposed to be the first 'goat-gland baby' fathered after treatment. Of course, the boy was named Billy!

Sporting a goatee beard and with a receding hairline in mid-life, Brinkley presented a memorable and larger-than-life personality. Influential figures travelled great distances to receive treatment at his clinic, including an editor of the *Los Angeles Times* and a Chancellor of the Chicago Law School. Brinkley flourished throughout the 1920s because animal organ grafts were not completely outside the credibility of orthodox science. Indeed, several medical centres and authorities were currently recommending them for all sorts of illnesses when conventional treatments had failed. He offered a refreshingly different kind of service to people who had reached the stage of last resort. And he craftily followed the old mountebank practice of insisting that patients give up alcohol and tobacco, for then a graft could at least be credited with the benefits from being abstemious.

On arrival at the clinic, patients would hear the bleating of young billy-goats penned close by. Punters could select their donor much as a diner chooses a lobster from a restaurant aquarium. Such highly professional roguery provoked many exaggerated anecdotes, though the facts about the Brinkley enterprise were hardly less colourful. On one occasion an elderly gentleman arrived from Boston with his own goat on the running-board of his car. Brinkley, offended at his full service being snubbed, asked why the man insisted on using his own goat for the operation. The gentleman answered, 'I know what that goat can do!'

As his reputation grew and his influence spread, the Doc came under increasing attack from the medical establishment, especially in the form of the tireless Morris Fishbein who vilified Brinkley as the apotheosis of quackery. In 1929 the Kansas Medical Board moved against him to revoke his licence to practise medicine, to which he responded by marshalling some dotards to testify in his defence. Patients who had just parted with a sizeable sum of money for a goat-gland operation were usually willing to defend their ram-parts by professing improved health or, better still, by physically demonstrating their vigour in the 100-yard dash. Nevertheless, Brinkley was forced to close his operation in Kansas and to move to more liberal states to continue his practice – until Fishbein's net trapped him there.

He played one further card that might have altered the fortunes of his rejuvenation clinic and the course of state history. On three separate occasions in the 1930s he ran for the governorship of the state of Kansas. He had a large popular following in the Depression years when the established political parties were held in disdain. So powerful were his political allies in the state capitol that they had decorated their celebrated citizen as an Admiral of the Kansas Navy (*sic*), giving him a bicorne hat, a natty uniform and a ceremonial sword. Despite his celebrity status, he tried to portray himself as a typical representative of the ordinary and decent man, though one who happened to be up against a medical Goliath. In the event, he narrowly failed on a technicality to get elected Governor.

Brinkley had been knocked down but not out. In the mid-1930s he was busily operating from Arkansas on patients with prostate-gland trouble. This had become better business than goat-gland operations because synthetic sex hormones were replacing transplants in popularity. He had observed that the decline of sexual power and testicular size were warnings of impending pathological enlargement of the prostate gland. He chose the Steinach operation with the aim of stimulating the Leydig cells and stemming further prostatic growth to avoid the risky operation of removing a diseased gland. His reasoning was faulty and the surgical work was futile – but it was very profitable.

The inquisitorial Fishbein pursued him across the country in a campaign of professional purification. In 1939 Brinkley responded by bringing a $250,000 legal suit for libel – and lost. By 1941 he was declared bankrupt by his own petition, though we all know that this need not mean a man is broke. The following year, while convalescing after an amputation for circulatory disease, he received a letter from the US Postal Service, which had filed a complaint against him for spreading false claims through the mail about goat-gland operations. The citation belatedly indicted him for collecting $12,000,000 from 16,000 patients. Rejuvenation therapy had moved a long way from the laboratory of the altruistic Brown-Séquard to the world of American enterprise culture.

• Monkey-Gland Business

A few orthodox doctors too were recommending animal organs for grafting. The surgeon who eventually assumed leadership of this field was a Frenchman of Russian Jewish extraction, Serge Voronoff. He had followed a fairly conventional medical career until middle age, when he switched to transplant surgery. While serving as a young doctor in a Cairo court he got the impression that eunuchs do not live as long as other men, and this set him thinking about the causes and treatment of ageing. A chance meeting during the Great War with another French military surgeon, Alexis Carrel, spurred his ambition to become a transplant surgeon after demobilization.

The appalling loss of the flower of French youth during the war had created a population imbalance and helped him choose his medical speciality. There was a national shortage of husbands, and many of those returning from the front had been mutilated by war injuries. Young women would have to look for suitors within the generation that had been too old to be called up for war service.

Voronoff proudly proclaimed that he was devoting the rest of his career to restoring the physical and sexual vigour of men to help the work of national reconstruction.

He began in 1917 by practising his surgical skills on sheep and goats. These experiments soon paid dividends. Within two years he was able to report preliminary results to the Société de Biologie in Paris and at the French Surgical Congress. He had grafted testes from young donors into 120 rams assumed to be hormonally deficient after castration or in old age. Grafted animals had increased in weight, grown stouter horns and produced half a kilo more wool per fleece. In those days there were no government grants for researchers but, with characteristic boldness, he proposed a national subsidy for his work which promised increasing wool growth to help pay the French war debt.

Soon afterwards he announced even more impressive results. Within two months of surgery, ten-year-old rams were more bellicose than before and successfully mated every ewe within reach. This could hardly be attributed to the psychology of suggestion! To counter once and for all any remaining doubts, he showed that the formerly weak condition of his animals returned when the grafts were removed. The grafts were apparently working well and secreting testosterone. Most dramatically of all, the rams enjoyed an increased lifespan: they were living at least a quarter longer than their normal span of twelve to fourteen years. People began to wonder whether human lifespan extension might be possible after all.

Government officials were sufficiently impressed that Voronoff was invited to try to improve stocks of sheep in the Algerian colonies. During one of his visits, he was asked to rejuvenate an old prize bull, Jacky, who was seventeen at the time and quite useless as a stud. This was an economically attractive proposition because it was costly to import replacements from France, but not without personal risk. In March 1924 Voronoff wrote:

> I grafted into him the testicles of a native three-year-old bull
> [under local anaesthesia] in front of a great number of breeders

... Although the animal was made to lie upon its side and was kept in this position by some ten Arabs, it gave frequent signs of impatience which resulted in the frequent upsetting of all the surgeons.

In June of the same year, Monsieur Nouvion of the Algerian Agricultural Society wrote to Voronoff, who had returned home to Paris,

The bull we operated upon is keeping very fit; its hair has become glossy, its eyes sparkling and ... [it] now seems full of ardour. During the last few days he was put with a cow that was on heat, and he covered this animal four times during the course of the morning, which number is quite a record.

A later letter recorded that Jacky 'scarcely ever ceased to exercise his reproductive functions save when it has been impossible to furnish him with partners'. Jacky produced six calves in 1925 alone, though he needed another graft three years later. Voronoff was satisfied that this was unequivocal proof of the value of gland grafting.

In 1921 he was appointed to the post of Director at the Experimental Surgery Department in the Collège de France. His encouraging results with animals convinced him that the time was ripe to embark on human testis grafts to follow-up Lydston's earlier success. He too encountered difficulty obtaining a supply of suitable organs. The legal prohibition of removing organs from accident victims was annoying, and waiting at the foot of the guillotine for specimens was both undignified and impractical. A few young men volunteered an organ but their charges were exorbitant, and the offerings of the elderly were rejected. Circumstances were forcing Voronoff either to drop human grafts altogether or to resort to animal donors.

Since the genetic gulf between farm animals and humans is great, he preferred to use chimpanzee donors until forced to switch to monkeys when the supply ran out. Under chloroform anaesthesia, each animal surrendered one testicle to patients whose scrotums were surgically opened so that the donor tissue could be stitched alongside the resident organs. A chimpanzee provided enough tissue for several men because it has relatively large testicles for its body size, like other highly promiscuous species. The smaller organs of monkeys were often grafted whole, which required burning holes through the capsule to let the blood vessels grow in – a procedure dubbed 'lanternization' in America. Imagine the scene in the operating room of man and monkey lying on adjacent tables – a picture of the brotherhood of creatures!

The performance of the grafts in Voronoff's first two patients, who had been castrated for tuberculosis of the scrotum, was disappointing and the beard of only one of them sprouted again. A third man, who was fifty-nine and suffering from memory loss and depression, declared he felt much better after his operation. The fourth patient, a famous man of letters who remained anonymous, was sixty-one and showing signs of senility at the time of his operation. He claimed to feel ten years younger afterwards, and was able to resume a heavy workload without fatigue. Voronoff seized an early opportunity for publicity and exhibited one of his patients at a medical congress. This seventy-four-year-old Englishman had been old and haggard, walking stiffly with a stick. Some months after grafting, his *embonpoint* restored, he was obviously stronger, more agile and jovial, and claimed to feel at least twenty years younger. One might easily have believed that portraits taken before and after his operation had been reversed.

In many other apparently convincing cases, mental health improved, flabby fat was absorbed, hair sprouted on the scalp, sexual and intellectual powers returned and heart conditions improved. All these successes were attributed to physiological refreshment by the sex hormones from the graft. Voronoff strenuously denied charges that his work was aimed at sexual rejuvenation but, as far as extension of the lifespan was concerned, he was willing to risk the wrath of professional colleagues by hinting at grand possibilities. He told a reporter from the periodical *Scientific American*:

> If we consider one year of a ram's life equivalent to six years of a
> man's, then we may estimate that by grafting we can add thirty

or forty years to a human life. We cannot tell yet just what results we will achieve, for we have been grafting glands successfully only for the last five years ... When a man will have lived to be 125, we will at last have found a path towards the abolition of old age.

Voronoff was enjoying his heyday, constantly in demand for prestigious lectures and hounded by reporters for news of his latest cases. Like other rejuvenators, he was a master of self-publicity, though his style was more suave than Steinach's and more sophisticated than Brinkley's. Many people who met him recalled he had the 'presence' of a great man. Although constantly embattled by critical peers in the medical establishment, his tall stature, deportment and elegant French manners impressed his patients and junior doctors.

While Voronoff was the acknowledged doyen of testicular grafting in Europe, his American counterpart was the Surgeon-in-Chief at the American Hospital of Chicago, Max Thorek. Together, they spearheaded the 'monkey-gland campaign' – so called because American journalists were prohibited at the time from publishing the word 'testicles'. Thorek was convinced that monkey-gland grafts were 'thoroughly successful' for overcoming symptoms of sex hormone deficiency and nervous disorders. During the years 1919 to 1923 Thorek's team performed ninety-seven monkey- and human gland transplants and claimed marked improvements in fifty-nine patients. He was extremely courteous towards the Frenchman but cautiously distanced himself from any claims that the transplants could prolong life. A difference of opinion also existed between them about the source of the sex hormones. Voronoff believed that the tubules were responsible for producing both sperms and hormones, and the fatty Leydig cells merely nourished them. Thorek concurred with Steinach that the Leydig cells were the source of testosterone. He was a better microscopist than Voronoff and had found that these cells survived better after grafting than the tubules, and he was eventually proved right.

Editors and proprietors of the more salacious newspapers on

167

both sides of the Atlantic milked the monkey-gland story for all it was worth. Tall tales began to circulate about taxi-drivers being waylaid and robbed of their glands for black-market sales to ageing million-aires. General ignorance of the principles of genetics encouraged speculation about the novel hybrids which might be fathered by men revitalized with monkey glands. These worries provided plenty of stimulating material for cartoonists and even playwrights. Bertram Gaymer wrote a popular spoof based on the monkey-gland business, called *The Gland Stealers*. George Bernard Shaw quipped that 'man will remain what he is in spite of all Dr Voronoff's efforts to make a good ape of him'.

Not long afterwards, a storm of criticism broke about the ethics of this medical breakthrough, much as it had after Brown-Séquard's declaration. In England, antivivisectionists, for once acting in unison with professional biologists (if with different motives), generated a climate of opinion that deterred introduction of monkey gland therapy into the country. Despite the social changes after the war, prudish attitudes to sexuality persisted and many people genuinely believed that rejuvenation was immoral – particularly if it depended on sex-organ therapy and opposed the natural decline. These feelings were reflected in an influential American book by Sylvanus Stall entitled *What a Man of Forty-Five Ought to Know*:

> If the wife is to lose her power to conceive and to bear children,
> it is but reasonable to expect that the natures, which had during
> the long years of wedded life been suited to each other as the
> different parts of a complex but perfect machine, should now
> find, both in the husband and in the wife such mutual physical
> changes as should continue to harmonize their lives during the
> remainder of their days.

This idealized view of married life was being slowly eroded as sexual problems were discussed more openly. Marie Stopes, the British pioneer of contraception, received a large correspondence from both sexes revealing that many men are anxious about their physical appearance and sexual capacity in mid-life. Gland grafting promised much for them – and for their partners too.

Despite knee-jerk opposition from traditionalists, the 1920s were good years for Voronoff and for the rejuvenation enterprise generally. Even the British medical establishment moderated its views. As a sign, the Royal College of Surgeons chose testicular transplantation as the subject of its prestigious annual Hunterian Lecture in 1924. The lecturer, a Dr Walker, declared the results 'distinctly promising'. Even the *British Medical Journal* commented favourably on Voronoff's second book:

> Dr Voronoff has been the victim of a certain amount of misrepresentation and prejudice, largely owing to the premature interest which the lay press has taken in his work . . . No doubt the use of monkey tissue for the rejuvenation of men – a return, as it were, to our ancestry for refreshment – has in it certain elements of humour which have not passed unrecognised . . . The testicular graft is something worthy of serious consideration.

Respectability at last!

• Nemesis

As the Depression years of the 1930s ushered in a more sober period, so the fortunes of the rejuvenators turned sour. Incomes were falling and the prospect of another European war loomed. The problems of old age were thought to be less urgent than the struggle to maintain basic living standards.

At the same time, controversy within both medical and scientific establishments over the value of rejuvenation therapy was reaching a climax. Voronoff's claim that gland grafting had commercial agricultural significance had been noted in several countries, and the authorities agreed that they warranted investigation. A group of leading scientists from the UK, France, Italy, Spain, Argentina and

Czechoslovakia was assembled under Dr Francis Marshall FRS, a Cambridge physiologist and the author of the standard work on reproductive physiology. In November 1927 the delegation sailed from Europe to meet Voronoff in Algeria.

On reaching Bou Ghellel, some twenty miles outside Algiers, the company was addressed by Voronoff in an opening lecture. He provided the visitors with a large research folio and demonstrated his grafted animals, including the bull Jacky. Voronoff accompanied the party to the research station in the arid southern territories where he was reputed to have produced 'super sheep' by gland grafting. There seemed to be no doubt that the grafted animals were heavier and healthier than the rest of the flock. One of the friendly Arab herdsmen took a British delegate aside to say, 'We always ensure that the Doctor is provided with the best animals.' Perhaps he wanted to bolster the reputation of the research or felt that too little credit had been given to the workers. If so, his intentions backfired because any selection of animals for quality would have biased the results. This possibility worried the British members for the remainder of the tour. We will never know for sure whether Voronoff was misled by well-meaning assistants in the way that Mendel's monks are suspected to have 'tidied-up' data collected during his historic studies of the genetics of the garden pea.

After returning home, the delegates prepared national reports and recommendations about the new methods they had witnessed. Only the British were critical. They did not openly ridicule the work but they were obliquely critical of the record-keeping and the selection bias towards prize animals. Jacky's case particularly troubled the group because any bull surviving to the age of seventeen must have been exceptional. Most bulls reach peak performance at about three and are well past their prime at ten. The report read, 'Whilst the case of Jacky supports the hypothesis so ably adumbrated by Dr Voronoff, it cannot, nor can the other cases recorded by him, be accepted as final and conclusive proof of the validity of his thesis concerning rejuvenation.' Voronoff was furious with the Britons. He accused them of being out of step with the main body of expert

The **male marsupial 'mouse'** (*Antechinus stuartii*)
quickly becomes old, balding and haggard during
the mating season because its only appetite is for sex.

By permission of Dan Irby

'The Bridge of Life' was commissioned by a statistician at the turn of the century to represent the increasing chances of dying as we grow older.

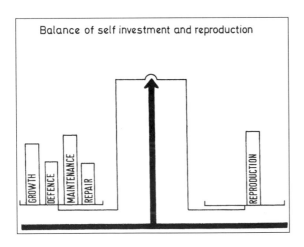

Balance of self investment and reproduction

GROWTH
DEFENCE
MAINTENANCE
REPAIR
REPRODUCTION

According to the disposable soma theory, living things have made a choice during evolution between investing in self-preservation and procreation, and the balance determines how quickly they age and their maximum lifespan.

George Dunnet, now retired from the University of Aberdeen, is an ornithologist who has studied fulmar petrels on Eynhallow, Orkney, for half a century. The first plate, taken in 1950, shows him with a bird he has ringed. The second shows him with the same bird in 1976. Unlike George, the bird hardly shows any signs of ageing.

The members of the international scientific delegation which investigated the claims of **Dr Serge Voronoff** (fourth from the left) in Algiers in 1927.

By permission of the Journal of Endocrinology

Opposite:

Charles-Edouard Brown-Séquard (1817–1894), Professor in the Collège de France and pioneer of hormone research.

(Inset) An advertisement for Brown-Séquard's Elixir from a pharmaceutical journal of the 1890s.

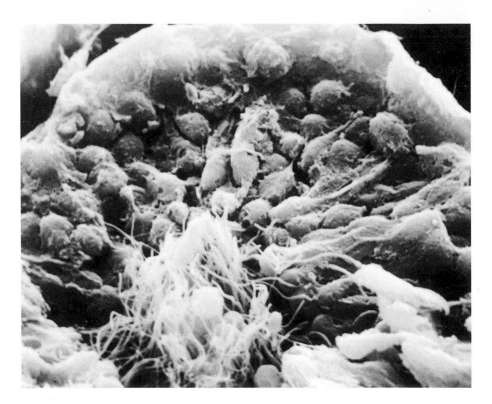

Electron micrograph of a testicle. The testis, shown here under an electron microscope, consists of tubes where the sperm are produced surrounded by cells which are responsible for testosterone secretion.

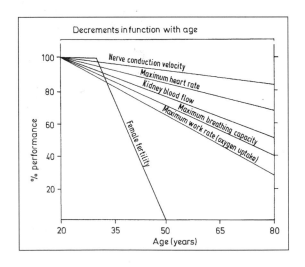

This graph shows the decreased performance of the human body as we age.

opinion. But the British establishment closed ranks and declared that Voronoff's claims were unproven.

Meanwhile a young biologist had entered the field with high hopes of clarifying waters that had been muddied by his elders. Carl Moore of Chicago wanted to satisfy himself that rejuvenation was possible in old rats, as Steinach had demonstrated. He tried both testicle grafting and tying the vas deferens, but neither gave a positive result.

When Moore inspected the testicles in the vasectomized animals, he neither found signs of the degenerating tubules reported before nor evidence of any change in hormone production. He investigated the discrepancy by hooking the testes out of the scrotum of other rats and securing them with a stitch in the warmer environment of the body cavity. This procedure mimicked what happens with undescended testes in men – or 'cryptorchidism'. Since sperm production abruptly ceased, it was apparent that it requires a slightly cooler environment than deep body temperature. Moore mused that a poor surgical technique may have prevented the testes of Steinach's rats descending to their normal site, and the much-vaunted claims were possibly just an artefact of heat damage. The Steinach operation may not have done any harm to patients, but the benefits were probably more psychological than organic.

Moore also singled out Steinach's belief in gland grafting for a withering attack. 'No organ within the body is stimulated to increased function by the introduction of products which it, itself, produces ... Why, in the face of ... negative evidence regarding other glands as well as the testis itself, should anyone postulate that testis hormone would revivify a so-called hypofunctional testis?'

Criticisms were coming thick and fast from many places, including the relative obscurity of French Morocco. News of Voronoff's work had reached a veterinary surgeon, Henri Velu, who tried to repeat it with his own flocks. He found lumps of hard tissue persisting at the graft sites – just as Voronoff had said. But, when he investigated them with a microscope, he found only scars remaining. Not a single cell from the original graft had survived more than a couple of weeks!

Velu's conclusions were not universally welcomed, especially by members of his own profession who had adopted gland grafting in their practices. But he dug his heels in and was eventually vindicated.

While the gland-grafting flotilla was sinking, another rejuvenator was rising in popularity. Paul Niehans attracted some of the world's richest and most famous figures to his exclusive clinic in Switzerland. It mattered little whether it was true that his patients included Somerset Maugham, Noël Coward, Conrad Adenauer and the Duke and Duchess of Windsor: the rumours were all the publicity he needed. His prestige became almost impregnable after being called in to treat the ailing Pope in 1935.

Niehans too had obtained poor results with the Steinach operation when he was a young doctor and he realized that new remedies were needed for the old problem. He developed 'Cellular Therapy', which was defined as 'a method of treating the whole organism on a biological basis, capable of revitalizing the human organism with trillions of cells by bringing it those embryonic or young cells which it needs'. One of his favourite cures for old age was to inject cells from sheep foetuses. Authority for this strategy rested largely on Alexis Carrel's experiments which showed (wrongly as it turned out) that cells could grow for ever *in vitro* when fed with embryo extracts. Niehans believed that substances produced from youthful cells are lost with age and need replacing. This was phoney science and did not help respectable gerontologists in their efforts to throw off the reputation the subject had gained for quackery.

The question of whether foreign cells could survive for long in a different body was beginning to surface at this time. Foetal and placental cells are genetically dissimilar to the mother and are tolerated throughout pregnancy, but this is a special case and does not answer for grafts at other times and of other species. For a long time there was a muddled notion that foreign grafts are tolerated if the body 'needs' them, but it was wishful thinking to expect a foreign organ to last just because the native one was absent or inactive. Gradually it was understood that the body rejects a foreign graft, just as Carrel had warned, but no one was sure what the limits of tolerance were. Someone without pecuniary interests in the results and with a fresh mind was needed to look beyond the myths and throw light on the natural laws of transplantation.

Shortly after the Second World War, Peter Medawar began to explore whether skin grafts might be used successfully to treat burn injuries. He found that skin from one strain of mouse was always rejected after grafting it to a genetically dissimilar strain. When the operation was repeated using the same donor as before, rejection came even swifter, showing that the immune system had a memory. The greater the genetic difference between the two, and the more often the operation was repeated, the more aggressively the host reacted – despite the graft being in its best interests. With the exception of identical twins and inbred animals, every individual is a genetically unique creation and mounts a hostile immune response to anything which is recognized to be different to itself. Medawar's work effectively quashed any remaining doubts about the fate of cells and organs grafted from one person to another or between species.

The rejuvenators had transgressed the basic rules of immunology as well as having misinterpreted their results. Glands grafted from animals to humans and from man to man would have died within a week or two at most – and repeats sooner still. With hindsight, grafts could not even be justified on the basis of releasing hormones to produce short-lived effects before they degenerated. Testosterone has to be produced continuously from a healthy human testicle because the organ only stores 1 per cent of what is needed each day by a normal man (seven milligrams).

By the 1930s the gland grafters were going out of business, pursued now by angry patients rather than the press. As evidence grew that their operations were not only worthless but perhaps harmful, compensation claims multiplied. Sores and abscesses were irritating reminders of having been duped into paying for false hopes, and some patients settled for substantial sums in compensation out of court. The surgeons were lucky to have avoided even hotter water. Donor organs had been obtained from apparently healthy men, but there was still a danger of transferring infectious diseases, especially to vulnerable sick and elderly patients. Monkey glands were no safer because they can transmit many serious diseases, including tuberculosis, hepatitis, Marburg fever and perhaps others.

Not all grafts deserve to have scorn poured over them, for where graft and host are genetically identical there is a strong chance that the graft will 'take'. In 1941 the testicles of an American who had been castrated in an industrial accident were carefully extricated from the machinery, minced, and injected into his belly muscle. It is hard to say whether the self-graft had indeed raised his testosterone levels, as claimed, but another operation carried out in St Louis in 1977 is fully convincing.

A policeman who was born without any testicles had a genetically identical twin who was willing to donate one after he had fathered children. A microsurgeon, Sherman Silber, transferred the organ to the brother's vacant scrotum and carried out the necessary plumbing connections on the free ends of the blood vessels and the vas deferens so that a circulation was restored and sperm could pass to the penis. The operation was soon judged a success and the patient's blood testosterone levels rose to normal in a few days. Sperm appeared in his semen and he has since fathered four children. The grateful man later returned to his surgeons with a request for a vasectomy – but they refused to undo their handiwork!

This technical feat marks a high point in surgical skill and fraternal charity, but it offers little hope to most sterile men and closes a chapter on testicle grafting. Organ grafting boasts many notable achievements, and many thousands of people are thankful for the gift of a grafted kidney, heart or other organ. While the donation from an identical twin is rarely possible, close matching to the host and suppression of the immune system have revolutionized the chances of organ survival. Were they alive today, the rejuvenators would probably want to take some of the credit for this progress, but the legacy they left to science was as barren as what they gave to their patients. They had recklessly tried operations before enough basic research had been done and had misunderstood the relationship between sex and ageing.

Ageing is far more complex than they had suspected, and we now know that not all symptoms are triggered by declining sex hormone levels – though some undoubtedly are. The rejuvenators had at best kept the ball rolling until science was poised for further progress. Chemical endocrinology eventually triumphed and confirmed inklings about the existence of sex hormones that had been around for centuries. The availability of pure, synthetic hormones has at last provided a powerful way not only of controlling reproduction and treating its disorders but also of alleviating some of the ills that the gland grafters had been pointing to all along. Not that progress on hormone replacement therapy has been without its controversies, and science has still to reach a final verdict on the role of sex hormones in the process of ageing.

CHAPTER 8

Hormones Come of Age

> Though you drink your fill of medicine, avoid the taste in swallowing it.
>
> An old Chinese proverb

• Nostrums, Potions and Satyricons

Herbal remedies are enjoying a revival in popularity after decades of neglect. We were becoming so familiar with synthetic drugs that we were almost in danger of forgetting that all medicines had natural origins until fairly recently. As yet, however, there is little sign of a resurgence in the acceptability of animal products, though they were an economically important component of the medicaster's trade and could yet play a role in modern medicine. What is beyond dispute is that animal preparations deserve some credit for launching research into hormones and their actions, which has been of immeasurable benefit to both humans and animals.

Brown-Séquard's Elixir for senility and impotence was one of the most important of these pioneering potions, though it eventually proved ineffective. The thinking behind it probably owed as much to ideas prevalent in the ancient world as to Victorian science. In the streets and market-places of Rome, preparations from the testicles of goats and wolves were peddled as remedies for all kinds of nervous disorder and for hastening recovery from sexual excess. Caligula and Nero were said to have used these *aquae amatrices* to obtain greater stamina during their debauches, and Messalina, the promiscuous third wife of Claudius, administered satyricons to revive her exhausted lovers.

Pliny the Elder, the Roman scholar who had a fatal curiosity to see the eruption of Vesuvius, made detailed records of the medicines prescribed in his day. Hundreds of different animal and human products were used in the formulations. Boiled brain of crows or owls was good for headache, ass's liver for liver pain, kidney of hares for renal pain, and a boar's bladder (including its contents) for colic caused by stones. Men were advised to eat animal testicles to overcome impotence, while the genitals of hares were prized for helping women to conceive.

Male organs figured largely in the *materia medica* of many cultural and religious groups. From the Middle East to China, desiccated or raw testicles of pigs, dogs and sheep were recommended for restoring strength and fertility. Like was treated with like – which is neither an unreasonable nor an unfamiliar principle. A millennium later, Nicholas Culpeper listed many animal products in his *Dispensatory* (pharmacopoeia) for the Royal College of Physicians of London:

> The lungues of a fox well-dryed (but not burned) is an admirable strengthener to the lungues. The liver of a duck stops fluxes, and strengthens the liver exceedingly … The yard of a stag helps fluxes, the bitings of venemous beasts, provokes urine, and stirs up lust exceedingly.

Animal sex organs were commonly prescribed to boost strength, improve fecundity and virility, and overcome frailty in the elderly. Testes were still mainstays for treating male problems in the seventeenth century according to this memorable entry in William Salmon's *Dispensatory*:

> Sperma hominis, semen, sperm. Of this Paracelsus makes his homunculus. Experience has proved it good against imbecility of the instruments of generation.

During the Renaissance the principle of using like for like was elevated to the status of theological dogma by the radical Swiss doctor

177

Paracelsus. In his human-centred universe he envisioned that, because the world was created providentially for us, every animal and plant carried an indication of its proper use. According to this 'Doctrine of Signatures', lungwort leaves were valuable for treating lung disease, the colour of saffron was for jaundice, and red wine alleviated blood disorders and anaemia. Its remarkable androgynous shape recommended the mandrake plant for sexual problems as far back as Old Testament days, and Jacob's wife, Rachel, fell pregnant after wearing one as a talisman. Infertility was as much – or perhaps more – a cause of anguish then as it is today.

We do not know who discovered that testes are needed for fertility and virility, but their exposed position must surely have inspired intelligent guesswork in prehistoric times. The effects on masculinity of either accidental damage to the organs or their congenital failure to descend to their proper place in the scrotum would not have gone unnoticed for long. An accurate physiological explanation came much later, but there was plenty of speculation. Aristotle knew that testes were essential for fertility, and suggested that they were needed as weights to hold down the spermatic ducts!

Once the beneficial effects of castration on an animal's temperament and on the flavour and fatness of its meat had been recognized, farmers used the operation commercially. This practice continues to this day. The same treatment was meted out routinely and without qualms to men in the ancient world, but this mutilation was not regarded so negatively as it is nowadays. Eunuchs held positions at almost every level of society – from slaves and servants to court officials and harem managers, even the occasional army general.

The ovaries, a pair of walnut-sized organs lying deep within the female abdomen, draw much less attention to themselves. They can easily be overlooked during dissection of the body, especially of an old woman. From the days of Aeschylus, if not earlier, the male was regarded as having the primary role in human reproduction, as in other important matters. Popular metaphors of the seed and fertile ground, which Aeschylus also accepted, belittled the mother's part:

> It is not the mother who begets the one called her child; she but nourishes the seed sown in her. The begetter is the man who fertilizes her; she – a stranger – safeguards a foreign sprout, when the gods do not injure it.

Some of the first microscopists in the seventeenth century even declared that they could see a little man or 'homunculus' in the sperm's head. The old myth may have been accepted uncritically at first by scientists, but they eventually scotched it. Later in the same century the significance of the 'female testicles' was realized by a Delft physician, Regnier de Graaf, though it was not until 1834 that the first mammalian egg was identified under the microscope. Soon it was appreciated that females actually make the larger contribution to the embryo. The principle of *omne vivum ex ovo* – every living thing starts as an egg – had been held for egg-laying species since time immemorial, and now science was raising the newly discovered mammalian egg to the same high status. Had the key role of the ovaries been suspected earlier, they would certainly not have been absent from the lists of ingredients in old pharmacopoeias.

The mountebank business, though hardly an honourable one, was more excusable before the advent of physiology and pharmacology, and some of the traders were probably taken in by their own advertising. Their modern counterparts know better, yet they still seek to profit from fear, naïvety and superstition. Most of us will grasp at straws when desperate, especially if conventional medicine fails. A New Hampshire woman, who had spent a lot of money on a string of doctors, recently rang for advice about the 'alternative medicine' she had been taking for infertility and oestrogen deficiency. According to the manufacturers, the capsules, which carry a fancy name, contain raw ovary, uterus, adrenal and pituitary glands plus vitamins, minerals and 'RNA powder'. We have no idea how this crude concoction would perform in double-blind clinical trials – and the suppliers ignored my enquiries. This little incident shows how the vulnerable and unwary still fall victim to smooth-talking pedlars.

The most that can be said is that this preparation probably did no harm to patients or animals. Unfortunately, this is not the case with the oriental trade in rhino horn powder and tiger bone wine, which are claimed to increase the sex drive and strengthen feeble constitutions. We can only hope that it will end before it pushes these wonderful animals into oblivion.

There is one nostrum that costs nothing, hurts no one and still has a few adherents – neat urine. A wee dram taken before bedtime has been said to preserve a long and healthy life. Urine contains precious little sugar, protein or other nutrients in healthy people and is the way in which the body maintains a correct hydrogen-ion balance and eliminates excess salt and waste products. It seems pointless and even folly to return what the body, in its wisdom, has seen fit to eliminate. Nevertheless, urinary products do have some virtues.

If the aim is to make good a deficiency of an important substance in the body, it is logical to recover it from those who have an excess. Postmenopausal women excrete large amounts of fertility hormones in their urine, which may be used to treat infertility, while they, in turn, can benefit from rich sources of oestrogen in animals' urine. Today there are millions of women taking urinary steroids daily in the form of Premarin tablets, so named because they are produced from *pregnant mares' urine*. We tend to regard hormone replacement therapy (or HRT) as a modern development, but its roots are older than most people realize and came to light only recently.

• A Chinese Remedy

Long before Western scientists had even begun to speculate about the existence of sex hormones, the Chinese were treating patients with oestrogens extracted and semi-purified from urine. The preparations were supposed to restore fertility, to help them beget sons and to promote long life.

Oriental science depended more on tradition and philosophy

than on empirical observations, and Chinese ignorance of sexual biology was as great then as in the West. It held that every organ contributes an 'essence' to the blood and so helps to maintain a healthy balance in the body to thwart the progress of ageing. Treatment with urine was thought to correct any imbalance. According to Taoist philosophy, harmony in the universe depends on a balance of opposites: passivity and activity, dark and light, female and male – which were symbolically represented by *yin* and *yang*.

This principle is not entirely alien to the Western mind and was taken up independently by some of the first physiologists. As one set of muscles contracts, its opposite set relaxes. Were it otherwise we would not be able to move at all, because our muscles would be at odds with each other. Such reciprocity also exists in the processes of reproduction and lactation, as well as in urination and ejaculation. A balance is struck between stimulation and inhibition, though this is not a permanent truce between opposing forces: it tips in one direction or another when the need arises. The agents of this balancing act are the hormones and the nerves, though even the Ancient Chinese did not have the foresight to understand how they worked.

Chinese manuscripts record that around the year AD 200 there were three practitioners who were 'all expert at following the techniques of Jung Cheng in commerce with women. They could also drink urine ... They were careful and sparing of their seminal essence ... and did not boast with great words of their own powers ... All these people lived to between 100 and 200 years of age.' So influential were they that the merits of taking urine became widely known and the practice lasted for centuries. By AD 1350 one of the most famous doctor-chemists of the day, Chu Chen-Heng, recalled, 'I once attended an old woman over eighty years of age who gave an appearance of being about half that seniority. In reply to my questioning she explained that ... she had been instructed to take human urine, and this she had done for forty years.' The benefits were rather general and to be enjoyed by both sexes. Two centuries later, Li Shih-Chen was advising patients to drink urine to 'keep the blood in motion, greatly help sexual debility, bring down heat, kill parasites and disperse poisons.' He was scathing of 'lascivious people, who use it to further their unrestrained desires; the result is that eremotic heat is set at large, . . . and the seminal secretion quite exhausted.' These claims are remarkably reminiscent of those made by Brown-Séquard and his retinue of rejuvenators more than 300 years later, though the sexual philosophy of the Taoists was not so pessimistic.

Chinese chemists set about purifying the active agents (*chhiu ping*) in urine – not for the sake of scientific curiosity but to satisfy wealthy patricians. Urine has an unsavoury taste, and the merchant classes were happy to pay to have it made more palatable. The methods used in the extraction process were considerably more sophisticated and successful than those used by Brown-Séquard for testicular extracts. They came to light only fairly recently, when Joseph Needham, the distinguished Cambridge biochemist and sinologist, translated ancient manuscripts showing that a veritable pharmaceutical industry existed between AD 900 and 1500 in China. Upwards of 200 gallons of crude urine were collected at a time from adults and were stored in huge vats. After standing for a while, the solids precipitated out and could be collected. They were then heated in a special vessel until they sublimated. The condensed matter was ground to a powder and mixed with dates to make into pills the size of mung beans.

Urine contains many steroids but most of them are at low concentrations and biologically inactive. The fate of many hormonal steroids in the bloodstream is to become linked to sulphate or glucuronate ions produced in the body, which render them more soluble and easier to excrete via the kidneys. Even so, it is more practicable to purify hormones from urine than from either blood, where very high concentrations of protein interfere with extraction, or glandular tissue, which may transmit disease.

Needham had lived through a period of revolutionary progress in steroid biochemistry in the 1930s. What excited him about these historical discoveries was the astonishing convergence of technologies from two very different traditions and philosophies. Long before empirical chemistry had begun in the West, the Chinese had some-how hit upon the right temperature for sublimating steroids. Their recipe would almost certainly have yielded some oestrogens which were active by mouth. And still more remarkably, by luck or perspi-cacity, they even used urine from pregnant mares and human placen-tas during the Ming period. These are spectacularly rich sources of oestrogens. Had Needham's revelations been made a century earlier, Berthold and Brown-Séquard might have made more progress with urinary extracts and the science of endocrinology might have been spared a difficult birth.

After such an impressive start, Chinese science stood still after the 1500s because it had not understood the connection between urinary products and the sex glands. Western research eventually triumphed because it established the sources of the hormones.

• The Mysterious Midwife of HRT

Even though their reproductive role took longer to uncover, the ovaries have long been known to affect behaviour and to shape the body. In his *History of Animals*, Aristotle recorded that 'the ovaries of sows are excised with the view of quenching in them sexual appetites and of stimulating growth in size and fatness'. These effects were so well known that 'sow-gelders' were in demand in farming communi-ties throughout the Middle Ages. But it was not until much later that it was suggested that the ovaries produced eggs, nor was a hormonal role suspected until Brown-Séquard came along. He assumed that 'invigorating substances' were produced by ovaries, but thought they were not very potent and advised women to take testicular extracts. His philosophy was that what was good for the gander would also be good for the goose!

This attitude may appear blatantly sexist today, yet he did encourage others to test ovarian extracts for relieving menopausal complaints. Appropriately enough, it was a couple of enterprising women who took the initiative, and they probably had better success with their treatments than he ever had with his testicular elixir. This episode, which opens the first chapter of the story of hormone replacement therapy, is recorded as little more than a footnote in one of Brown-Séquard's papers. He briefly mentions that a Parisian midwife tested ovarian extracts on women, some of whom were relieved of menopausal symptoms. Unfortunately, that is all we know about the mysterious midwife of HRT.

A larger trial was carried out by a certain Mme Augusta Brown, who was no relation of the professor. Middle-class Victorians tried to shelter their womenfolk from the trials of business and professional life, and most medical schools barred them from their lecture and dissecting rooms. The first British woman doctor qualified in Edinburgh in 1812 only by disguising herself as a man, known as James Barry. She was sufficiently convincing to become a distinguished army medical officer and Inspector General of hospitals, and only after her death was her true identity uncovered. Others succeeded later in obtaining a medical qualification by grit and determination, and then only at first in one of the more progressive medical schools in France or Switzerland. The enigmatic Mme Brown may have been the victim of male prejudice for, although she was said to be an American graduate of the Parisian medical faculty, her medical thesis could not be traced during a search of the archives, and she did not publish her experimental trial in a learned journal. With the notable exception of Brown-Séquard, most commentators of the day referred to her work in rather dismissive tones.

Mme Brown prepared extracts from adult guinea-pig ovaries by the *méthode séquardienne* and injected them into several dozen middle-aged women. Many reported that they both felt and slept better. One who had lost a fine voice claimed that her larynx was strengthened by the treatment, though this was one of the less plausible claims.

It is difficult to assess the true benefits of Brown's efforts because her clinical trial was flawed by the omission of a control group. Menopausal symptoms are notoriously sensitive to the placebo effect, so we cannot be sure whether the benefits were more imaginary than real. Even so, it is likely that her ovarian extracts contained oestrogens and might have had some effects. Had she used alcohol instead of water to extract the glands, the preparations might have been more potent. She was lucky that the ovaries have a ready supply of oestrogen in the follicles. These are fluid-filled sacs looking like blisters bulging from the ovaries' surfaces, and each contains a single precious egg. She correctly assumed that the menopause and its symptoms are due to a deficiency of the ovaries, and her argument that ovarian replacement therapy would reverse some of the problems of underactive ovaries was compelling.

Like so many innovations, the launch of organ extracts was controversial. Manufacturers sprang up in France and elsewhere selling dubious products with little or no hormonal potency. They had no idea about the chemical composition of the products which were rarely what they assumed or hoped. Little did they know that they would have been more justified in marketing ovarian extracts as anti-cancer agents because the corpus luteum which forms from each follicle after ovulation is rich in vitamin A-like carotenoids. (The corpus luteum is also called the 'yellow body', though it is not in fact yellow but looks like a cherry in humans.)

There was no shortage of raw material for an industrial scale of manufacture. Pig and cow ovaries that had formerly been thrown away with other waste matter at abattoirs now found an eager market. They were ground to a paste in water or glycerine or alcohol to make extracts suitable for injection. Since hypodermic needles were even more fearsome then than now, oral preparations were devised too. After desiccating the tissue, the powder was compressed into pastilles which were coated with sugar to make them more palatable. Brand names such as Ovarine, Ovaraden, Oophorin and Ovowop enjoyed wide popularity for a while. People with stronger stomachs took their hormone treatment raw in the form of freshly minced ovaries in a sandwich.

There is now such a profusion of hormonal formulations and delivery systems that we take them all for granted. Yet HRT has become arguably the greatest preventive health care measure for women since the defeat of epidemic diseases. It is staggering that the perceptive midwife of HRT and Mme Brown have gone unrecognized for so long.

• The Heroic Age of Hormone Research

In experimental medicine it is often a moot point whether it is the patient or the doctor who is the more courageous, but in the early 1930s chemists were unquestionably the heroes of hormone research. They transformed the dubious quest for sexual therapies into an enterprise which made hormones available for all.

The process of discovering and purifying a new hormone was arduous and often disappointing. Starting with a crude extract of a gland or a body fluid, successively purer fractions were prepared laboriously. At each step in the process, hormonal activity had to be tested to check that it had not been lost, otherwise the effort would be wasted. When successful, the reward was just a few precious crystals of pure hormone, though the final goal was to determine its molecular structure and to try to synthesize it, otherwise there were only slim prospects of applying the discoveries in medicine. In the days before sophisticated laboratory equipment, these feats required plenty of inspiration and perspiration.

Rapid progress had been possible around the turn of the century with adrenalin and thyroxine because these hormones are stored in large amounts in the adrenal and thyroid glands respectively. They also turned out to be relatively simple molecules derived from amino acids and therefore easy to synthesize. Insulin proved to be more difficult because it is a protein, and only limited amounts are present in the pancreas. By the 1890s pancreas malfunction had been implicated in diabetes, but repeated attempts to isolate insulin from this organ failed because it was inactivated by enzymes during the extraction process. Knowledge of the role of the pancreas did little, then, to help the large numbers of patients who were waiting for a remedy. Eventually persistence and youthful optimism paid off, and in 1923 Frederick Banting and Charles Best of the University of

Toronto managed to produce a semi-pure preparation which lowered blood-sugar levels in diabetic patients. Diabetes research never looked back. The time seemed ripe for tackling another of endocrinology's most tantalizing secrets.

By 1906 Francis Marshall, then in Edinburgh, had deduced that the ovary produced sex hormones, and he even considered extracting them but did not have either the means or the experience to carry this to fruition. Another seventeen years passed before there was a major step forward. An American biologist, Edgar Allen, and a chemist, Edward Doisy, joined forces to extract hormones from animal ovaries. Four years later no pure hormone was yet in sight, although the researchers had found an effective way of testing the potency of their preparations. When castrated female animals are treated with oestrogen, they become sexually receptive again and the cells of the vaginal wall thicken and dry out to protect against abrasion during mating. The discovery of this natural response opened the way to testing the potency of hormonal preparations in the days before chemical methods were available.

Allen and Doisy were wise to avoid blood as a source for extracting oestrogen, because it contains vanishingly low concentrations of this phenomenally potent hormone. Levels during the menstrual cycle fluctuate around an average of only 100 picograms per millilitre of blood (i.e. 10^{-10} grams per millilitre), but even these are ten times higher than in most domestic animals. To get some impression of how little this is, a lump the size of a sugar cube would have to be dissolved in a large swimming pool to get the same concentration. That sugar solution would not taste sweet even to the most discerning tongue. But the cells of the vagina, uterus and breast can detect even lower concentrations of oestrogen since only 1 per cent in the bloodstream is biologically active, the rest being bound to proteins. The extraordinary sensitivity to hormones depends on special receptor molecules in the cells in question. Each hormone molecule has to engage its corresponding receptor like a key in a lock before it can gain access to the nucleus and exert its specific biological effects via the genes. Each sex hormone opens a particular part of the genetic treasure chest, and other hormones have their own receptors and actions, otherwise their language would degenerate from clear signals into a confusing babble.

The rediscovery of the medicinal virtues of urine proved to be a turning-point for oestrogen research for it had only been used for diagnosis rather than as a major therapeutic agent in the West. Its colour and sediments would sometimes be examined by a physician for omens of health and disease, like a medium searching her crystal ball. The breakthrough was made in 1928 when two German doctors, Bernhard Aschheim and Selmar Zondek, found large amounts of oestrogen in both human and equine pregnancy urine. This was the lucky strike that the chemists needed. By switching from ovaries to human urine, the first member of the oestrogen family was quickly discovered by Doisy in 1930. This hormone was oestrone, and just one milligram of the pure steroid was enough to bring 10,000 mice into a state of sexual frenzy! Meanwhile other researchers were relieving pregnant mares of urine, which had been found to contain large amounts of oestrogens, some of which are unique to horses (equilin and equilenin).

Shortly afterwards, Guy Marrian, beavering away in the bowels of University College London on a shoestring budget, succeeded in isolating the second member of the oestrogen family. This hormone was produced by the placenta and, although less potent, was the most abundant of the oestrogens in human pregnancy urine. It turned out to be peculiar to our own species and became known as oestriol. The jewel in the crown lay undiscovered until 1935. A few milligrams of crystalline oestradiol was the reward for the immense effort of extracting four tonnes of ovaries collected from the carcasses of about 100,000 sows from American meat-packing companies. It is the dominant oestrogen of the menstrual cycle and the most potent (and least abundant) member of the oestrogen family.

About the same time that Doisy discovered oestrone, a rather different 'female' hormone was discovered in the corpus luteum by Willard Allen and George Corner in the United States. Whereas oestrogen was needed if animals were to become sexually receptive and achieve pregnancy, the new hormone was essential for the embryo's gestation within the womb and, appropriately enough, was called progesterone. It has since been recognized as the archetypal member of a small family of hormonal steroids called progestogens, with related actions.

All of these were exciting discoveries of momentous significance for women's health and for controlling the reproductive process. In due course they led to the development of oral contraceptives and to better treatments for infertility and the menopause.

The rejuvenators were more interested in research into male hormones, collectively called androgens, of which testosterone is chief of the tribe. Pregnancy urine had proved to be a suitable source for oestrogens, so men's urine seemed a sensible source to search for androgens. Chemists were by now in a hurry, as they anticipated – rightly as it turned out – that Nobel Prizes would be awarded to the winners of the international race to find the most potent male hormone. Obtaining a sufficient supply of urine from men was a key factor, and Adolf Butenandt, one of Germany's most brilliant young chemists, shrewdly enlisted the police barracks in Berlin. Whether the officers were selected on the basis of their professional discipline or supposed virility is not clear, but by the end of his study they had provided him with 25,000 litres of the golden liquor. There must have been intense relief all round when, in 1931, the tank had been reduced to a few crystals and the odour of stale urine about the laboratory became a thing of the past.

The rejuvenators had been satisfied if their patients had experienced relief from non-specific symptoms of ageing, but Butenandt insisted on a more objective test for the male sex hormone. Berthold's studies in Göttingen of eighty years earlier suggested a technique, and the laboratory was soon furnished with a chicken house to provide capons for testing the potency of purified hormones. Pure androgens should cause their combs and wattles to regrow, just as Berthold's testicular grafts had done. The rejuvenators, who had been kept at arm's length by the chemists, must have awaited the outcome with bated breath – and no doubt crowed in triumph when positive results were announced. Disheartened by being beaten to the finishing-line, most of Butenandt's rivals now let the scent go cold on the testosterone trail.

But one of the bloodhounds had not completely given up the chase. Another German, Ernst Laqueur, was still busily at work in Amsterdam making extracts from a hundred kilograms of bull's testicles. This was wise, because urine contains a cocktail of hormones and their breakdown products, but very little of the all-important one, testosterone. In fact the hormone, which Butenandt called androsterone, has little hormonal activity, and his claims that he had found the main male sex hormone were premature. Many testicular substances were found to have hormonal activity, but which one made the cock crow loudest? In 1935 Laqueur succeeded in isolating testosterone itself, but the race to synthesize the pure hormone was a photo-finish with Butenandt and a group in Zurich, and the Nobel Committee split the prize between them. Afterwards, when the heat of competition should have been cooling, an unseemly row brewed up between pharmaceutical companies about who had the right to exploit the discovery of the king of the sex hormone realm.

Rumours began to spread that 'dynamite drugs' were about to be unleashed on an unprepared population. Testosterone was regarded as especially dangerous, and cartoons illustrated how it could turn men into monsters. Rejuvenation was all very well, but what about the costs? Newspaper columnists were poised to run sensational stories: 'What kind of spectacle would human oldsters make of themselves . . . prancing about under testosterone's hot influence?'

While this drama was being played out, the rejuvenators waited in the wings for news that might help to reverse their dwindling prestige. They hoped that elixirs and grafts would be replaced by a new generation of more reliable treatments based on pure hormones. The chemists donated some of their precious hormone crystals to physiologists who tested them first on animals and later on humans. It quickly became apparent that Brown-Séquard's hunch that sex hormones are the same in all mammals was quite correct. Testosterone and oestrogen are just as active in a gorilla as in a goldfish. They also dramatically hastened puberty in juvenile rats and mice of the corresponding sex, and reversed some of the effects of castration in adult animals. But did they significantly extend longevity or increase vigour? The answer was a resounding *no*.

With hindsight, it is odd that the sex hormones should ever have been regarded as panaceas for old age. Senescence has many causes, unlike classical hormone-deficiency syndromes such as hypothyroidism or Addison's disease. The muscular weakness of eunuchs does not signify early ageing, and their resistance to disease and their lifespan may actually be greater than normal. And the natural absence of sex hormones in some species of animals, such as worms and insects, and in most plants, does not make them any weedier or shorter-lived. The sex hormones are required for fertility and for making biological gender distinctions, but they do not prolong life. On the contrary, a price may have to be paid for living as a sexual being.

The 1930s were the heyday of steroid chemistry. Whenever a new hormone was identified by its effects, studies of its chemical composition and its role in the body followed. One of the most remarkable facts to emerge about steroid hormones is that they are very similar in structure despite widely different, and sometimes opposing, actions. The molecules are all based on a pattern of four rings of carbon atoms. The steroid hormone group also includes some substances without any specific actions on the sex organs, namely vitamin D and the heart drug digitalis. The sex hormones differ in the numbers of double chemical bonds they have and in the length and nature of their side branches. Seemingly trivial modifications of structure, such as the lopping-off of a branch here or bending one there, can make enormous differences in biological activity. All steroids belong to the lipid family of molecules and are therefore much more soluble in oil than in water. Brown-Séquard had assumed that watery extracts of testes would contain the vital principle he was seeking, but water cannot hold pure sex hormones in solution any more than olive oil can be dissolved in the vinegar of French dressing.

He had fooled himself as his extracts contained only a crude mixture of protein and carbohydrate with traces of vitamins and minerals – hardly a tonic.

Extraction of hormones from natural sources is troublesome and costly, so, wherever possible, synthetic substitutes have been sought. Once an important steroid had been identified and patent rights had been reserved, pharmaceutical companies were eager to develop saleable products from the new discoveries. Besides, chemists can sometimes tailor steroids to have particular characteristics, such as the ability to be active when taken by mouth. A minor modification of the structure of one substance could provide a useful product which was cheap, pleasant to take and much more potent than the original.

At one time, synthetic drugs or hormones were highly regarded for their supposed modernity, but attitudes are now changing in favour of natural products. Equating 'natural' with 'safe' as a principle is, however, quite irrational, because some of the most toxic substances known are produced naturally by living things. Besides, cells do not discriminate between two chemically identical hormone molecules just because one has been extracted from the body and the other was synthesized in a chemical laboratory. Yet one still hears murmurs against some drugs simply on the grounds that they are 'synthetic'.

Steroid synthesis gained a boost through the serendipitous discovery of the structure of cholesterol in the 1930s. As the grandmother of the steroid family, among other things, it does not deserve its malign public image. It was used as the starting-point for making several hormones, though the oestrogens were still obtained from abundant natural sources.

The manufacture of sufficient quantities of progesterone for treatment purposes proved difficult at first. This hormone is relatively weak-acting, so large-scale production was necessary to make enough for alleviating menstrual and fertility problems. The difficulty was overcome during the Second World War by a brilliant American recluse. Russell Marker had no time to waste on lectures and never completed his PhD degree, preferring to trust his intuition to steer a career in chemistry. After completing some important studies on the 'knocking' of gasoline that led to the concept of octane number, he turned his attention to steroids.

He began work on soap-like substances obtained from the rhizomes of yams belonging to the genus *Dioscorea*. He was particularly interested in one which was used by Indian fishermen to stupefy fish without making them inedible. This apparently esoteric project was later to have a worldwide impact when he realized that this substance, called diosgenin, could be converted to progesterone. The problem was to obtain enough rhizomes, and in 1943 Marker set out on a botanical expedition into the jungles of Vera Cruz in Mexico to track down the plant in the wild. He could hardly speak a word of Spanish and would bawl out its local name to the natives, '*cabeza de negro*', hoping for some directions. On one occasion he was nearly murdered by an Indian who took this as a great insult.

He survived, and found enough plants to prepare three kilograms of pure progesterone. This was worth $250,000 on the open market at the time and represented by far the largest stock anywhere in the world. His achievement opened the door to the founding of a major industry producing a range of steroids for gynaecology and contraception.

Oestrogens, androgens and progesterone were now in the bag, but the natural steroids carried certain disadvantages. They lose much of their activity when taken by mouth. Those that are absorbed in the intestines have to pass first through the liver where a powerful group of enzymes reduces their biological activity. An alternative route for administering hormones is via the skin, using patches and pellets from which the steroid can be absorbed directly into the bloodstream without having the 'first pass' problem. While these are excellent methods of delivery, pills offer greater flexibility and reassurance. We now know that oestrogen becomes orally active when ground to a fine dust, or 'micronized', but in the early days efforts were made to alter steroid molecules in the hope of making an orally effective compound without losing hormonal activity.

The first oestrogen to meet these requirements was not a steroid but a substance called stilboestrol (or diethylstilboestrol). It was discovered in 1938 by E. C. Dodds at the Middlesex Hospital in London almost by chance as an impurity during the preparation of another compound. It surprised everyone that the opening of two of the four carbon rings of the oestrone molecule should produce such a highly potent oestrogen that was effective by mouth and cheap. Even more amazingly, further modifications of the molecule reversed its activity so that it now antagonized the action of oestrogen. In this form it later found a use, somewhat paradoxically, in treating infertility.

Shortly before the Second World War the Schering Corporation in Europe began trials to modify the oestradiol molecule in the hope of finding a product that could be taken as a pill. Addition of an ethinyl group at the C17 position of the steroid rings was remarkably successful in achieving oral activity and boosting potency at the same time. Meanwhile Carl Djerassi at Stanford University, California, and Russell Marker were theorizing that splitting off the methyl group from the progesterone molecule at position C19 would increase its potency ten-fold, and so the commercially important 19-norsteroids were born.

These developments underpinned the introduction around 1960 of a revolutionary contraceptive that was almost 100 per cent effective and which we universally know as 'the pill'. For years it had been known that ovulation is inhibited during pregnancy by progesterone through the suppression of the pituitary hormones, LH and FSH. Gregory Pincus, who was at the Worcester Foundation in Massachusetts, tested combinations of oestrogens and progestogens in the hope of mimicking the natural inhibition of the hormones in non-pregnant women. That he succeeded so well is one of the major triumphs of twentieth-century biology, though he was mistaken in believing that the Vatican would sanction the wedge being driven between sexual enjoyment and procreation.

Rather less controversial was the adoption of synthetic and natural steroids for the clinical treatment of menstrual disorders, infertility and sterility. It even became fashionable in some circles during the late 1940s and the 1950s for healthy women to take oestrogens, but only in the 1960s did massive popular interest in oestrogen replacement therapy mushroom. The numbers of women reaching mid-life were rising everywhere, and there was striking evidence that many of them could benefit by restoring oestrogen levels to what they had been before. HRT promised to end vaginal dryness, osteoporosis and hot flushes and to provide a mental tonic. It was even reputed to have cosmetic benefits. If she wished, a woman could take sex steroids in one form or another more or less continuously from puberty to the grave.

It is rather more difficult to justify routine testosterone treatment for older men. Menopause is an unambiguous milestone in a woman's life and signifies the début of a low-oestrogen phase of life. Although there is no exact equivalent in males, we shall see in the next chapter that some men undergo a change that could be called an 'andropause' when testosterone levels fall. Just how many is hard to say, and whether they are really in need of treatment or are best left alone is debatable. It is hard to be sure whether testosterone treatment will catch on in a major way, but I suspect that it will.

The idea of using androgens for treating elderly men has been around for over a century. What was once a crude and ineffective remedy for old age has become a potent agent which can be conveniently taken as a pill or a patch slapped on to the scrotum. On the positive side, testosterone is said to conserve protein in the body and to increase muscle bulk. This anabolic effect may be beneficial in thin individuals and may help to reduce painful bedsores in older patients. There is, of course, concern about abuse of the hormone by the fit and healthy who want to increase their libido or are determined to get an unfair competitive edge in their sport. We now know that boosting sex hormones above normal levels for a long time is not without its risks. Testosterone is regarded as the 'dangerous hormone', but oestrogen should also be treated with respect. My laboratory fridge contains bottles of oestradiol and testosterone, both of which carry bold warnings printed in red. This naturally raises the question of whether we are at risk from the hormones we make in our bodies.

• Sex Hormones – Friends or Fiends

Almost as soon as the first oestrogen was synthesized, alarm bells began to ring. This was no idle foreboding. From the 1950s, more than 5 million women in America and Europe have been treated with stilboestrol to prevent recurrent miscarriages, and we have only recently learned at what cost. The effects of the drug on their own health was not so much in question as those on their children. The stilboestrol molecule bears a sinister resemblance to substances that are known to cause cancer. The incidence of vaginal cancer, normally rare, was much higher than usual in the daughters as they reached adulthood, and they also had more fertility problems. The sons too were affected by the treatment their mothers had received. Undescended testicles were more common than normal and, as the boys reached manhood, fertility problems loomed for many of them. If one type of oestrogenic agent can have such dire effects, we should be cautious about others too.

Few drugs have been screened as thoroughly as the contraceptive pill, which is a combination of oestrogen and progestogen, and rarely has any been so dogged by scare stories in the press. When an elderly person dies suddenly of a stroke or a heart attack no one is particularly surprised, but the freak death of a woman in her twenties or thirties warrants investigation. In 1968 the Royal College of General Practitioners launched a study of 23,000 British pill-users and controls. A slightly higher death rate was found in the users, and so, a decade later, the College repeated the survey. This confirmed their suspicions, although the high-risk group was mainly among women over thirty-five who had used the pill for more than five years or had high blood pressure or smoked. Women over thirty-five were advised to use another form of contraception, though this is no longer considered necessary for non-smokers. The accusing finger has usually been pointed at the oestrogen in the pill, but the progestogen has come in for some stick too because its weak androgenic activity could have undesirable effects on blood lipids. In response to these revelations, manufacturers lowered the dose of oestrogen by more than half, which has improved the pill's safety without compromising contraceptive efficiency.

The last great scare was in 1983 when it was claimed that the pill increased the risk of breast cancer. Since this is such a common and feared disease, many women stopped taking the pill, but the story was scotched by further research which mostly showed that the pill actually reduces the risk of disease. Besides providing contraceptive protection and controlling irregular or heavy periods, it reduces thyroid problems, rheumatoid arthritis, peptic ulcers and fibroids. What is more, it protects against cancer of the ovaries and the uterus. The degree of protection is small for short-term usage, but amounts to a 70 per cent lower risk after seven years, and the benefits last for at least ten years after stopping taking oral contraceptives. The advantages of the pill now appear to outweigh the risks, and it deserves credit as an ally in disease prevention.

These benefits suggest that the monthly process of ovulation and the associated bombardment of the breast and reproductive organs by high levels of oestrogen and other hormones may carry some risks in later life. In the process of ovulation, a tiny wound is opened on the surface of the ovary so that the egg can escape in an oestrogen-rich fluid from a follicle, and this may encourage a malignant change. The cyclic production of sex hormones from the ovary stimulates the uterus to repeat cycles of growth and shedding unless or until the woman becomes pregnant. A modern woman will typically experience 450 menstrual cycles and ovulations in her lifetime – three times as many as our ancient forerunners and the remaining bands of hunter-gatherers in Africa today. The average !Kung tribeswoman has about five or six pregnancies spaced at intervals of four or more years by breast-feeding. By carrying the baby with her throughout the day and sleeping beside him or her at night, suckling is much more frequent and effective at inhibiting ovulation. A combination of less exposure to oestrogens and fewer ovulations with the reproductive system lying dormant sets these women at a much lower risk of breast disease and other gynaecological cancers. Matters are made worse for

197

the Western woman by the prosperous lifestyle which encourages an earlier puberty and a possibly later menopause, which add up to another fifty or so menstrual cycles and more oestrogen exposure. So it is perhaps not too far-fetched to claim that we would do well to discourage the number of cycles a woman will have in her life.

A balancing act has to be performed to ensure that a postmeno-pausal woman is not put at risk by the oestrogen in HRT. On balance, the treatment is more beneficial than harmful because the dose is much less than during the menstrual cycle. Perhaps the greatest plus is a halving of heart disease, according to a nationwide study of American nurses. One of the main ways in which oestrogen helps to protect against heart disease is by affecting the levels of cholesterol and its disposal. It maintains more of the protective high-density lipoprotein (HDL) in the bloodstream, which carries cholesterol away from the vessel walls. At the same time, it reduces low-density lipoprotein (LDL) and so avoids the deposition of cholesterol in the walls and elsewhere. Testosterone acts in the opposite direction, putting men at more risk of heart attacks and strokes. Why cholesterol metabolism should differ between the sexes is not clear, though evolution has presumably tolerated this arrangement for good reasons – males being the more disposable of the two sexes. The solution is not for men to take oestrogens – not only would they be feminized, but studies show that those who were treated with oestrogens after a heart attack died sooner than those who were not.

When given alone, oestrogen stimulates growth of the womb and increases the risk of uterine cancer, which is reason enough for giving it only to hysterectomized women. Others need to have oestrogen combined with a progestogen for part of the month, to moderate the stimulating effects of oestrogen and allow periods to prevent any build-up of unhealthy cells in the uterine lining. Proges-togens have had a bad press because they sometimes produce unwel-come side-effects, but there is a variety of doses and formulations of HRT and new generations of progestogens with fewer side-effects to try. To be sure, there could be a risk that oestrogen will increase breast cancer because the progestogen in HRT fails to protect the breasts, but the evidence suggests that the treatment is safe for at least five to ten years, and possibly much longer. Since a woman is five times more likely to die of a heart attack than of breast cancer, she would be wiser to embrace HRT for the sake of her heart and arteries.

Men have no reason to be smug as their wives juggle the pros and cons of HRT. They have fewer options – none of them particularly rosy. They seldom suffer from breast cancer, but prostate cancer is a greater scourge at later ages. One in four will contract it by eighty years of age, and virtually all who live long enough will have an overgrown gland making the passing of urine more difficult. As the population ages, this disease is reaching epidemic proportions throughout the Western world. Ten million Americans are estimated to have microscopic 'seeds' of malignancy in their prostate gland, although 'only' 100,000 cases are clinically diagnosed with cancer each year. Mass screening is needed to nip it in the bud – just as women are offered breast examination.

The organs most susceptible to cancer tend to be those in which growth continues throughout life into old age. That is why the breast and the prostate are at higher risk than, say, the vagina and the penis, which grow little if at all beyond early adult ages. It is questionable whether the sex hormones actually cause cancer, but once an aberrant cell has emerged they encourage it to grow. The only animal that shares our tendency to prostate disease is man's best friend, though a dog's tumour seldom turns malignant.

During the 1930s the Chicago surgeon C. A. Huggins noticed that prostate tumours shrink after men have been castrated, and he came to the conclusion that they are aggravated by testosterone. Castration is hardly likely to catch on as a prophylactic measure because, quite apart from loss of virility, hot flushes and osteoporosis, it has to be done before thirty-five to forty years of age to avoid the build-up of hormonal effects over the years. Age can be a saving grace! His curiosity aroused, Huggins found he could achieve this benefit of castration with oestrogen, which antagonizes some of the effects of testosterone and shuts down hormone production from the testes. This was a much easier remedy than radical removal of the prostate gland, despite the side-effects. Unfortunately, it is often only palliative because the tumour becomes recrudescent when it eventually grows independently of hormones.

There are now better ways of overcoming the harmful effects of testosterone using an enzyme antagomist to prevent conversion into an even more potent androgen called dihydrotestosterone which is mainly responsible for driving the prostate gland in health and disease. The existence of the enzyme, 5-alpha reductase, was dramatically revealed in a few families in the Dominican Republic who carry a mutant gene which cannot make an active enzyme. Its absence causes boys to be born looking like girls, but they change at puberty into indisputable men – a condition known in Spanish slang as *guevedoce* or 'penis at twelve'. Their testosterone alone is too little and too weak to masculinize them until levels shoot up in their early teens and partly compensate for the lack of the more potent dihydrotestosterone. Men with this enzyme deficiency are unlikely to contract prostate disease in old age.

Drugs that inhibit the enzyme abolish the effects of dihydrotestosterone while allowing testosterone to continue its direct effects on other organs, notably the penis and the brain. In essence, the treatment should help to avoid the negative effects of androgens in men without diminishing their ability to make love or causing them to look less virile. The drugs were developed to stop further growth of prostate tumours in their tracks, but it is too early to say whether they are safe to take over long periods as a preventive measure.

Castration has swung from being claimed to be a cause of ageing to apparently being its best prevention, but no one has clarified its effects more than the late James Hamilton. In the 1940s and 1950s he studied patients at an institution in the state of Kansas who had been involuntarily castrated many years ago when this was still accepted for managing some types of mental handicap. On average, these men lived to sixty-nine years compared to fifty-six for the other patients, which is a far larger gap than expected. It must have been a freak result because the eunuchs lived even longer than women residents, and if castration really added fourteen more years to life it might have caught on!

To be sure, castrated animals do live a little longer than normal, and this is true of females as well as males. They avoid the costs of sexual activity and reproduction and the diseases encouraged by sex hormones. Arteries become narrower in rats bred at the maximum rate, and the bones of broiler chickens become brittle through much egg-laying. The sex hormones even carry risks when animals are forced to be unnaturally celibate. Virgin female rats and mice often develop tumours in the uterus, pituitary and mammary glands during their second year of life, because they have cycles of oestrogen provocation every few days. This is reminiscent of the hazards of repeated cycles in women. Oestrogens may be necessary for some diseases to develop, but they are not a sufficient explanation in themselves. Some breeds of animals are more vulnerable than others, showing that genetic factors also play a part, just as they do in breast cancer in women.

Pregnancy is a mixed blessing because it carries special risks, but a reduction in certain kinds of cancer is one of the benefits. The protection is due more to progesterone counteracting the effects of oestrogen than to the fact of carrying a baby. Even when conception is prevented by pairing a mother rat with a vasectomized male, she is protected by the string of pseudopregnancies that are triggered by mating. This condition reduces the number of ovulations and the levels of oestrogen at the same time. A woman cannot gain this protection from a vasectomized husband because she does not become pseudo-pregnant, but if she chooses to become pregnant early enough in life she too will reduce her chances of disease by moderating the harmful effects of repeated menstrual cycles.

For the sex hormones to encourage cancer in the very organs needed for procreation seems perverse considering the high importance of reproduction on every creature's life agenda. But cancer is not the only adverse effect that sex hormones have late in life. Repeated cycles of oestrogen stimulation abolish the ability of the pituitary gland to release the spurt of LH that is needed for ovulation and fertility, if only in laboratory rats and mice. Follicles still ripen in the ovaries but, in the absence of a hormonal trigger for ovulation, they persistently produce oestrogen which aggravates disease in the other organs of reproduction. We are fairly certain that oestrogen is the culprit because the system remains more 'youthful' in spayed animals. Young ovaries grafted into castrates can reinitiate ovulatory cycles long after the time when they are effective in normal animals because the pituitary gland and the parts of the brain controlling it are biologically younger. If the adverse effects of oestrogen build up over time, a large dose should speed up age changes, and this appears to be the case. Animals given a large dose of the hormone in infancy stop cycling earlier and develop pathological changes sooner. These effects do not apply to every species, and in humans it is the number of eggs in the ovary rather than the number of cycles that fixes the upper limit to reproductive life. Another contrast between species is that there is some good news to tell about the effects of oestrogen on the human brain.

Women have a somewhat greater risk of developing dementia of the Alzheimer type than do men of the same age. We cannot be sure, but it seems likely that oestrogen may help to maintain the vitality of some brain cells until the menopause. Recent unconfirmed studies in America suggest that cognitive performance is improved in female Alzheimer sufferers using HRT, but this is still a long way from prevention of a terrible disease.

The sex hormones have, by turns, been viewed as elixirs of life and as agents of disease. The truth of the matter is that they have both benefits and costs. This may seem paradoxical because we expect that natural selection will weed out harmful effects, but we should not be surprised since George Williams's theory of pleio-tropic gene action predicts a mixed bag of effects. In fact the sex hormones present some of the most convincing evidence for his theory.

However we regard these hormones, reproduction would be impossible without them in higher animals. They not only help eggs and sperm to ripen but also have actions on many somatic cells around the body which assist directly or indirectly in the process of becoming pregnant. Without their effects on bone and muscle, the body would not assume its mature shape or such a robust construction. Without their effects on behaviour, the sexes would never get together. And without hormones to stimulate the growth of the sex cells, there would be little point.

Evolutionary selection has finely honed reproductive performance over countless generations. Genetic mechanisms have evolved which improve the chances of successful reproduction, and the sex-hormone signalling system has been adopted to ensure the appropriate timing and strength of action. Whether other hormones might have evolved to fulfil the sex hormones' role is beside the point because the genes they act upon have been just as subject to natural selection as the hormones themselves. In Chapter 5 we saw that when deterioration later in life conflicts with reproductive fitness when young, youth wins over age. Evolution has turned a blind eye to the adverse effects of sex steroids in mid- and late-life because, when only a minority of individuals survive long enough to be affected, natural selection fails to cut out undesirable traits that are reproductively neutral.

On balance, we are better off with sex steroids than without them – even late in life. Nobody in good health and sound mind seriously considers a prophylactic castration. Not all hormonal effects are necessarily pleiotropic in Williams's sense, and many are good for all adult ages. Yet hormone replacement therapy for menopausal women and testosterone for some older men are not entirely free from side-effects, and that is why the subject is able to generate headlines after a century of research and still leaves many people confused. The jury may still be out, but most of its scientific members are in little doubt about the verdict. The sex hormones are guilty of misdeeds, but they do more good than evil. The challenge is to adjust the balance to our best advantage and minimal risk.

The debate over whether to use HRT or not has often centred on the question of whether menopause is a change for the better.

There are many points of view. Sociologists and feminists regard menopause from the perspective of a woman's changing role in the family and society. Epidemiologists weigh up the risks and benefits of keeping oestrogens artificially high. But for biologists the question of menopause is essentially an evolutionary one, which deserves a chapter of its own.

CHAPTER 9

The Meaning of Menopause

The menopause is . . . a colossal bit of biological sabotage on women.

John Studd, a London gynaecologist

• The Biological Egg-Timer

The English biologist Jane Goodall has been studying troops of wild chimpanzees in Gombe National Park, Tanzania, for more than thirty years. Her work has become one of the classics of twentieth-century field biology and has transformed perceptions of our closest living relative – and of ourselves at the same time. Through winning the trust of the apes, she has enjoyed the privilege of witnessing every detail of their private lives.

One of the chimps, whom she called Flo', had successfully mothered several children. Like any other adult female chimp, her hindquarters would swell and blush for a few days every month, giving a clear signal to males up to 100 metres away that she was available. The sex skin advertises the fertile time of the cycle and the female's readiness to accept any interested male in the troop. This is because it is highly sensitive to oestrogens which peak around the time of ovulation. Flo' had been flagging up invitations to males since she was a teenager, but when she turned forty-three she ceased to do so. Temporary loss of menstrual cycles had happened in the past when she was pregnant, but this was a permanent change. She had reached the menopause.

Flo' was an old lady, and few chimps live longer than her in the wild. In captivity, a fiftieth birthday can occasionally be celebrated, but the constitution of chimps at this advanced age is weak and equivalent to human beings in their late eighties or older. We are so biologically alike that humans and chimps share many of the same diseases and disorders of old age, possibly including those triggered by the menopause. Chimps may even have hot flushes and emotional swings in their forties. It may not be too ridiculous to wonder if they will one day use sign language to tell psychologists how they feel during 'the change'.

The menopause and its symptoms – sometimes called the climacteric – had been regarded as a uniquely human trait. Its existence in apes breaks down another barrier we had thought separated us from animals. Even so, it is still remarkable for occurring so early in the human lifespan. A woman can expect to have her last menstrual cycle within five years of her fiftieth birthday – barely halfway to the maximum human lifespan. The chances are high that over a third of her life will be dominated by menopausal physiology. This fact is all the more important these days because unprecedented numbers of women are reaching this stage and asking themselves and their doctors about the significance of menopause – why it happens and whether it is a change for better or worse.

Most women feel the menopause is a mixed blessing. For some it means a release from worries about contraception and the nuisance of periods. In some societies, menopause even opens the door to a higher social status: Rajput women in India are freed from the cultural and religious constraints of purdah so they can join the company of men and the supposed privileges that go along with it. Attitudes towards the menopause are more negative in the West with its youth cult. The change is a discomfiting reminder of the inner clock ticking away and a gloomy foreboding of organic decline. No other normal change in the adult body is quite so abrupt and explicit, and few physiological phenomena have provoked more speculative theories.

Like most things connected with human procreation, the whole subject has become obfuscated by myth and superstition over the centuries. But ignorance is no longer a defence. For the better part of a hundred years we have known why menopause occurs, and the change is now better understood than almost any other aspect of ageing. What has remained controversial is its after-effects. The pioneer hormone researcher Eugen Steinach contended that 'at the moment when [sex hormone] activity ceases the well-spring of life runs dry, and the ailments of old age commence'. He rather overstated the case since we have seen that ageing begins at puberty rather than in mid-life, but the decline in sex hormones still holds a morbid fascination for doctors.

Menopause is a much-abused term derived from an old French word meaning that monthly events have ceased (*'la ménespausie'*). A period is the end-product of sloughing off the uterine lining, and this rather unusual fertility cycle is found only among the apes and monkeys of the Old World. Most species do not have periods, and even American monkeys have a different kind of cycle. Strictly speaking, neither a marmoset nor a moose nor a mouse can have a menopause. The expression 'male menopause' is something of a misnomer too, but looks set to stick as something of a wisecrack.

A state of irreversible ovarian failure is almost unheard of in nature. With the exception of the occasional chimpanzee and pilot whale and an invertebrate or two, wild creatures breed for as long as they live. Nor is there any hard-and-fast upper limit for fertility in most domesticated animals or in birds, although there may be some tapering off. Broiler hens lay less often after three or four years, and cats and bitches older than ten come into heat less regularly or even stop completely. Even so, their ovaries usually contain a few eggs and a trace of oestrogen may still be produced. Only in a few breeds of laboratory mice do we find universal ovarian failure at a little over a year old, which is middle age for these animals. Comparisons with the human menopause are misleading though, because their sterility has a different genetic basis. It is an artefact of inbreeding and can be reversed by outbreeding for just one generation, whereas menopause is one of the heritable characteristics of being human.

The early age at menopause in humans is not only unusual, it is an enigma. The evolutionary success of a species is weighed in terms of the numbers of offspring that are produced. Any gene that makes an individual less fertile than her peers will set her and her descendants at a disadvantage because they will produce fewer offspring in the next generation. In time, the numbers carrying it will be swamped by those of more fecund females. So, any gene that calls a halt to breeding halfway through life is biologically perverse. Or is it?

Such a gene would be permitted if it had a sufficiently heavy compensation to balance the disadvantages. For example, were it not for the menopause, there would be more complications of childbirth and genetically abnormal babies than already exist. With modern obstetric care and antenatal diagnosis, these are less likely than they were for primeval Eve. The efforts she had given to bearing children when she was young would be wasted if she died before they had reached an independent age. Besides, an older woman has less energy for the demanding job of motherhood. Sadly, that was the case for Flo' whose last child, Flint, died in infancy. Perhaps she too would have been better off with an earlier menopause.

The geneticist George Williams offered a similar theory for menopause when he was formulating his theory of ageing. He argued that it may pay an older mother to retire from the business of reproduction in favour of helping to raise her relatives' offspring. Such a trade-off would have freed Flo' from risk so she could have devoted more time to her grandchildren, nieces and nephews. Genetic brownie points would accrue if this gave her kin a better chance of survival, but nannying children of other families would undermine any competitive edge. If this strategy worked and the family became more reproductively efficient, menopause might drift down to younger ages over the course of many generations until it reached the point where it started to cut into some of the most fertile years, when it would halt.

There is so much negative talk about the menopause that finding something positive to say about it is rather appealing. But, to hold water, this theory has to assume that sufficient numbers of women were surviving past fifty in the remote past for natural selection to work. They left no tombstones or biographies behind, and most estimates of the lifespans of palaeohumans are guesswork or based on fragmentary information at best. As far as we can tell, life was much briefer than today and averaged no more than twenty years. A few tough females may have survived much longer – perhaps to age fifty or even more – but they would not represent a sufficiently large evolutionary carrot to feed a trend to an earlier menopause. For the trait to gain a genetic foothold in the species, the supposed advantage of grandmothering would have had to recur generation after generation.

Another problem with the theory is that it is doubtful whether our forerunners would have been in sufficiently good shape to make adequate nannies at fifty. If chimps are anything to go by, old age was far from rosy for the first humans. An animal completing its quota of years is likely to have worn-down teeth, joint disease and even cancer. Living with infirmity in the wild is a struggle even to keep going, and the ageing individual is unlikely to be an asset to younger family members – rather the reverse. What is more, the lack of oestrogen after the menopause aggravates the problems and difficulties of old age and increases the risk of fractures and heart disease. Studies of American Seventh-Day Adventists, chosen for their abstemious and healthy lifestyle, show that women who have an early natural menopause are more likely to have a shorter life than those who reach the change at fifty or later. The physiology of menopause is more a handicap than a benefit, and the gynaecologist John Studd goes so far as to call it 'biological sabotage'. We should beware of idealizing the change; after all, the likes of Jane Fonda – lean, fit and energetic – are products of modern and prosperous times.

It seems to me that menopause is more likely to have crept on to the stage by default, like most other aspects of ageing. Since it is reached after the age when most of our predecessors would be dead, natural selection failed to oppose it. A negative explanation is, admittedly, less engaging than a positive one, but it frees us from evolutionary rhetoric and the temptation to endow the change with some value. We are then able to concentrate on how it occurs rather than straining to discern its purpose.

Jim Nelson and his former colleagues at McGill University in Montreal have counted the number of eggs remaining in the ovaries of middle-aged women to find out whether the Achilles' heel of a woman's fertility is in the ovaries or in the pituitary gland which produces hormones required to keep these organs going. They collected ovaries donated by patients undergoing routine operations and cut them into thin slices with a microtome, a laboratory instrument resembling a bacon-slicer. Almost without exception, the ovaries of women past the menopause were already barren. Women who had been cycling regularly had ten times as many eggs as those of the same age who were already in the throes of the change. These results confirmed the suspicion that the state of a woman's ovaries counts for more than her age when it comes to the drying-up of periods. The menopause occurs simply because the ovary runs out of eggs.

The ovary is like an hour-glass containing a million grains of sand, each grain representing an egg cell. This clock has a running time of about fifty years and starts at birth with a full chamber. Time slowly runs out as the sand slips through the narrow waist into the lower chamber. In the ovary most eggs go to waste – they (and their follicle envelopes) die before reaching maturity – and only one, or occasionally two, is ovulated each month. Consequently the egg-timer is hardly affected by ovulation events and runs on regardless of fertility and without interruption from birth until middle age – or until the egg store is exhausted. Unlike an hour-glass, the ovarian clock cannot be turned upside down to start the process over again.

It is tempting to lapse into teleological language and say that the ovary is programmed to last only so long. In many respects it ages faster and becomes senescent earlier than any other organ in the body, but this need not be so. Red blood cells only live about 100 days, but they are continuously replenished by stem cells in the marrow. Why doesn't the ovary follow this wise strategy of retaining the ability to make new eggs? In fact it does in some species. The ovaries of rockfishes off the Canadian west coast look as young at a hundred years old as they did at twenty, and they never have the piscean equivalent of the menopause. And, although less long-lived, a large codfish becomes more productive as it gets older and larger, spawning as many as 100 million eggs in a season.

These species have kept stem cells to make new ones because they need to shed enormous numbers of eggs into the sea where the embryos will have to fend for themselves and most will be gobbled up by hungry predators. Mammals and birds have evolved from prodigious egg-producers like them, but economies could be made when they adopted wombs and nests in which to nurture their embryos. Humans have lost the ability to make more eggs after birth but are still over-endowed because only a few hundred are needed for ovulating once a month over the course of a reproductive lifetime. Why the ovary makes a million more than required is hard to say, although some eggs are undoubtedly abnormal and better eliminated. Until the 1950s it was thought that new eggs are made continuously until middle age. Lord Solly Zuckerman's rebuttal of this error was perhaps his finest hour, though he is mostly remembered nowadays for his wartime research on injuries caused by bombing and as a Chief Scientific Adviser to HM Government. Nowadays the fixed endowment of eggs at birth is held as a central dogma in biology.

The egg that pops out of the ovary halfway between periods has an amazing history behind it, as befits a cell of high importance. The progenitor cells are formed early in life and are first seen when human embryos still look like fish. These germ cells are not yet in the future gonads nor even in the embryo: they are found in the yolk sac, which is like a primitive placenta. Why they should start in this site is odd, unless it is a way of conserving their unique identity while the rest of the body is undergoing tumultuous changes of shape and destiny. Female and male germ cells look alike at this stage and it is impossible to tell whether a gonad is going to be an ovary or a testis until later.

The primordial germ cells multiply in the yolk sac and afterwards make a long march to the gonads. They are rather like the Children of Israel migrating through deserts and across seas to the Promised Land – but there is no Moses at their head. Each cell follows a chemical trail leading into the embryo, along the wall of the

211

future intestines and towards the vacant gonads. Some lose their way and die in the wrong environment. The successful ones soon settle after they have arrived in their proper home, but the rest of the story depends on the sex of the gonad. Germ cells in the testes become dormant and don't reawaken until puberty and, since some of them survive as stem cells, the male organs need never be wanting for new sperm. In the ovaries, however, the germ cells give up the ability to renew themselves; they turn into eggs with the ability to be fertilized and make new creatures.

By midway through pregnancy, the number of eggs in a female foetus has climbed to 7 million, which is more than there will ever be again, but falls to a million by birth. The making of an egg cell is a complicated process that is prone to error, and many of the eggs being lost are probably weeded out to avoid a later miscarriage or a baby born with a birth defect. Some children form fewer or lose more eggs than others and will probably have an earlier menopause in consequence. Children born with an abnormal set of chromosomes generally have fewer eggs than average. For example, girls who are born with Turner's syndrome and have only one of thier two X chromosomes are often barren at birth and the ovary is unable to make any oestrogen. Failure of their eggs to thrive denies them the experience of a natural puberty, let alone motherhood.

An early menopause sometimes comes out of the blue, but women with a history of autoimmune disease or chemotherapy, both of which destroy eggs and hasten ageing of the ovaries, should be prepared for one. Whenever eggs are destroyed, the age of the ovaries is advanced – as if sand was decanted from an hour-glass to speed up time. Some historical evidence suggests that menopause was some- what earlier in the past, and this is still the case in parts of the developing world. Tribal women from the Highlands of Papua New Guinea become menopausal around the age of forty-three – some four years earlier than the better-off lowlanders. Since the average age for the menopause around the world today is fifty to fifty-two years, it is unlikely that the differences are genetic even among tribes which have lived in fierce isolation for untold generations. Malnutrition and disease no doubt play a part, but the differences may also say something about the diet and health of the mothers during pregnancy. Organs that stockpile cells before birth cannot make up for early deficits if conditions improve afterwards. An early menopause may sometimes be a sign of poverty in the womb – we are in a sense what our mothers ate.

The menopause is such a pivotal event in life that if it became possible to offer a cheap and safe way of predicting it ahead of time many women would doubtless subscribe. Perhaps this will one day be possible, since forecasting does not lack a sound theoretical basis so much as a practicable way of counting the egg store. With 250,000 eggs in the ovary at puberty, a woman has about thirty-five years of cycles in prospect, but when numbers have fallen to 25,000 this is down to fourteen years, and when only 1,000 remain the menopause is just around the corner. There is no easy way of estimating the number of eggs in the body because the vast majority of them are dormant and far too small to be seen by medical scanners. Over 90 per cent of the oestrogen produced during a menstrual cycle is from the single large follicle destined to ovulate, and so hormone measurements are also useless for estimating the numbers remaining in the store.

At present we can estimate the biological age of an ovary only by removing it and laboriously counting the eggs in tissue slices. My late colleague and Zuckerman disciple Esther Jones developed a permanent squint after long hours of peering down the microscope. She found that the numbers of eggs in the mouse ovary are fewer than in almost any other species and halve every three months. This rapid rate of depletion is commensurate with a short life. The longer-lived the animal, the bigger its endowment and the slower the ovarian clock runs. Humans are no exception, and our ovaries fit into the picture exactly as predicted for an animal of our size. But what provides a good safety margin for sheep and big cats that live for little more than twenty years is inadequate for ourselves.

The number of eggs in a young human ovary halves every seven years, which is close to our actuarial rate of ageing and therefore consistent with our biological deterioration overall. This is another reason for thinking that the ovary is not so much out of step with a woman's physiology as with her extraordinary longevity. Perhaps we should be asking why we outlive the function of our ovaries rather than why the menopause occurs so early.

We had thought that ovarian time runs as steadily in humans as in animals, but we were in for a shock. Malcolm Faddy at the University of Queensland has found that the rate at which eggs are being lost speeds up after age thirty-seven: the numbers halve every three years instead of every seven. With hindsight this is less surprising: had the rate remained constant, there would be at least 10,000 eggs remaining at fifty, which is far more than Nelson has found. Accelerated ageing brings the ovary to the brink of sterility at a little over fifty years of age rather than at seventy. Whether the last eggs in the ovary are programmed to undergo suicide is hard to say, but they do appear to have passed their 'sell-by-date' by the time a woman reaches her late forties. Besides, we already know that the quality of eggs deteriorates with age because older mothers have a much higher risk of conceiving a Down's syndrome baby. For a species that for aeons has rarely lived long there was no point investing in longer-lasting eggs.

• The *Yin* and *Yang* of Endocrinology

The ovaries do not have a life of their own but require hormones in the bloodstream before they will ovulate and produce sex hormones. In 1928 the Zondek-Aschheim research team in Germany was the first to show that the necessary hormones are released from the pituitary gland after puberty and for the rest of life. The gland is well hidden in the body, lying between the palate and the floor of the brain. By the late '20s Philip Smith in the United States had devised a clever operation to remove it, whereupon the gonads became quiescent, as if time had been reversed and they were immature again. These experiments were among the most important ever published in reproductive biology, and opened up new avenues for research and the treatment of infertility. The operation, which became known as hypophysectomy, is used to remove a pituitary tumour and has even been used as a desperate measure to reduce the production of oestrogen in women with advanced breast cancer.

We encountered the two gonadotrophic hormones, FSH and LH, in an earlier chapter. Produced by the pituitary gland, each has a distinct and complementary role in fertility. Neither acts directly on the egg but rather on the layers of cells that envelop it to make a follicle. A group of about twenty growing follicles compete for the limited amounts of FSH in the blood at the beginning of a woman's cycle, shortly after she has finished a period. Normally only one of them is successful and this comes to dominate the rest, which soon die unless the woman is given more hormone. The chosen follicle produces nearly all of the oestrogen until a spurt of LH causes it to burst and release its egg into the adjacent fallopian tube. That is only the end of a chapter for the follicle because it is resurrected as a corpus luteum which, for the next two weeks, produces progesterone and oestrogen to make the uterus receptive to an implanting embryo. The length of the menstrual cycle is fixed by the lifespan of these bodies – the follicle for the first two weeks and the corpus luteum for the second two. The waxing and waning of these bodies goes on for cycle after cycle unless the woman falls pregnant. If she does, the life of the corpus luteum is extended so that it can continue to produce hormones for several weeks until the placenta takes over responsibility.

None of these events occurs before puberty because levels of FSH and LH have not risen high enough to stimulate the ovary. Afterwards, they see-saw up and down with the levels of sex hormones in what appears to be a struggle for supremacy but is in reality a dialogue between the pituitary and the pelvis. The aim of the dramatic hormone swings is to achieve the central event in the cycle – ovulation – and, if conception fails and the corpus luteum undergoes pro-grammed death, to ensure that another crop of follicles begins the cycle all over again. This is usually a harmonious process which continues from puberty to menopause more or less indifferent to the woman's age while her egg store lasts. When the supply of growing follicles gets short, her cycle becomes irregular, rather like an automobile firing intermittently as it runs out of petrol until it eventually halts. The analogy breaks down at this point, however, because the store of eggs or follicles cannot be replenished.

Follicles serve the functions of the ovary by nursing the growth of eggs and producing hormones that help the eggs achieve their destiny. They wrap each egg up in a spherical bundle of cells containing a large watery bath in which steroid hormones accumulate before being released into the veins. But, just as patients provide employment for nurses, so the nurse cells need eggs for their own survival. There are few better examples of symbiosis anywhere in physiology. The significance of this arrangement is that when one cell type disappears, so does the other; consequently the end of fertility and loss of ovarian hormones go hand in hand at menopause.

As the ovary gets older, the pituitary gland senses that something is amiss because the ovary fails to send back messages in the form of oestrogen and progesterone. The frustrated gland tries to force the ovary to resume the dialogue by releasing more FSH and LH and synthesizing them in longer-acting forms. But the postmenopausal ovary cannot respond because it no longer possesses the cells needed for hormone production. Nevertheless, the pituitary does not give up and increases its output of FSH and LH – but to no avail. So characteristic are these high hormone levels that they are used for testing whether the ovaries are barren. These hormone levels remain elevated after the menopause until old age, and large quantities are filtered out of the blood by the kidneys and into the urine.

There is a twist in the tail to this story because what is waste to a postmenopausal woman can be a boon to a younger one whose ovaries are normal but who has insufficient FSH of her own. According to legend, the first source of the two gonadotrophic hormones for testing and commercial production in the 1950s, was an Italian convent – presumably on the assumption that nuns' urine is purer and less likely to be contaminated with pregnancy hormones. Whatever their origin, these hormones were certainly effective, and they have become mainstays of fertility treatment because they help to control patients' cycles and allow more eggs to be harvested for *in vitro* fertilization. Ironically this is a technique which the Vatican now frowns upon.

After the menopause the ovaries gradually shrivel, though never to the point of vanishing – even in a centenarian. The first to draw attention to this was the Delft physician Regnier de Graaf who discovered the role of ovaries. 'The size of the female testicles [*sic*] varies not a little according to age ... In a woman of advanced age and the decrepit they become smaller, harder and more dried-up, gradually withering more and more but never entirely disappearing.' The cells that remain after the menopause are fibrous and, although they produce traces of androgens, the ovaries are as good as finished in the eyes of most gynaecologists. Since they are no longer working, their removal does not compromise a woman's oestrogen levels any further and, given a suitable opportunity, the ovaries are often taken out as a precaution against cancer.

After the menopause, oestrogens fall to less than 5 per cent of menstrual cycle levels and the main oestrogen is no longer oestradiol but a less potent one, oestrone. Most of this steroid is produced by cells that are not conventionally regarded as glandular, the most important being fat cells because of their abundance. Each fat cell contains a trace of the enzyme aromatase, which converts oestrone from the weak androgens which are released into the bloodstream by the adrenal glands. There may be little enough of this oestrogen, but every molecule helps to avoid menopausal problems – and plump women produce more than thin ones. Oestrogen is not the only type of ovarian hormone to fall after menopause, but it is the most important one because virtually all the symptoms of menopause stem from insufficiency.

As long ago as 1933, one of the first big surveys on the subject, by the Council of Medical Women's Federation, reported that only 16 per cent of women remained free from menopausal symptoms in mid-life. Most complained of hot flushes and sweating but headaches, palpitations, insomnia and giddiness were also common. The situation remains much the same today. Yet treatment of the symptoms continues to be controversial, and only some 10–20 per cent of women in developed countries are taking HRT, fewer still elsewhere. One of the reasons is that we are not dealing with a classical deficiency syndrome as not every woman suffers during the change. And the worse effects, which are on bones and arteries, develop insidiously and don't show up until a couple of decades later – long after a woman has forgotten about hot flushes and the like.

Menopausal symptoms are all too often lightly regarded by those unaffected by them. After all, they are usually transient, do not threaten life, and psychological and sociological factors play a part in an individual's experience of the change. Japanese women, for instance, are said to cope better with them than Westerners. Nevertheless, the discomfort and embarrassment of flushing and sweating can be distressing, particularly at a time of life which is often strained by domestic and other pressures. Women should not have to suffer in silence, and their feelings need to be taken seriously at that time.

Symptoms often begin a year or two before the last menstrual period at the first hint of lower oestrogens and continue for a similar time afterwards. A hysterectomized woman will often have them slightly earlier than others and, since she cannot have normal periods, they are the only sign that her ovaries have ceased to function. Some people get off lightly with just the odd episode, but unlucky ones may flush every hour or two or on and off for a decade or more. The hot flush – or flash, as it is more often called in America – can be triggered by a sudden drop in oestrogen levels at any age or by drugs that stop the hormones entering their receptor keyholes and exerting effects on cells. People get hooked on their sex hormones and it takes time for them to come off.

Each episode of flushing is a ten- to fifteen-minute surge of heat, felt mostly on the chest, shoulders and face. Heat-sensitive cameras reveal that temperature elevation occurs across the whole surface of the body, but women are generally unaware of its full extent. The heating is due to a sudden rush of blood to the skin and is usually accompanied by sweating. These strange events are often triggered unexpectedly while resting at comfortable room temperatures, though stress may contribute and women will sometimes have a premonition of an attack. Flushes are the result of the body trying to adapt to lower levels of oestrogens. The brain fires signals along the nerves to the skin – inappropriately as it turns out – to allow more blood to flow to the surface and so radiate more heat, in much the way that we glow after a hot bath or vigorous exercise. The problem lies in the erratic behaviour of the body's thermostat.

The main thermostat lies in the floor of the brain, the hypothalamus, and it may be no coincidence that this is close to the nerves that control the output of pituitary hormones. Gonadotrophic hormones surge in synchrony with flushes, though they are not responsible for them. More significant is the resetting of the thermostat to a fraction of a degree lower. We would not feel such a small change in a domestic heating system, but the effects in the body are detected by a biochemistry that is sensitive to tiny temperature changes, as we know from our responses to a febrile illness or jogging, though these have different causes. There are precedents for hormonal effects on the thermostat for it is set fractionally higher in women after ovulation and during pregnancy as a result of actions of progesterone on the hypothalamus. We can appreciate why a higher temperature and basal metabolic rate may be desirable for reproduction, but it is difficult to discern any purpose in a hot flush.

Fortunately, HRT provides early relief from these unpleasant and embarrassing symptoms. But the treatment is effective only while it is being taken, and those who give it up are advised to reduce the dose gradually, to allow the body to adjust and so avoid the old symptoms surfacing again. Many women do not persevere with HRT for a variety of reasons. Some suspect that it is responsible for weight gain, others do not want even light periods to return and still more say they get sore breasts and feel nauseous. Were they to experiment with different preparations they might hit on one that is more acceptable, but some people are understandably suspicious of what they see as overmedicalization of the change, which is managed mainly by male doctors.

Some women are indignant that the problems of mid-life biology seem to fall more heavily on females. But do males really get off scot-free?

Men may pride themselves on having sex organs that are engineered to complete the course, but can a sixty- or seventy-year-old testicle be the same as when it was twenty? If so, it would be uniquely immune to ageing. Men do not have hot flushes unless they are castrated or treated with drugs to suppress their hormones, and then only for a while. They get off lightly because their testosterone levels do not normally plummet, though there are fewer reasons to be sanguine than many suppose. This hormone has the reputation for remaining constant day in day out, year after year. This makes for a much less interesting biological story than the spectacular surges of a woman's hormones, although one study showed that young Parisian males have lower testosterone in the spring than at other times! The explanation for the greater placidity of this hormone is that sperm are produced continuously rather than in monthly bursts, so the hormone is needed all the time.

Sperm develop in spaghetti-like tubules in the testes where they are bedded down with nurse cells which are responsible for nourishing them but produce little in the way of sex hormones themselves. The male hormone is made by the Leydig cells, which are like the sauce spread between the strands of spaghetti. These cells have a direct dialogue with the pituitary gland, regardless of whether sperm are being produced or not. Pituitary LH stimulates them to make testosterone, which in turn feeds back to stop too much LH being released, so keeping a suitable *yin–yang* balance. Sperm production hardly enters the equation. That is why you cannot distinguish a man who is fertile and another who is sterile by appearances. In the ovary, hormone and egg production are firmly linked and so, inequitable though it may seem, only females suffer the double blow of losing their sex hormones and their fertility at the same time.

Men would suffer from menopausal symptoms either if the pituitary failed them or if they lost their Leydig cells, because either event would cause a catastrophic fall in testosterone. The Leydig cells are long-lived and fairly robust, and there is no reason to expect their numbers to fall with age – in fact we know that they don't in rats, and numbers even increase in stallions. However, perhaps because of a dwindling blood supply, the numbers of these cells in an average man of sixty are only half what they were when he was thirty, and they continue to fall in old age. The ability of the male organ to make hormones consequently tapers off, though never so completely as in the ovary. This is as close as a man gets to the state of menopause, and it is stretching matters to call it an 'andropause'.

Just as women reach menopause at different ages, changes in male hormones vary a great deal from man to man. If the results of the Baltimore Longitudinal Study were generally applicable, men would have good cause for satisfaction for it showed that testosterone levels in middle-class Americans can be as high in an eighty-year-old as in a young man. These were, admittedly, a highly selected group in excellent health, and other studies in America and elsewhere have shown that the levels are lower on average in old men, and lowest in those who are less than fully fit and harbouring diabetes and cardio-vascular disease. Men who take care of their health are probably safeguarding their sexual functions too.

The appearance of the testes betrays little about changes in hormone production or sexual potency, so the male ego can go unruffled deep into old age. Urologists estimate testicle sizes with a reference set of 'beads' on a string, called a Prader orchidometer – a normal adult organ is about eighteen millilitres throughout adult life, though racial differences exist. Hormone levels should be more informative than size, but high levels of testosterone do not necess-arily mean high biological activity because only a small fraction in blood is active. Most of the hormone is bound to the blood protein SHBG, and is not immediately available to the cells. Older men have more SHBG as a result of a battle between the sex hormones because their slightly greater amounts of oestrogen stimulate production of SHBG, just as they do in women. The surfeit of SHBG mops up a greater fraction of the testosterone, and it is tempting to suggest that this is in the interests of reducing the risk of prostate disease.

Regrettably for this theory, the difference could threaten to speed up the loss of calcium from the bones, which only goes to show that any simple biological theory of ageing that is particularly pleasing should probably be discarded at once.

Before closing this section, I feel bound to declare my belief that it will be possible to do something to stem the tide of ageing, especially in the ovary. Given that the organ stockpiles eggs before birth and uses them rather prodigally for the next fifty years, the idea of extending ovarian life by reducing egg wastage is not science fiction. If the egg store could be eked out until seventy years old, the pituitary gland would still be able to produce enough FSH and LH to stimulate the ovary and keep menstrual cycles going. Menopause would be postponed into old age or even abolished altogether. Whether this is desirable is another matter.

When oral contraceptives were introduced in the 1960s, some doctors wondered whether women who suppressed ovulation for long enough would be saving their follicles for another day. A moment's reflection should have been enough to dismiss the notion that the ovaries of pill-users age more slowly. For one thing, there would be an economy of only the one follicle that ovulates per month compared with the score that die every day, so the effects would be trivial. For another, we would expect that women who have many pregnancies, and therefore fewer ovulations, would reach menopause later, which is not so.

Considering its biosocial significance, it is surprising how little we know about how the rate of ovarian ageing is controlled. Discovering a way to slow the process could lead to the biggest revolution affecting women's ability to control their reproduction since the dawn of steroid contraception – which might be sufficient cause for some people to discourage scientific exploration of the possibilities. But there is good reason for ignoring the largely imaginary fears that this would encourage very late motherhood. Besides, there are plenty of women at risk of a premature menopause who would welcome a way of slowing down their ovarian clock to achieve a pregnancy before it was too late.

How this can be achieved is still a matter of speculation for no one has discovered the time switch that lies at the heart of the ovary and sends each egg towards ovulation or, more often, oblivion. A fact that is often misunderstood, even in undergraduate textbooks, is that neither the pituitary hormones nor the hormonal steroids have any influence over the rate at which the ovarian clock runs. Their role is downstream of the main switch and is to control which follicles that are already growing will eventually succeed in ovulating and to condemn the rest.

Lateral thinking comes no more easily to scientists than to anyone else, and it may take a fresh mind to make a breakthrough. The follicle is noted for being the fastest-growing structure in the body, and it is natural to concentrate on hormones that stimulate this process and easy to forget that growth can also be controlled by suppression. More examples of inhibitory hormones are coming to light, and an inhibitory strategy would make sense in the ovary because there is a danger of exhausting the follicle store too soon and ovulating more eggs than the uterus can cope with. We can at least be certain that whoever discovers the key to ovarian time will be quickly followed by others who are mainly interested in making money from it.

The fact that we are even considering how the menopause might be postponed goes to show that this particular milestone does not strike a happy chord with everyone. Rather than celebrating with a coming-of-age party, we view the change gloomily and it is a risky subject for polite conversation at parties. Menopause marks the close of the child-bearing years and heralds the onset of fresh problems, but it certainly need not be the end of life as a sexual being.

• Sexual Asymptote

In biomedical parlance, the word 'menopause' simply means the last menstrual cycle, but in popular usage it has come to represent many of the negative aspects of mid-life. Often it is used as a poisoned dart

223

to fire a person, of either sex. As if the problems of growing older are not enough, those in their sixth decade and beyond are assumed to be less of the woman or man than they were, and probably 'past it'.

Writing about the effects of age on sexual interest and capacity is not something that a biologist can feel totally at ease with. I would rather have bypassed these quicksands and passed on to the story of the physical effects of sex hormones in the next chapter. It is difficult to find a subject that is more speculative or intractable to study. Our sexual behaviour stands apart from that of animals in its great variety and intensity and in the way that it is engaged in for recreation – not that play has been a trivial factor during our evolution. Plenty of authors have suggested that the cementing of the pair-bond by regularly making love throughout life has contributed to the success of our species.

Gender is so important to humans that it is the first thing we are told by the midwife when a baby is born. From that moment onwards, the child is treated in a particular way and, for better or worse, is canalized into a gender-specific role for the rest of its days. Our gender identity is so ingrained and profound that most of us find difficulty in imagining being otherwise. That is why aspersions about a woman's sexual receptivity or a man's prowess can be so cruel. Alex Comfort has often championed the sexual dignity of older people and challenged the assumption that older people don't – and shouldn't – engage in sexual activity. So entrenched is this view that in some parts of India couples go into voluntary sexual retirement after the birth of grandchildren. Setting cultural obligations aside, this need not be. We are no less a woman or a man for being older. Our gender fate was genetically stamped at the moment of conception, confirmed by the emergence of a body with either ovaries or testes and reinforced by the formative effects of sex hormones on the organs. The most fundamental of these imprints are not reversed by age. So much for sex – but sex and sexuality are not the same thing.

Sexual interest and capacity certainly do wane with age, and these are among the first changes to occur as men get older. Some ancient Greeks even made a virtue of having 'at last got rid of the sexual instinct, which incessantly disturbs man up to that time, just as if they had succeeded in escaping from a maddened and wild master'. Everyone becomes aware sooner or later that their sexual longings are moderating, but for a long time the subject was taboo and there was no more solid information than mere anecdotes. Until the late 1940s nobody had seriously tried, or dared, to scrutinize human sexual decline.

A research team led by Alfred Kinsey at the Institute for Sex Research at Indiana University was the first to inquire into the sexual habits of Americans. After sifting through thousands of replies to a questionnaire, they concluded that, for men, 'The high point of sexual performance is ... somewhere around sixteen or seventeen years of age. It is not later.' The performance rating was based not just on conjugal acts but every other sexual outlet reported, and so the decline could not be blamed on the sex drive or age of the man's partner. The human male may deny it, but his sex drive reaches a peak in adolescence and starts to taper off almost immediately. A man may say he is in the prime of life in his forties, but his biology says otherwise, even if he thinks his interest in the opposite sex is undiminished. Responsibility for this change cannot be laid at the door of testosterone, which remains at adequate levels in most men until their sixties or later. Libido would be a good biomarker of ageing were it not for the confounding effects of physical and mental illness and the problems of finding satisfactory, not to say acceptable, means of measuring it.

The Kinsey report did a service by scotching the myth that the male libido abruptly ends in mid-life. It records that 'at no time did old age suddenly enter the picture'. The vicissitudes of health make the downward slope bumpy for some individuals, but the average trend is a gentle descent towards the bottom. The slope for the whole population should properly be called 'asymptotic' in mathematical parlance because it never touches zero. There is always the rare individual who claims to be still sexually alert and potent long after his peers.

Several years passed after the first report before Kinsey published the results of a large survey of sexual activity in women. This told a rather different story. He concluded that 'The incidences and frequencies of marital coitus, and of coitus to the point of orgasm, do not provide any evidence that the female ages in her sexual capacities.' Since the sexual activity of single women was unchanged up to menopausal age, suspicion about who was responsible for the decline in marital sex fell on the husband – which no doubt reinforced the anxieties of men with voluptuous wives. The biology of ageing is often perverse, and never more so than in sexual matters. Conjugal relations are less harmonious across the lifespan than the picture of biological tandem idealized a century ago by Sylvanus Stall. Try as we may to rationalize a man's decline on the grounds of more satisfaction and less premature ejaculation, there is no question that the sex drive peaks at different ages in men and women.

This must have been long suspected, but it took the Kinsey study to make it official. Its corollary is that women are better matched to younger husbands. Such partnerships are often regarded as farcical, but this betrays a prejudice against older women which has still not been shaken off. One of Shakespeare's contemporaries, the Rev. Robert Burton, summed up the attitude of his day: ''Tis not held fit for an ancient woman to match with a young man.' Whether there are any theological grounds for forbidding such unions I doubt. Suffice to say that Burton had no qualms about officiating at marriages where the man was a lot older than his bride. His faith in this arrangement was pseudo-biological because he thought that a young woman had the capacity to reawaken sexual ardour and reinvigorate an old man. 'Ancient Men will dote in this kind sometimes as well as the rest; the heat of love will thaw their frozen Affections, dissolve the ice of age, and so far inable them, though they be 60 Years of age above the Girdle, to be scarce 30 beneath . . .' This was no prudish clergyman: he recognized the power of the novelty factor in sexual relations long before Kinsey announced it. One of the famous prescriptions for ailing burgermasters made by a contemporary of Burton, the Dutch physician Boerhave, was to lay each old man between two maids. The liaison did not necessarily require actual physical engagement, as a girl's 'vapours' were sometimes enough to spark an old gentleman into life. A precedent for this was set in the Bible, for when King David was given the Shunamite maiden Abishag in his declining years 'he knew her not'.

Few researchers have probed into the physiology of human copulation, and fewer still have considered the effects of ageing. In some studies the researchers have been their own subjects, in the worthy belief that the human sexual response is best studied within the intimacy of an established relationship. While the motives are clear, the arrangement is far from satisfactory because those who choose to make a laboratory out of their bedroom can hardly represent Mr and Mrs Average and are likely to grow weary of recording the slow advance of age.

The greater openness of the 1960s helped to launch more intrusive studies into what had been regarded as a private matter. A pair of sexologists in St Louis became renowned for recruiting paid volunteers in order to study the physiology of sexual responses under laboratory conditions. While some people were offended by the methods used by Masters and Johnson, others were outraged at reducing lovemaking to a number of stages and physiological reflexes, like any other bodily function. The justification for such studies, then and now, is that sexual problems can cause misery in relationships, and active therapy is more likely to be restorative than passive acceptance.

Perhaps the findings were less surprising to the subjects than to the researchers. Healthy people over fifty were found to be able to enjoy as much sexual satisfaction as younger ones, and both the man and the women were capable of a full sexual response, even if the climax was delayed and its intensity diminished. As might be anticipated, those who gained the most satisfaction from sex tended to be active more regularly.

Animals are little different from humans when it comes to sexual ardour in old age. Male laboratory rats gradually lose interest in copulation, and females remain receptive as long as they continue to have cycles. So a principle is emerging that the female stays the course while her ovaries are still functioning, which is consistent with the evolutionary arguments set out earlier. It is in the interests of a male to reproduce as soon as possible after puberty and to invest his genetic capital in the next generation once he has reached full size and strength. There is no advantage in delaying reproduction, particularly for a species that is as vulnerable in the wild state as a rodent. Pregnancy is an investment that a female can make only a few times in life, and it pays her to be careful with whom she mates and to be keen to take a late reproductive opportunity.

In animals, sexual receptivity is much more bound to the cyclical rise of oestrogens than in humans. A female will accept a male only when she is in a state of oestrus, and he, in turn, will detect signs that his partner is ready. As any pet-owner knows, an oestrous bitch gives off aphrodisiac odours to advertise her sexual state to every dog in the neighbourhood. These pheromones are volatile confederates of the hormones inside the body and serve to increase the chances of reproductive success. The quest to find human pheromones has been difficult and frustrating because, if they exist at all, our responses are likely to be vestigial, and the relatively insensitive nose of a man is overwhelmed by a blanket of perfumes and deodorants. Unless men make a deliberate effort to find out, they have no idea of the days in the month when their wives are most fertile – nor, indeed, do most women know.

Women are more emancipated from their sex hormones than animals. Apart from an occasional ovulation pain, or *Mittelschmerz*, most are oblivious of when they are ovulating, which is surprising because the bursting follicle is the size of a grape. So secretive is this process that until the 1930s it was widely believed that the most fertile time was during the periods rather than between them. This error grew out of a false analogy between menstruation and the seepage of vaginal blood in dogs at oestrus, and gave the rhythm method of contraception a bad reputation from the start.

Unlike virtually all animals, women do not lose their sex drive during the non-fertile part of their cycle; they will also engage in sexual activity, albeit less enthusiastically, during pregnancy and breast-feeding when ovulation is suppressed. Some long-lived animals, like gorillas and elephants, may go for a year or two between copulations, but humans are different. If feelings of sexual longing in women fluctuated with their oestrogen levels, sexual activity should peak about fourteen days after the beginning of periods, but there is remarkably little evidence that this is generally so. Most studies have shown that there is no day of complete sexual abstinence except when required by religious taboos. A slightly higher frequency of sexual intercourse has been found near the middle of the cycle in some studies, though in others the peak has been on an earlier day, or even during periods. Oestrogens appear to hold little sway over decisions when and how often to make love.

Human biology is more complex than we are sometimes wont to believe, and men are not the slaves to testosterone that some people make out. The castrate who is not taking androgen replacement therapy is not totally uninterested in the opposite sex and is able to copulate, even if less inclined to do so and unable to ejaculate semen. Likewise, compulsory castration for sex offenders is no guarantee against recidivism, and the argument to reintroduce this is motivated more by a desire for punishment than justified as a therapy. Testosterone is also held responsible for a lot of human aggression, and the problem of adolescent thuggery is given as the main evidence. This is a gross oversimplification though, and human aggression is more socially conditioned and less hormonally determined than is popularly supposed. Has anyone who doubts there is more to aggression that testosterone never met an irascible female hamster or a snarling bitch at the gate?

Were the sex drive as dependent on oestrogen in humans as it is in animals, conjugal relations would evaporate at the menopause because spayed female animals are frigid. Kinsey showed that this is far from the case in women, though more recent research has shown that the change has some impact on sexual feelings. Studies in Sweden

229

and Australia show that menopause has a much greater effect in damping ardour than ageing *per se*, which pours cold water on the old myth of 'autumnal fires'.

The most plausible explanation is that lower oestrogen levels are unable to maintain the thickness of the mucous lining of the vagina and the nether regions of the urinary system. The tissue consequently gets drier and more easily damaged and infected. Penetration during intercourse can be painful and membranes may inflame. Fortunately the cells are as responsive to oestrogens as they were before, and these problems are ameliorated by oestrogen-containing creams or HRT pills and patches.

The state of a woman's mind is likely to sway her sexual feelings much more than a dry vagina, however, and this is more difficult to treat. A study of Australian women in the Melbourne area revealed that a sense of well-being was rather more important for satisfying sexual relationships than taking HRT. The formula for sexual satisfaction was good health and fitness, no smoking and a good relationship with a partner. Those who are fortunate in all these respects are generally the ones who graduate more serenely at the menopause and later on.

Whether HRT has any effect on a woman's sex drive is controversial, not least because the question enters the cross-fire of sexual politics. The confounding effects of changes in hormone levels and of ageing are not easily disentangled, but some evidence that libido can be increased by oestrogen has come from studies of younger women after a surgical menopause. A small dose helped to maintain a normal sexual interest, but increasing amounts had no additive effect. Since spiking oestrogen with a little testosterone is said to boost an ebbing libido, people have wondered whether the greater fall in oestrogens than androgens after the menopause will also make women more assertive and sexually receptive. But this is an unwarranted fear – or wishful thinking – for reasons that have already been given.

Just as a woman may need a trace of oestrogen to maintain sex drive, each man may require a threshold level of testosterone to be 'turned on'. But hormone levels are not everything, as castrates know.

A larger dose may not increase the sexual drive proportionately or cause priapism and satyriasis – and could be harmful. Hormone levels in most men leave a safe margin at young ages so that, provided the threshold does not drift upwards, a man still has enough even if the levels fall slightly when he is older. Anyone unlucky enough to have a high threshold and low levels of testosterone may be in jeopardy of becoming undersexed when he is older. But it is more difficult to measure the hormonal threshold in a man than his hormone levels, and most men would probably prefer to remain blissfully ignorant on this count. Trials now underway in America to test the anabolic effects of testosterone in older men provide an unintended opportunity for enlightenment and for ending a century of speculation about the relationship between hormones and a flagging libido.

Impotence is rather uncommon in healthy men until late middle age, and, when it does emerge, the problem can usually be blamed on ill health or the side-effects of medication. Age alone is an unlikely cause, and erectile impotence is not caused by insufficient male sex hormone. Once regarded as mainly a psychosexual problem, impotence more often has an organic origin. Nocturnal events throw some light on the cause. During sleep, dreaming episodes recur every ninety minutes or so. Muscles become rigid, eyes twitch, and the penis of a sexually healthy man becomes tumescent – irrespective of the content of the dream. A man will often find that he has an erection on waking, and wonder why. In fact it is the man who is consistently flaccid who should be wondering about the state of his organ for this is a sign of physical impotence. There are many possible reasons. Alcohol and some prescription drugs, such as antidepressants, are well-known anaphrodisiacs, though their effects are reversible. Often the cause is an illness because sexual health and general health go hand in hand.

The human penis does not contain a bone, or *os penis*, as in some animals, but has remarkable powers of extension due to engorgement with blood. This process is triggered by nerve impulses which cause the artery wall to relax and allow more blood to flow into capacitance

231

vessels in the shaft, or corpus cavernosum. As the vessels become distended, the veins draining blood from the organ become compressed, as if a tourniquet had been tied around the base of the organ. Failure of erection in diabetics and paraplegics occurs because of nerve damage, whereas the problem in men with circulatory disease is due to their inability to deliver enough blood via clogged arteries.

Where spinal nerves have been severed and the organs and blood vessels are otherwise healthy, erection and ejaculation are still possible by electrical stimulation or drug treatment to mimic the normal firing of nerve impulses. This was another area in which self-experimentation proved fruitful. A London doctor tested a number of drugs on his own penis. The most dramatic result was obtained by injecting three milligrams of an alpha-blocker, or muscle relaxant. His penis was soon far from relaxed and remained stiffly at attention for two whole days despite his best attempts to distract mental attention by reading Plato's *Republic*. The effects eventually wore off, but antagonistic drugs are available for making a penis quickly go limp. This pharmacological balancing act may seem to be a very comical joke and to make a mockery of lovemaking, but if it helps an injured party to fulfil a proper sexual role, why not? No doubt the present range of drugs and electrical devices for alleviating sexual dysfunction will become more discreet and sophisticated, but their effectiveness will depend on having well-preserved blood vessels, and that can be a problem in older men.

Attitudes to people who enjoy regular sexual activity deep into old age have been ambivalent. Sometimes sex has been regarded as health-promoting, although it is rather a sign of good health than a cause of it. More often it has been frowned upon, and the historical view has been a pessimistic one. Some 450 years ago the religious reformer Richard Taverner wrote, 'Green ivy, which catcheth an olde Tree, maketh quicke worke for the fire: and the imbracements of a faire woman, hastneth an olde man to his grave.' Old fears die slowly. A reader recently wrote to a woman's magazine for advice about her sixty-seven-year-old husband, who was twenty years her senior. They were making love two or three times a day, and she was worried whether this might be bad for his heart. The agony aunt seemed to have dismissed the possibility of a hoax and wisely reassured her and congratulated her on her luck in having a husband in such good shape. There is no age bar to sexual fulfilment, particularly when both partners are healthy. There may be problems, of course, when one wishes to continue and the other to retire from conjugal activity, but, in today's society, it would be a pity if what was for so long a taboo should become a requirement. A trusting bond between partners of any age adds up to much more than a successful physical union.

The sexual dichotomy of life is one of the fundamentals of nature and is not defeated by either age or the menopause. We cannot ignore the toll of years on the body, but we can at least reflect blithely on our degree of independence from sex hormone changes – at least in the realms of behaviour. The menopause is a milestone in a woman's life and, although men may go an extra mile, hormone changes eventually catch up with them too. There is no biological *purpose* in having lower oestrogen or testosterone levels later in life, but plenty of significance. The steroids that helped to shape us from the beginning of life have actions that continue and extend far beyond the immediate needs of reproduction. Why this is so, and with what consequences for old age, we shall see in the next chapter.

CHAPTER 10 **The Shape of Steroid Action**

Now Jove, in his next commodity of hair, send thee a
beard.

> Clown to Viola (dressed as a youth) in Shakespeare's
> *Twelfth Night*

• *Vive la Différence!*

Boys are born with bigger brains in proportion to their size than girls,
but during childhood the girls edge up and overtake them at puberty.
Make what you will of this observation, there is no denying that many
other organs differ between men and women too. A woman's liver is
relatively bigger than a man's throughout life, and she has a larger
spleen from an early age. These differences turn out not to be innate
but depend on the balance of sex steroids prevailing before birth and
afterwards.

    All this seems to be rather puzzling at first sight because these
organs are mostly engaged in activities other than reproduction. It is
understandable that testosterone and oestrogen should affect the sex
organs because the *raison d'être* of the uterus and fallopian tubes in
females and the penis and prostate gland in males is to serve the needs
of reproduction, but it comes as something of a surprise to find that
most of the body is far from indifferent to these hormones. Liver,
spleen, brain, kidneys, heart, lung and skin, among others, differ
between males and females, and the gulf is sometimes large. The
salivary glands in male mice are two to three times heavier than in
females, though it is the other way around in hamsters. Such
differences in size are often matched in biochemicals. It seems that

the entire body serves the needs of reproduction to some extent and, to this extent, all parts are 'sexy'. The significance of this is that the body fabric can change in response to hormone fluctuations the worry is that any changes might affect not only our appearance but also our health.

Rising levels of hormones in adolescence help to enlarge, strengthen and shape the body for its future reproductive role. They also make it more attractive to members of the opposite sex and *la beauté du diable* is prized all the more for being transient. Sex hormones may produce a very appetizing dish at first, but make a less than tempting recipe later on. This is often a direct result of falling hormone levels, but unwelcome changes sometimes come regardless because biological time does not stand still. Some of the concerns are cosmetic and are shared by both men and women – too much hair or fat in one place and not enough in another. Other changes cause the bones and perhaps the muscles to grow weaker. Finally, there are those that pare down the lifespan by encouraging cancer to develop or blood clots to jam in narrow vessels and provoke a heart attack or a stroke.

We have already seen there is no biological rationale for these changes other than the fact that only the early years of life are at the sharp end of evolutionary selection. Natural selection has little or no power to prevent decay and a whole gamut of undesirable changes from creeping on to the final scenes of life. That is why we are fittest and most vigorous in the bloom of youth. Although evolutionary theory links senescence with reproduction, it is far from true to say that all the problems of old age are related to our sexual physiology, past or present, but some are. This chapter attempts to explain what these are, why they are often different in men and women, and how they might have evolved.

Once the dust had settled over the evolution controversy, Darwin pondered why the sexes of some, though not all, animals appear so very different from each other. If a primary distinction between male and female gonads is enough for some species, why do others go to the trouble and expense of making special adornments and weapons? Since species can change over the course of time, it was a short step for him to accept that there is nothing permanent about the physical similarities and differences between the sexes. But why did they evolve in the first place?

Males feel the pressure of competition because it is only those that compete successfully for partners that pass on their characteristics to the next generation. The losers in the mating game leave no genetic legacy, and their unique combinations of genes are evolutionary culs-de-sac. Darwin called the pressures on males 'sexual selection'. It is a counterpart to natural selection, the overall driving force for evolutionary change. He put it this way:

> when the females and males of any animal have the same general habits of life, but differ in structure, colour or ornament, such differences have been mainly caused by sexual selection: that is by individual males having had, in successive generations, some slight advantage over other males, in their weapons, means of defence, or charms which they have transmitted to their male offspring alone.

By the end of the 1860s Darwin's days of globe-trotting were long past, but he did not have to recall any exotic creatures from his travels to make his point. There were good examples of sex selection in his backyard. Peacocks' tails are as much products of sex selection as wings are the handiwork of natural selection. Each gives its owner an edge in the wily game of courting a mate and thriving in a tough and competitive world. Since reproduction is the alpha and omega in Nature, almost any part of the body can be made to serve its purpose if need be. Tail fans and antlers were not always so distinctive in males and females. In their new role, the tissues have become more sensitive to sex hormones, so that they can keep in tune with the gonads and improve the chances of success with a mate.

An appealing body surface and a large frame are winning ingredients for sexual success. Skin and bone and their appendages are some of the more important targets for hormones because their signals can be seen clearly by onlookers. Cocks with the gaudiest plumage and stags with the strongest antlers gain a reproductive advantage over rivals and so contribute more genes to posterity. The brain is also a target for sex hormones since shrewd courtship behaviour can count for as much as elegance and physique. Suitors that give the most impressive displays, revealing plumage in pristine condition and free of parasites, will make the best fathers of the hen bird's chicks. Likewise, a bellowing stag is reassuring the hinds in his harem that they have a strong protector. Behind the secondary sexual characteristics of a species lies a history of struggling males and choosy females.

Polygamous species face the stiffest test because the stakes are highest for them. A few choice males manage to establish a territory and gather a harem to the exclusion of all on-comers. The winners take all. Darwin knew 'that some relation exists between polygamy and the development of secondary sexual characters'. The greater the competition, the more pressure there is on males to exaggerate their virility symbols. War-torn bull elephant seals are an extreme case, the 'beach-master' dwarfing his cows in size and ferocity. The size gap between the sexes can even be used to gauge the degree of polygamy in different species. This rule fits rather well in primates and confirms what we know about the significant tendency to polygamy and marital infidelity in our own species.

But an evolutionary arms race between males cannot go on unchecked for ever without threatening the success of the individual and the good of the species. Elephant seals have taken sexual selection to the point where their bulk and aggressiveness begin to undermine the reproductive advantage they had won. Their lumbering gait severely restricts the size of their territory, and they sometimes trample their own pups in defending it. So there are limits to the extent to which the most powerful members of a group can monopolize females and feeding places. Successful animals have to balance on a knife-edge between natural selection and sexual selection.

There is no better-known, or more sickening, symbol of the pressures of sex selection than cock-fighting. Given no way of escape, the males have to fight it out, more like gladiators than contestants in a male beauty contest. Animals have evolved all sorts of gestures and displays to try to avoid the folly of locking in mortal combat. Even so, pulling rank can still carry a price. Social baboons achieving high rank have higher levels of corticosteroids compared to those lower down. These stress hormones from the adrenal glands may be natural and beneficial in some ways, but they diminish breeding efficiency. Peacocks and other dandies of the avian world must watch their step too. If they become too conspicuous or ungainly they will be more vulnerable to predators. Likewise, the streamers of the male great-tailed grackle from Mexico hinder his aerial performance in strong winds. Though this male's mortality rate is twice that of his mate, sex appeal must have outweighed the poorer survival prospects, otherwise his adornments would not have lasted. But there is no law of nature that insists that costly trade-offs always have to be negotiated to gain a reproductive advantage. Pheasants boasting larger spurs are more attractive to females, produce more offspring and even live longer. Spurs are the avian equivalents of padded shoulders and snazzy ties, but apparently carry no hidden price tags for the wearer.

In matriarchal societies, the shape and physiology of females can be subject to sex selection too. The female spotted hyena is both heavier and more aggressive than her mate, and may even fight and kill her sister while they are still cubs. Virilization and its costs are not always the prerogative of the male. The female hyena's clitoris is as bulky and erectile as her mate's penis, and her labia are fused into a scrotum-like pouch. Despite these obstacles, she still manages to mate and give birth through the hole at the end of her endophallus. This unorthodox behaviour and physiology is due to the extraordinarily high levels of androgens for her sex, even before birth. Evidently the sex hormones are not strict respecters of gender.

Women who produce abnormally large amounts of androgens from their ovaries or adrenal glands become hirsute and masculinized – and suffer from male diseases too. Conversely, a male who has never been exposed to testosterone has only a shadow of his full potential, and his somatic development is closer to the normal female form. There are exceptions on both sides. Stallions produce large amounts of oestrogen, which is ironic considering that these beasts have always stood as one of the great symbols of virility. They are not feminized by their female hormone levels, though a human male will be if he receives such a large dose of oestrogen. Males and females produce and respond to both androgens and oestrogens, and the difference between them depends largely on the balance of hormone concentrations and actions.

If we were designing a new species from scratch and chose to create females and males, there would be two theoretical options open to us. We could lay out thousands of genes to specify every distinction we wanted to make between the somatic cells of the two sexes. Sex genes would be required for assigning all the details of the genitalia and other parts of the body where differences, major or otherwise, should exist. Alternatively, we could give both sexes the same set of genes except for a unique type designed to act as a gender switch for one of them. We would not need divine wisdom to choose the second option, for this is the more economical plan. The difference between a man and a woman starts with the flick of a switch in the embryo. Afterwards, hormonal signals get down to the business of instructing the body to be moulded one way or another.

Details of how the switch operates vary between groups of animals, but the principle is universal. In mammals, the baby's sex is decided at conception, depending on whether the fertilizing sperm carries an X (female) or Y (male) chromosome. The gender decision is nevertheless kept secret for the first six weeks of life in the womb. The gonads remain ambisexual and vacant as they await the arrival of primordial germ cells, which are the progenitors of eggs or sperm.

Strangely, it is not the immigrating germ cells but the resident somatic cells that decide whether the gonad will develop into an ovary or testis. If the future nurse cells carry a Y chromosome, a gene called *SRY* is briefly switched on to instruct cells to make tubules suited for nourishing sperm. In the absence of a Y chromosome, the nurse cells form rings of granulosa cells which clasp around the future egg cells to make follicles. If nationality were decided on the same basis as sex, our family origins would matter less than the country of adoption.

The importance of the *SRY* gene for gender is proven beyond doubt. Injecting the gene into fertilized mouse eggs that are genetically destined by two X chromosomes to become females turns them into males with incontestable testes. Once the sex of the gonad has been pointed in the direction of either a testis or an ovary, the gender fate of the rest of the body is decided.

The late Alfred Jost in Paris showed that the testes are the more influential of the gonads when it comes to deciding the gender shape of the body. He castrated the foetuses of pregnant rabbits and swapped the ovaries and testes between others to investigate the effects on future body shape. Eliminating the testicular hormones before birth had an even more dramatic effect than afterwards as it prevented development of parts of the male genital tract as well as abolishing sexual behaviour when the pups grew up. The females were more indifferent to removal of their ovaries and remained in a permanently immature state. A testis graft made a lasting mark on the female body. It blocked formation of a uterus and fallopian tubes and caused the development of a vas deferens instead, and generally encouraged the development of male 'character'. Long ago, a natural experiment was drawn to John Hunter's attention by a farmer who complained that cows carrying twins of opposite sex were producing masculinized female calves. The culprit for these sterile 'freemartins' was not testosterone on that occasion but another testicular hormone, but it confirms the dominating effects of the testis. Since male hormones leave an almost indelible imprint of body structure, biologists have called females, rather pejoratively, the 'default sex'. Put more diplomatically, the basic plan is a female one and male characteristics are optional extras. Either way, it is a far cry from the myth of Eve being created from Adam's rib.

Jost's experiments put paid to any notion that the gene enabling cells to respond to testosterone is on the Y chromosome. Females can be as subject to this hormone as males. The receptor molecules for the androgens are encoded by the X chromosome so that everyone can respond to male hormones – or almost everyone. Imagine the dilemma faced by a doctor who is called to examine an infertile, married woman and discovers that 'she' has a short, blind vagina and no uterus, normal male levels of testosterone and a pair of undescended testicles! This condition, called pseudohermaphroditism, is fortunately very rare and happens when the gene for androgen receptiveness is blighted by a mutation. As males have only one X chromosome, and therefore only one copy of the gene, they have nothing to fall back on in this case. No matter how high their testosterone levels rise, they still look like females.

The flaws of nature can sometimes reveal as much about the actions of genes as years of laborious experiments, though this is of little comfort to those affected. Another case that recently came to light shows that the small amounts of oestrogen produced by men are probably essential. A twenty-eight-year-old American male had reached a height of 204 centimetres and was still growing when he volunteered for investigation. He had reached puberty more than ten years earlier, though his bone age was still the same as a boy of fifteen. During the adolescent growth spurt, the long bones elongate under the combined action of the sex steroids and growth hormone, but on reaching full strength the steroids cause the growth zones at both ends to ossify. This sets the ceiling on height. This man's bones had not reached this stage but, to everyone's surprise, his testosterone levels were normal and the underlying problem turned out to be a lack of the oestrogen receptor. He was totally unresponsive to the hormone. The textbook story of bone growth may have to be revised in the light of his case, which suggests that oestrogen is more important than testosterone in this respect.

Puberty is not only the beginning of the reproductive phase of life but a milestone in the development of body shape and appearance as well as of physiology and outlook. From then on, the sexes increasingly diverge. Steroid hormones produced by the gonads are the agents of change and affect nearly all parts of the body to some degree. Androgens from the testes stimulate hair follicles on the beard

241

to produce long (terminal) hairs instead of fine (vellus) ones, and activation and infection of their sebaceous glands often produce unsightly eruptions of acne. In girls, glandular and adipose (fat) tissues in the future breasts are responsive to the rising oestrogens from the ovaries, causing the nipples to elevate into mounds. These are but some of the familiar changes. Whenever there is a consistent difference between the sexes, we can be fairly certain that one or other of the sex steroids is behind it and that the target cells have the necessary receptors to respond. The evolutionary roots of these gender characteristics lie in the sex selection pressures which operated for millions of years.

One of the fears about menopause and ageing is that falling levels of sex hormones will reverse these differences. This harks back to the notion that ageing is like a form of castration, and there is a little truth in this. None of the organs that were built up in youth is completely spared from the effects of sex hormone withdrawal in mid or late life. Even the skeleton feels impoverished afterwards. These are the changes that the rejuvenators were trying to stem. Although they wrongly put all the weakness down to hormone deficiency, they were right to assume that an old body is equal to a young one in its ability to respond to hormones. Even at the end of our lives, cells still contain good numbers of receptors for sex steroids and other hormones. Were it otherwise, it would be futile even to attempt to replace oestrogens or androgens.

Tissues with the most receptors are first to feel the draught of hormone withdrawal – and are the most responsive to HRT. The lining of the vagina is extremely sensitive to oestrogen and so, after the menopause, the shrunken cells provide less protection from abrasion during intercourse, hence the pain which doctors call dyspareunia. The little remaining lubrication is less acidic than before and not so effective at discouraging infection because carbohydrate stores in the cells have fallen to rock bottom. Even the passing of water can be uncomfortable because the urethral tube is lined with cells that are responsive to oestrogen. All these changes are quickly reversed by oestrogen treatment. If the effects of sex hormones were as dramatic on every other cell type in the body, the wildest dreams of the rejuvenators would have been fulfilled, but it is clear that no sex steroid, nor any other hormone, is the elixir of life.

While many changes are going on within the body, its surfaces easily betray our biological age. Being an organ of communication, the skin responds to sex hormones, albeit unevenly. Hair follicles in the beard, armpits and pubic triangle are sensitive to androgen, as are those in the scalp – though events there turn in the opposite direction. Other areas of the skin are less sensitive, and responses are variable between individuals. Androgen levels normally remain high enough to maintain the density of sexual hair until old age, and, oddly enough, the covering of body and face is more luxuriant in mid-life than ever before.

The effects of oestrogen on skin are more subtle than those of androgens and less well understood. There was a lot of conjecture about the origins of women's beauty in the early days of evolutionary theory, which is now deservedly forgotten. Whether the effects of oestrogen were ever subject to sex selection in Darwin's sense is dubious because in nature it is a rare female that is left without a mate.

These days the speculation is over the role of oestrogen as a cosmetic. Whether oestrogen creams enhance beauty only the eye of the beholder can judge: biologists are wiser to keep silent on this question and to distance themselves from pseudo-scientific advertising of skin products. All we can say with any certainty is that after the menopause the skin gets thinner as its cells divide less frequently and its fibres become sparser and less elastic. Skin undergoes a sort of dermatoporosis akin to osteoporosis in bones. It is true that oestrogen receptors are present in skin as in bone, though this by no means implies that oestrogen can restore what is lost or improve appearances. Those who have high expectations of the cosmetic effects of HRT are in for a disappointment. Blemishes and wrinkles appearing by middle age have many causes – exposure to strong sunlight in particular – but they are neither prevented nor reversed by HRT. The Victorian love affair with pale skin created the parasol, which preserved more faces at less expense than any hormone presently on offer.

• Apples and Pears

The bulkier layers of fat and muscle below the skin give the body its contours, and they too are discriminators of sex hormones. Unfortunately, any discussion about these cell types is likely to be hijacked by considerations of self-image. The general attitude is that the more muscle a man develops the better, whereas attitudes to fat in a woman are quite the reverse. No healthy tissue is more maligned than fat or adipose, but, when the dictates of fashion leaders are set aside, biology reveals the fat cell in new light – it is the *shape* of fatness that really counts.

Humans are a very fatty species as a whole: we carry as much adipose as domestic pigs and far more than any wild animal except whales. Fat is a valuable tissue since it serves as an insulating layer against the cold and is a highly efficient way of storing energy. In calories per gram, it is more than twice as economical as carbohydrate or protein, which means carrying less weight around. Fat is worth celebrating – though not to excess.

Yet fat has got a bad name. Most of our adipose cells were formed early in life and lie in reserve until called upon to store surplus energy. Their capacity is so large that human obesity can run to well over 50 per cent of body weight. Obesity is a sign of plentiful food or a sedentary lifestyle or, more often, both. We are not well adapted for excess weight because our forebears, like hunter-gatherers today, were lean and had to scrape for a living. Not surprisingly, excess weight is linked with a number of diseases, such as diabetes and heart disease, to name only two. Long ago the philosopher Francis Bacon had an inkling that body shape and appearance can be portents of ill-health: 'Leanness, where the affections are settled, calm and peacable ... [indicates] long life, but corpulency in youth foreshadows short life; in age it is a thing more indifferent.'

No matter how hard the Twiggy era tried to repress natural curves, a modicum of fat is good for us. Too little fat, as well as too much, can lead to problems later on, but the quota for optimal health is considerably larger for women than for men. At 25 per cent of her body weight, or some fifteen kilograms, the average modern woman has almost twice the fat stores of a man the same age. This has nothing to do with dietary choice, as the ditty about Jack Spratt and his wife would have us believe: her more generous helping depends on her hormones. It is possible, if difficult, to resist the build-up of fat by the discipline of a strict diet and regular exercise, but fertility suffers if a woman's fat stores fall as low as those in a young man. Ovaries often shut down and periods dry up in professional ballet dancers and athletes, and the acute deficiency of oestrogen from the ovaries is aggravated by a lack of fat, which normally makes a minor contribution to topping levels up. Hormone deficiency in a young woman invites problems later on, especially for those who are eating poorly and exercising infrequently.

Fat was biologically more important in the past as a buffer against cycles of famine. Adipose cells load up with fat during times of plenty; when food becomes scarce, hunger triggers the release of hormones which stimulate enzymes to release the stored energy. Fat was an insurance policy which helped people to survive in a fickle environment, and the average woman survives starvation longer than a man. She needed more reserves to bear the additional energy costs of pregnancy and breast-feeding. Plumpness was once a virtue, and still is in some quarters. The Cro-Magnon artist of 25,000 years ago who carved massive breasts and buttocks on his statuette of the 'Venus of Willendorf' was saying as much. Even more recently, when it was still deemed essential to provide a partner with an heir, it was considered to be unattractive to be thin. As the Book of Common Prayer proclaims, 'They [such as are planted in the house of the Lord] also shall bring forth more fruit in their age: and shall be fat and well-liking.'

Girls and boys have a roughly similar quantity and distribution of adipose tissue until their gonads stir in adolescence. Oestrogens, along with other hormones, then define the future shape of the woman by acting on her fat cells, as well as on her bones and metabolism and reproductive organs. Much of the extra fat is deposited in the breasts, buttocks and thighs, and these regions are given an even larger helping if she becomes pregnant. Unless already overweight, it may be unwise to thwart nature's generosity because the fat gained in pregnancy may still be important even in our well-nourished society. This fat is unwelcome because she may fear that it will be difficult to get rid of it afterwards. This attitude may be understandable, but the problem is largely an artefact of modern living and especially of the fashion for bottle-feeding. Mother's milk is not only best for the baby but is the natural way of slimming after pregnancy, so breast-feeding is in the interests of both mother and child. Some of the hormones released during lactation act on her pregnancy fat and release additional calories for feeding her baby.

Men start off with less fat than women, because it will never be called upon to bolster a pregnancy, but we face the same uphill struggle to keep lean as we get older. This has less to do with any changes in sex hormone levels than with difficulty in adjusting our lifestyles, and almost every surplus calorie ends up in the adipose layers. As we age, we ought to be reducing our dietary intake to take account of less physical activity and a gradual reduction in basal metabolic rate. The same applies to pets if they become less active after castration.

'Male fat' accumulates later and in different parts of the body compared with the female fat of puberty, and is epitomized by the paunch. Men put on weight rather higher in their bodies than women: their centre of gravity is around the waistline, whereas most females are larger around the hips and thighs. The shape of fatness in a man has been likened to an apple and is called 'android', whereas the classical appearance of a woman is pear-shaped or 'gynoid' – as in Goya's picture of *The Naked Maja* which so incensed the Inquisitors. There is no sharp dividing line between these body forms, and their dependence on sex hormones implies that there is nothing permanent about them. When male transsexuals are given pills containing oestrogen, more fat accumulates in the lower body, whereas the opposite is the case when testosterone is given to females. Fat distribution follows a hormonal recipe.

Not until the 1950s was it realized that the distribution of fat counts for more in health terms than the amount. Jean Vague, a Marseilles doctor, discovered this important fact during the course of routine hospital work, but his findings were at first overlooked by the anglophone scientific community because he published them in French. He noticed that the majority of his patients who were suffering from diabetes, cardiovascular disease or gout had an android fat distribution, irrespective of whether they were male or female. We no longer doubt that male fat should have a health warning pinned to it.

Weight-watching should be replaced by shape-watching. Doctors have used the so-called body mass index or BMI (weight/height^2) as a crude gauge of body fatness, but this is a weaker indicator of future health than the ratio of waist to hip circumference. The bigger the ratio, the bigger the paunch and the greater the risk. Women who have a more android fat distribution have more than their gender's fair share of male-type diseases on top of their own gynaecological ones. Their problems often stem from producing too much androgen. Sometimes they turn up at fertility or endocrinology clinics because of difficulty in conceiving or because of having too much hair on their face and body and too little on their scalp. More immediately concerned about their appearance, most do not realize the risks of disease they will run later in life, nor that they could improve their prospects if they lost weight or could get pregnant.

Only one of these options is open to a man who wants to shed some of his male fat. If he succeeds, he will reduce his chances of a number of diseases that Western men are especially prone to – high blood pressure, stroke, cardiovascular disease and a type of diabetes. These are the fiends that are most likely to rob us of years, if cancer does not get us first. Gerald Reaven of Stanford, California, has called this cluster 'syndrome X', as a token of current ignorance. One thing we know is that the resistance of fat cells to insulin and the consequent increase in both blood insulin and glucose levels are probably triggers of these diseases. In the early stages we may have some leeway to reverse their harmful effects on the circulation by living more prudently. Whether any reduction in testosterone would help after the onset of an illness is doubtful.

David Barker in Southampton noticed a tie-up between these diseases and those that people with a low birth weight tend to contract later in life (Chapter 3). He has offered the alternative name, 'small-baby syndrome', to draw attention to those who are most at risk. Matters are unlikely to be quite as simple as that, for, were low birth weight the sole cause of heart disease, stroke and diabetes, these would be plaguing the developing world rather than being mainly the diseases of affluent populations.

Muscle is another tissue that occupies a large proportion of the body and which, like adipose, is complex and not indifferent to sex steroids. There are three types of muscle, each responding differently to these hormones depending on the site in the body. Smooth muscle and heart muscle are not under our conscious control but are subject to a number of hormones as well as to nerves. The muscles wrapping around our reproductive parts are highly sensitive to oestrogens and androgens and, in some cases, progesterone. They become less active and shrink after castration and the menopause, though so reversible is this that a postmenopausal woman receiving hormone treatment can carry a pregnancy again if she is given a donor's egg. Smooth muscle cells in the intestines and blood vessels are less affected by the sex hormones, and any actions of HRT are likely to be subtle at most. Heart muscle is said to be sensitive to sex hormones but, though this carries a romantic ring, research has yet to show us why or how.

The third type of muscle is called skeletal muscle because it animates our bones and is under our conscious control. Its strength shows little sign of tailing off before middle age, and even this can be reversed by exercise. Oestrogens may play a minor role since there is a slight drop in hand-grip strength at the menopause which is partly restored by HRT, according to some recent studies.

248

Muscles grow when androgen levels are rising during adolescence in boys, but there the certainty ends. Stories about abusers of the anabolic steroids like testosterone so regularly command newspaper headlines that the reputation of these steroids has got ahead of the facts. Few independent researchers are busy in this seedy area, and we have mainly the wrathful sports authorities and their advisers to go by. Nobody questions the dramatic effects of these hormones in boys or women or hormonally deficient men, but claims that they make much difference to brute strength and aggression are still unproven. Steroid abuse may have much less effect on muscles than on public opinion, but it still brings some sports into disrepute. Worse still, the culprits run the risk of toxicity and of suppressing their fertility with high-dose treatment. A pair of shrunken testes on a beefy weight-lifter should be sufficient to raise suspicions even if drug tests prove negative.

Testosterone is the least respectable hormone, but may be about to become rehabilitated. The National Institutes of Health in the USA are currently exploring its possible use for stemming muscle and bone loss in elderly people when levels have fallen low. Wastage of muscle contributes to bedsores, and osteoporosis puts a frail old man at risk of broken bones. A dose of testosterone might relieve the pain and restore a little self-esteem. Some of these effects might be credited to growth hormone since testosterone helps to boost a flagging pituitary gland. Whether it is better simply to administer growth hormone in the first place is one of the questions under investigation.

All this is beginning to sound reminiscent of the claims made by Brown-Séquard some 100 years ago. Yet we still do not know for certain what the side-effects will be, including those on sexual interest and potency. We can only say that the reputation of testosterone generally runs ahead of the facts. A healthy man who wants to build up his muscles would do far better to take plenty of exercise with a nourishing diet. The message is plain – if you don't use it you'll lose it, and this is equally true for older people. Sex hormones have striking effects, but no amount can compensate for a sedentary lifestyle or backtrack to lost youth.

• Bushy Beards and Bald Pates

A disproportionate amount of human pride is invested in the few grams of protein adorning our scalps. Considering the sums of money spent on hairdressing compared with health-care, an extraterrestrial visitor might wonder what dread diseases we are warding off with our combs, cuts, curlers and conditioners. That imaginary visitor would also be intrigued by the distribution of hair on the human body, which is more obviously uneven than in any other species. Even scientists are not agreed on what biological purposes hair now serves, if any.

At one time hair must have had insulation value against the cold and afforded some protection from sunburn. These benefits became redundant once people started wearing clothing. Yet some hair still clung on – but only in patches and in particular areas. Most patches are the same in men and women, but some differ and presumably served as adornments for attracting a mate. But therein lies a great deal of speculation.

One of the first signs that a pet is unwell is that the coat loses its glossy condition. With us, a so-called good head of hair represents vitality, beauty and youth and is a token of the qualities of parts of the body that cannot be seen. A fine beard flags up its owner's gender, and hirsutism in a young male is equated with tough independence. In the Bible, Esau was 'a cunning hunter' and 'a hairy man', whereas his brother, Jacob, was mild-mannered, 'dwelling in tents' and 'a smooth man'. Both shaving the head and sparing it are used as expressions of religious commitments and vows. The draining of Samson's strength after he was shorn symbolized a weak faith that had succumbed to infatuation.

By middle age, men have usually lost some hair from the scalp and, as with women too, what remains begins to turn white (not 'grey'). In old age, hair on the rest of the body follows suit, but more slowly and in both men and women. Many people find these changes depressing because they are harbingers of old age. Like other early signs of ageing, they have sometimes been regarded as punishments for indiscretions. Aristotle is responsible for indicting bald men for excessive sexual passion, and some men revel in the unwarranted reputation. This hair loss is just a consequence of being sexually mature and affects celibate and promiscuous males alike. Monkeys too can go thin on top, but seldom ever as white as humans.

A few white hairs start to appear on Caucasian scalps between thirty and forty years old, and most have some by sixty. The rate of change varies enormously between races and individuals, and has more to do with genetics than with anything else. Hair 'greys' because pigment cells fail to invade its roots, but no one knows why this happens. There is a silver lining, however, because men with dark hair who grey early tend to be spared from balding. This puzzling link may have something to do with the greater wiriness of unpigmented hairs, and the same explanation can be given for people turning white from shock. Thin coloured hairs cannot blanch overnight, as Brown-Séquard had thought, but fall out preferentially compared with their unpigmented neighbours. Early greying may not be such a good omen for women. It is said to be a biomarker for ageing, because the individuals affected have thinner bones and an earlier menopause to compound the risk of osteoporosis. It is odd if any association exists between hair and bone unless vitamin D is the common factor, but HRT and vitamin supplements should be taken as a precaution.

Male-pattern baldness carries no known health risks, but it is a bigger blow to pride than going grey, and more difficult to hide. The lately fashionable Mohican 'plumage' sported by some teenagers is a slap in the face to any middle-aged man because this is the site on which he has greatest difficulty keeping his hair. Skin is an organ of communication in humans as well as in animals, and hair is part of its vocabulary.

A middle-aged man can at least take comfort in the fact that his hair is growing more vigorously than ever before in other places, though not always welcome ones. It is paradoxical that, as his crowning glory recedes, his beard, just a few centimetres away, is still extending its range and increasing in luxuriance. He might be forgiven for wondering whether the one is growing at the expense of the other, but this cannot be true. Each hair follicle has a destiny of its own which is influenced by hormones, and those that are awakened at puberty grow more vigorous with time. Once again we see that not all age changes lead inexorably downhill after puberty. A follicle which was relatively dormant, with only a fine vellus hair hardly protruding from its pit, now produces a long and often wiry terminal hair. Such hairs sprout on the torso and limbs and even out of the nostrils and ears. Since sex hormone levels are fairly stable in men, we must look elsewhere for an explanation.

Intriguing though these changes are, few serious scientists have studied hair growth. Government agencies and medical charities are reluctant to fund what they perceive to be cosmetic research which panders to vanity. Perhaps this is unduly cautious, since history is full of examples of esoteric research unexpectedly finding practical applications. Whatever is responsible for triggering the activity or inactivity of follicles could be involved with other age or hormone changes. Besides, balding can cause real misery. Until there is more encouragement, hair studies will remain thin on the ground, and any discoveries will probably be locked away in the confidential files of a few cosmetic and pharmaceutical companies. The average academic egghead knows little more about the biology of hair than his hairdresser, though a few facts are agreed.

Hairs need follicles like eggs need ovarian follicles, and both are formed in limited numbers before birth. There are about 100,000 follicles in the scalp at first, and they undergo cycles of activity and rest. Each has a biological clock that runs for two or three years before becoming dormant and allowing the hair to fall out and starting all over again. The rate of growth varies from hair to hair but is about 0.2 millimetres per day on the head. The maximum length to which a hair can grow therefore depends more on the duration than on the rate of growth. It follows that the differences between the lengths of scalp hair and eyelashes are more a result of how long the hair follicle clock runs than of the rate of growth.

Every day, each of us produces about forty metres of hair on the head – or a little less at my age. About 100 hairs are shed each day and are replaced by an equal number of new ones sprouting from follicles becoming active again. The ravages of time and androgens may increase the daily loss to say 110–120 without a corresponding increase in the replacement rate. The slight imbalance in the equation may not be obvious in the shower tray, but it will become apparent in time in the form of a receding hairline and/or thinning on the crown. Like the fall of autumn leaves as the seasons change, hair loss occurs gradually, giving us time to adjust to an altered self-image. To this extent we are treated far more gently by ageing than by many diseases which can strike like bolts from the blue.

Baldness is so common among men that it hardly raises an eyebrow. I am told that the hairline is not the first thing that a woman cares about, or even notices, in a man. But baldness is unusual in women and a much more serious problem – socially if not biologically. If the pattern of balding in a woman is like a man's and her scalp is healthy, it is probably a sign that she is making too much male hormone or has been treated at some time with a hormone with androgenic side-effects. Either way, the hair loss is just as irreversible as in men, and she must fall back on her ingenuity to avoid drawing attention to the problem which she usually does with more success than a man.

High levels of androgens are necessary but not sufficient for male-pattern balding to develop: a man has also to inherit a gene that makes his hair follicles susceptible to them. As this is a dominant gene, balding requires only one copy present for it to be effective, and it therefore does not tend to skip generations as commonly happens with recessive genes. A quick scan of the heads of older male relatives gives a young man a rough guide to his chance of keeping his hair. It is more difficult to tell whether a gene for baldness is being passed down on his mother's side because she will not express it unless she is producing more androgens than she should.

Baldness is not one of the ineluctable changes of ageing because it can be prevented if the main source of androgens is removed before matters have gone too far. Not one of Jim Hamilton's fifty-four eunuchs had become bald by mid-life, and their skin was less oily or prone to acne than usual. If castration is carried out before puberty, sexual hair fails to develop, as Chaucer accurately observed: 'as small as any goat's his voice would come, yet no beard had he nor would ever have. But all his face shone smooth as from a shave.' If done afterwards, the beard grows less, but does not disappear completely. Other hair follicles, such as the eyebrows, are unaffected and similar in both sexes, like those in the armpits and the lower pubic triangle. These areas are sensitive to the weak androgens that are produced after puberty by the adrenal glands, even in children who are sterile.

At first all hair follicles in a foetus were probably much alike, but later on they are programmed according to the specific surface they are growing on. Some grow faster and thicker and longer than others. For this reason, the type of hair in a patch of skin from one part of the body will not change after grafting to another. Follicles from the chest and pubic area still produce short and curly hairs after grafting to the bald pate – and are stimulated rather than inhibited by testosterone. The genes responsible for these striking differences are either distinct ones or the same ones controlled differently, and when the cause has been tracked down new treatments may be available to cultivate hair growth. Then balding and shaving could become things of the past.

But what are the chances of restoring hair once lost? A bald pate is not quite so lifeless as it seems, but is somewhat reminiscent of a beach after the tide has gone out – it conceals an army of tiny hairs lurking like worms in their holes. The great challenge of hair research is to find ways of bringing the tide in again so that they may re-emerge. This may be feasible before the follicles have receded too far, but there is a point of no return. As Uncle Remus put it, 'No 'pollygy aint gwine ter make h'ar come back whar de b'ling water hit.'

Patent hair-restorers have been a favourite stock in trade of mountebanks because there have always been plenty of gullible customers. According to an Ancient Egyptian papyrus, a mixture of equal parts of crocodile, lion, hippopotamus and serpent fats is recommended as a remedy against hair thinning. The more outlandish the recipe, the more convincing it sounded to the hopeful purchaser, though none have stood the test of time. By the Middle Ages it was said that men were resorting to arsenic and prayer, presumably in desperation. Culpepper revived the idea of using parts of hirsute animals for a while: 'bears grease staies the falling off of the hair'. Each generation has been fond of its own particular remedy. During Prohibition in America, neat alcohol was applied to the scalp, perhaps in the expectation that a forbidden fruit would do the trick.

This potted history might be enough to make us determined sceptics, but not all claims are bogus or wishful thinking. It is possible to prevent hair recession – provided it has not gone too far. Hair follicles under the influence of testosterone become progressively miniaturized to the point of extinction. At that stage they can no more be restored to the skin than eggs can reappear in a barren ovary. For those who cannot resign themselves to nature's way, a hairpiece may be bought or discs or flaps of skin may be grafted from the better-endowed parts of the scalp which are resistant to androgens. Not every customer will be satisfied with the results.

We might suppose that the lure of profit would keep every pharmaceutical company alert to the commercial possibilities of a product for curing baldness. Not so. The American manufacturer of minoxidil recorded extra hair growth as an irritating side-effect of its new drug for high blood pressure and did not bother to protect the discovery. A couple of enterprising dermatologists spotted the potential, took out a patent and proceeded to sell the rights back to the same company! The original name was unappealing and a new one had to be found. They apparently overcame the temptation to use the euphonious title 'Regain' (by association with a former President with an excellent head of hair for his age), and now market the product under a not-so-dissimilar name on national television. Nobody doubts that it works, but there are drawbacks as it has to be administered continuously and hair sprouts in unwanted places.

The effects of androgens on the scalp can also be defeated with drugs that have anti-testosterone activity. At worst, this is chemical castration and the user stands a chance of devirilizing himself and perhaps reducing his libido and triggering hot flushes. Treating the scalp with creams containing oestrogens is not advisable for men either because the hormones can be absorbed into the bloodstream, causing feminization elsewhere in the body. Besides, the female sex hormone has been shown to retard hair growth in some animals, which is not a very good recommendation for humans.

A more promising remedy is the drug that blocks the activity of the enzyme 5-alpha reductase in the skin. This is the enzyme that converts testosterone to its more active form, dihydrotestosterone, which is mainly responsible for hair and prostate growth but leaves sexual interest and capacity unaffected. So the drug only attacks unwanted effects of androgens, unless the man wants a full beard. The drug is showing some promise as a suppressor of excess body-hair growth in hirsute women, but the eyes of the cosmetic world are more firmly fixed on the male scalp. The first trials in humans and monkeys have produced some encouraging sprouting on top, though falling far short of restoring pride in a full head of hair.

Cures for balding were hardly dreamt of by the Victorians, though they were familiar enough with ineffective patent medicines. Whether Charles Darwin envied his friend Thomas Henry Huxley's mop of hair is not recorded, but it is looking as if baldness is not something that future generations will have to put up with.

• The Dowager's Hump

The bones of a skeleton hanging in an anatomy museum give little impression of how metabolically active they were in life. What remains after death is mainly the mineral superstructure, but living bones have a blood supply and are teeming with cells like construction workers continuously busy on a building site. One set of cells is etching bone away here and there while another group goes around filling in the gaps with new bone. They may seem to be working against each other, but it is only by constant renewal that the fabric stays strong and deterioration is postponed. In theory, this arrangement should keep bones strong as long as necessary, but unfortunately that is not the case.

Bones reach their maximum strength early in adult life and have started to weaken by middle age in women or rather later and more slowly in men. The menopause is a particularly important staging-post in bone ageing because the process of wastage steps up dramatically at this time. For a year or two either side of her last period, a woman may lose 2 to 3 per cent or even more of all her bone mineral mass every year. Afterwards the rate settles down to 1 per cent for the rest of her life, though this is far from trivial. If she becomes menopausal at the usual age of fifty, she will have lost a quarter of her skeletal mass by age seventy, and a centenarian will be down to half. Women who have an early menopause are more jeopardized because bone loss begins correspondingly earlier and the consequences later on are all the more threatening. A Turner's syndrome woman is in the worst predicament because her ovaries were barren from the start and, at age forty, she might have the skeleton of a woman twice her age. The constant erosion of bone mineral changes what was dense bone with internal bracing struts into something resembling a Swiss cheese. No wonder this condition is called osteoporosis.

Osteoporosis sets in when the balance between the bone-dissolving and bone-building cells tips slightly in favour of the former. Calcium is slowly lost from the skeleton and leaves the body via the urine. The outer or cortical bone gets thinner, but it is the erosion of the inner struts that counts for more. Needless to say, weaker bones are much more easily fractured. Percentages of bone mineral loss translate into pain, immobility and even accidental death for the older woman.

This is true of animals too and has welfare implications. Each year, 40 million chickens are slaughtered in the UK and an estimated 30 per cent have broken bones by the time the carcasses reach the shops. Laying hens need two grams of calcium every day to maintain a balance within their bones, but even dietary supplements fail to fend off the hazards of osteoporosis – they are walking on eggshells. In hens this problem is due more to an existence for which they are not well adapted rather than to oestrogen deficiency; for the modern woman, both of these apply for osteoporosis.

Falling is serious when bones are brittle and is far more common in older people because they are less steady on their feet as a result of poor eyesight, joint disease and the soporific effects of some prescription drugs. Only in the past couple of decades have the gravity and scale of the problem become fully appreciated. In America alone, 20 million people are affected by osteoporosis, causing 1.5 million fractures per year – mostly among postmenopausal women. All in all, the costs to the community are measured in billions of dollars by health economists – and in untold suffering.

Fractures of the wrist are the first to increase a few years after menopause. Hip fractures start a little later, but by the time women reach their eighties a third of them will have had one. Fatal complications set in within a few weeks in 15 per cent of cases, but many of those who survive never regain full mobility. An osteoporotic woman does not even have to fall to break bones: vertebrae in the neck and spine can collapse spontaneously under the weight of the body once the bracing struts have been seriously eroded. This causes pain if the bones crush nerves at their exit points from the backbone, and it shortens stature. The spine can become noticeably deformed in the process, producing the 'dowager's hump' – known in medical circles by the ponderous name 'thoracic kyphosis'.

Considering that we are living through an epidemic of osteoporosis in the Western world, it is surprising that a connection with the menopause was not made until 1941. Fuller Albright, who made the discovery, was a Harvard endocrinologist whose brilliant career came to an untimely end when experimental neurosurgery for Parkinson's disease went tragically wrong. It was already known that other hormones and vitamins affected the composition and strength of bone, but his was the first inkling that oestrogen should be added to the list. He wrongly, though understandably, assumed that oestrogen was needed to maintain bone growth. Only recently has it become clear that this hormone inhibits the cells engaged in nibbling bone away. Testosterone has an equivalent effect in men, though this is less obvious because hormone levels tail off more slowly if at all with age. Men's bones don't become osteoporotic until a decade or two later than in women, unless there is another underlying cause.

Oestrogen is not the only hormone whose level changes at menopause or after removing the ovaries, but it is the crucial one as far as the bones are concerned. Hormone replacement therapy provides the clearest evidence, for osteoporosis is almost stopped in its tracks when HRT is given. Some studies even show a slight increase in bone mass, though the full strength cannot be restored. The effect is dramatic and prolonged oestrogen treatment can reduce the fracture rate by as much as 70 per cent. There is some sparing of bone substance even if HRT is taken for just a few years, and virtually everyone who is able to take it can benefit.

Evidence for the protective effects of HRT is now watertight, yet only a minority of women are availing themselves of the opportunity – perhaps because the dangers of broken bones or heart attacks are not perceived when they are still far off. A mixed response to HRT is understandable, given the controversy which surrounds it. Experts do not always agree about the balance of pros and cons and point out that not all the blame for osteoporosis should be laid at the door of oestrogen deficiency. Besides, osteoporosis is a complex problem and can be aggravated by a poor diet and lack of exercise as well as by hormone deficiency.

Certainly oestrogen cannot be the whole story, because a woman's bone mass starts to decline when she is in her thirties, some two decades before menopause. And the risks of osteoporosis vary because some people start with stronger bones at puberty than others. Women of Caucasian and Oriental descent are at most risk, Blacks least, and Asians somewhere between. The amounts of bone that individuals build up when they are young may account for much of these differences. This helps to explain the greater strength of men's bones in old age because bulkier bones will withstand greater mineral loss than thin ones before they reach the point at which they become brittle. This is another illustration of how the ills of ageing are rooted in earlier life. Plenty of exercise and a good diet while young will help women to build up mineral reserves and stand them in better stead later on. What the consequences will be for those who have gone in for strenuous slimming and taken up smoking in their teens no one dares to predict.

Signs that fragile bones cannot be entirely blamed on the menopause came to light during recent excavations in the crypt of Christ Church at Spitalfields in London when a large number of skeletons of Huguenots buried between 1729 and 1852 were exhumed. X-ray analysis revealed surprisingly little bone loss by mid-life. What is more, the rate of loss afterwards was less than it is today. The reason for the historical differences seems to lie with lifestyles rather than with hormones. In those days women walked a great deal more, and pregnancy and breastfeeding were more common. These are all beneficial for bone. Fish, meat and milk figured importantly in their diet, all of which are rich in calcium; and it is thought that the Huguenot women neither smoked nor drank much alcohol.

So the greater risk of osteoporosis in women today seems to be a consequence of our consumer choices and a sedentary lifestyle for which we are not fitted. Women can help themselves by enjoying a good diet and exercising while young, and by boosting calcium and vitamin D intake after the menopause. Unfortunately these simple steps are not enough to compensate for all the lifestyle factors. It is a mistake to think that dietary adjustments alone can prevent bone loss. One of the leading authorities, Claus Christiansen in Copenhagen, has shown that oestrogen is still by far the best remedy for preventing osteoporosis, which is one of the strongest arguments in favour of taking HRT.

An equal amount of space could have been devoted to the effects of sex steroids on other tissues, but I chose hair and bone as chief examples because we worry about the first and should be concerned about the second. In either case, the outcome depends on the balance of hormones over a long period of time. The details are complicated and, in the case of hair, paradoxical, and it is not always possible to predict what the effects of withdrawing and replacing the hormones will be. The main principle to emerge is that the cells most dependent on these hormones in youth will probably change most after the menopause in women or during a decline in a man's androgens. Replacement of male and female sex hormones is a successful story of controlling ageing, but it should not blind us to still more dazzling possibilities that will one day be achieved by tinkering with our genes.

CHAPTER 11 **A Very Infertile Species**

> And when Rachel saw that she bare Jacob no children,
> ... [she] said to Jacob, Give me children, or else I die.
>
> Genesis 30:1

• Where the Buck Stops

From time to time I receive pleas for help from people for whom the best efforts of conventional medicine have proved fruitless. This letter from a forty-two-year-old woman in the West Midlands is fairly typical:

> After years of infertility and ten unsuccessful attempts with *in vitro* fertilization, I had almost given up hope of a child of my own. Our home and marriage seem empty without children. Last year, my doctor advised us not to make any further attempts, and we can scarcely afford another treatment cycle anyway. A newspaper report of your research gave us a ray of hope ...

Estimates vary, but recent studies in Bristol and Aberdeen showed that 1 in 10 young couples will have a fertility problem at some time, although only about half of them turn out to be permanently and involuntarily sterile. Many are willing to undergo uncomfortable and even risky treatments with but a slim chance of success. Achieving a pregnancy can become an all-consuming obsession. Having a baby is a major life event, and those who cannot may feel bereaved and cheated.

In the past, the reproductive process was regarded as profoundly mysterious, even divinely inspired, though this has not always inhibited even godly folk from engineering human solutions. Jacob's love for the beautiful Rachel is one of the great romances of the Bible. But her womb was barren and she felt that life was not worth living without a child. Jacob irritably rebuffed her desperate cry for help with a *non mea culpa* because he had already impregnated his first wife, Rachel's sister Leah. Not to be outdone by her elder sister, Rachel offered Jacob her handmaid, Bilhah, to carry a child on her behalf.

A precedent for surrogacy had already been set by Jacob's grandparents. Abraham and his wife 'were old and well stricken in age; and it ceased to be with Sarah after the manner of women'. Sarah offered her Egyptian maid, Hagar, to her husband who was then aged about eighty-five. He rose to the challenge and entered into a liaison which produced Ishmael. But the intrusion of a third party into the relationship was to have repercussions. We cannot be sure of Sarah's age, nor whether her ovaries were strictly menopausal or just lying dormant, but she apparently had a late ovulation. Even more luckily, she managed to conceive a son, Isaac. This was bad news for Hagar and Ishmael, whom she drove into the desert, and descendants of these women remain at loggerheads to this day.

Women not only bear the burden of pregnancy but have usually carried the responsibility for an infertile union. Until modern times it was impossible to tell whether it was the woman or the man who was infertile unless one or other had struck up a productive partnership with someone else. The legendary midwife of eleventh-century Salerno, Trotula, was one of the first to refuse to lay blame automatically on the female:

> If a woman desires to conceive, it must be first ascertained whether she is able to have her wish, to know if there is any fault in either one of them or both. It may be ascertained thus: Take two little pots like mustard pots, and in each ... put wheat bran ... the man's [urine] in one ... the woman's in the other. Let

263

the pots stand nine or more days. And if the fault is in the man
... you will find worms in the urine and a terrible smell. And if
the fault is in the woman, you will find the same proof. And if
worms appear in neither pot of urine, the condition of the man
and the woman can be remedied.

Equality did not extend to the treatment stage for infertility since
Trotula required only the woman to take the antidote – dried hog's
testicles! At least Trotula had tried to understand the problem and to
find a solution. Before we pour derision on her crude laboratory test,
we should consider how posterity may come to regard our own
technologies. After all, the standard pregnancy test in hospitals until
recently required injecting the woman's urine into toads to see
whether they would ovulate. Trotula was right to be suspicious of the
assumption that the causes of infertility always lie in the woman. It
turns out that the female is responsible in only a third of cases, in
another third her partner is to blame and the remainder are classified
as mutual or unexplained infertility.

The process of reproduction is so complex that it is amazing
that it ever succeeds at all. Almost every imaginable problem has
turned up somewhere. And it is not just a matter of the abundance
and variety of diseases, for human fertility leaves much to chance even
under the best of circumstances. There is no oestrus in women to
ensure that mating occurs at the best time for conception, so a ripe
egg may miss its moment for fertilization and go to waste. Mating is
like a game of Russian roulette and is as successful as it is only because
there are many rounds of play. In most animals and birds, however,
the first shot usually finds its mark.

I learned this lesson the hard way as a child, and that experience
may have been the spark that ignited a lifelong fascination with the
reproductive process. When I was twelve, a neighbour gave me two
'brother' rabbits as pets. As far as we could tell, they were identical,
so we happily housed them in the same hutch. All went well for the
first month. Then one morning my younger brother came running in
from the garden, obviously distraught. Reading between the lines of

his scrambled sentences, we realized that he had witnessed the appalling scene of a pet's innards herniating on to the floor. But horror changed to humour when we discovered ten naked pups lying in a nest in a corner of the hutch. In those days the facts of life were largely unknown to youngsters of primary school age, but this incident was far more memorable than any lesson.

Once the buck rabbit had been identified, he was removed to bachelor quarters which we rapidly constructed next to his sister's hutch. We were well pleased with our handiwork but had quite underestimated the strength of his drive to mate and the sharpness of his incisors. Two months later he made a nocturnal raid on her hutch, and thirty days afterwards another twelve babies were delivered. Worse still, the whole cycle was repeated yet again, even after reinforcing his cage. Our parents took a dim view of the population explosion occurring in our backyard. We boys were more amazed that the buck's urge to reach the doe was stronger than any wish to chew his way to freedom and the kitchen garden.

The rabbit's reputation for lust and fecundity is legendary. At most times of year females are as ready to mate as males because they remain constantly in oestrus until they fall pregnant. Each ovary contains a ripe set of follicles from which oestrogen leaks into the bloodstream until the hormonal signal for ovulation arrives. That signal does not occur spontaneously on a certain day of the month, as it does in humans, but is sparked by nerves which have been stimulated by the act of mating. Trains of nerve impulses ascend from the vagina and cervix along the spinal cord and reach the brain where an intermediary messenger (gonadotrophin-releasing hormone or GNRH) causes the pituitary gland to spurt the hormone LH. It is LH that makes the follicles burst to release their eggs into the fallopian tube, where they are greeted by the awaiting sperm. The ovulation reflex in rabbits is as predictable as our knee-jerk reflex, though taking twelve hours to complete. The process is wonderfully efficient at arranging the meeting of spanking fresh gametes every time mating occurs.

Not surprisingly, many other species have adopted this arrangement too. Ferrets, voles and cats are reflex ovulators to varying degrees. Even white rats, which normally have oestrous cycles lasting four or five days, will convert to reflex ovulation if laboratory lights are inadvertently left on all night. The boundary between cyclic and reflex ovulators is not an absolute one, and some small animals can choose the best of both worlds according to circumstances. It has even been suggested that intercourse can hasten ovulation in humans (which would certainly put the cat among the pigeons for advocates of the rhythm method of contraception), though there is no evidence for this.

Reflex ovulation cannot be an incontestable advantage otherwise natural selection would have seen fit to ensure that it became universal. Its indubitable value could become a drawback for survival in the long run. A doe rabbit that stays virgin is at risk of contracting uterine cancer because she does not produce enough progesterone to moderate the continuous bombardment by oestrogen from her ovaries. This problem is usually avoided in the wild by frequent pregnancies, but it helps to explain why most domestic animals and humans have evolved ovarian cycles at the price of being fertile for only a day or two at a time. This built-in waiting time might seem to set short-lived animals like rats and mice at a reproductive disadvantage, but their cycles are brief and mating scores almost every time.

Reproduction is a serious business because the genetic future of the individual is at stake. In a world full of hazards and where the next meal is not guaranteed, animals cannot afford to spend time on recreational sex. If they lose their chance, partners may not be granted a second bite at the cherry. So great is the pressure to succeed in producing heirs that fertility has been honed by natural selection to a high degree of reliability.

The all too common fertility problems of zoo animals and even some pets appear to contradict this picture, but they have many causes and most are artefacts. Animal-breeders have blunted the sharp edge of natural selection by imposing their own values and fitness criteria. The qualities of a prize dairy cow, a racehorse or a Cruft's champion can be at odds with optimum fertility. As for zoo specimens, we still have much to learn before we can husband them in captivity as well as they can look after themselves in the wild. And, without due care, repeated inbreeding can lead to a genetic bottleneck which causes fertility to taper off.

There is a good example close to home. The fierce, semi-wild herd of cattle on the estate of the Earl of Tankerville, just south of the Scottish border, was enclosed around AD 1225. After surviving for centuries untainted by new blood, the herd fell to just thirteen animals after the harsh winter of 1947. Recovery has been slow because fertility is poor and rather variable. The bottleneck is even tighter than the actual numbers suggest because one male fights for the rights to all the females.

Until relatively recently, most people married their neighbours and relatives. This practice is continued by choice or simply cannot be avoided in some closely knit communities to this day. Charles Darwin wed his first cousin, Emma Wedgwood, and, although they produced enough children, family health problems aggravated his hypochondria about the family bloodstock. Nowadays, as people move around the world and choose unrelated partners, the problem of inbreeding is diminishing. We might expect human fertility to be improving, but it actually remains stubbornly low, making us possibly the most infertile species in existence. To a large extent this is by choice and partly as a consequence of the insults to which our generative organs have been exposed. But even when these are set aside there is a lot of infertility to explain, which makes us wonder whether our biological make-up and our evolution are the main factors and infertility is the price we pay for being what we are.

A long-lived and strongly *K*-selected species (Chapter 5) can afford to allow sexual encounters to fail occasionally because there is plenty of time to try again. It may even be desirable to be less than a perfect breeder if this disadvantage is offset by a corresponding survival advantage and a longer-lasting body. To my knowledge, no one has investigated whether a good human stud will have a shorter lifespan than the average male, though this theory of sexual pessimism appealed to the rejuvenators. Details are sparse, but there is some evidence to substantiate the idea that the infertility trait is shared by other members of the *K* club. Chimps require on average three or four monthly cycles to achieve pregnancy despite a highly promiscuous nature, and pregnancy loss is more common in most primates than in rodent species.

It is hard to estimate the fertility of the typical human being because we are so variable and often deliberately try to thwart conception. A super-fertile man and woman sharing a bed might find it all too easy to breed like rabbits and come to doubt my assertion that we are so infertile. But let them wait until their forties and they will probably see what I mean. By and large, choosing a mate is a lottery. Appearance and lineage are poor criteria for selecting a fertile one, as King Henry VIII discovered. One highly fertile partner can partially compensate for a less well-endowed one, but the odds are stacked against a couple when both have problems. Even today's much-vaunted fertility treatments provide but a small chance of success for the doubly disadvantaged. The effects of ageing on fertility, apart from the exhaustion of the egg store at menopause, are many and add to any existing problems.

For healthy young couples engaging in regular, unprotected intercourse there is much less than an even chance of falling pregnant during a cycle. A study of French newly-weds showed that only 50 per cent conceived in the first three months. This is the reason why doctors postpone a thorough investigation and treatment of couples anxious to have a baby until they have been trying for a full year. Couples in their thirties and forties must expect to wait longer to conceive spontaneously but, as time is running out for them, they need medical help sooner.

A positive pregnancy test is no guarantee that a healthy baby will follow, because a fair proportion of embryos come to grief. About 1 in 6 pregnancies results in a miscarriage in young women, and up to twice as many in older ones. This rate seems high, but even more embryos die at such an early stage that the woman may not even realize that she has fallen pregnant. Ultra-sensitive tests have shown shortlived increases of the pregnancy hormone HCG before periods, revealing that an embryo had existed and implanted, albeit briefly. The full toll of lost embryos may be greater than 50 per cent, which is far more than that ever encountered in a healthy wild animal. Miscarriage is a sad experience, but it is nature's way of eliminating imperfect embryos that might otherwise be born with a serious physical or mental handicap. Were it not for this winnowing *in utero*, far more babies would be born with genetic diseases.

In the past it was impossible to say why so many embryos die, but light is now being thrown on this question by studies of embryos conceived in the test-tube. Ros Angell in Edinburgh has shown that many of these are chromosomally abnormal, and the same could apply to conceptions within the body. We don't know how often genetic defects occur in the embryos of other primates, although a Down's syndrome-like condition can occur in chimpanzees. In laboratory rodents, where much more research has been possible, fewer than 1 per cent of those conceived are abnormal, so human reproduction is far more prone to error.

For sexually active young people, genital infections are one of the major causes of infertility. Even when the bugs have been successfully treated with antibiotics and other drugs, scars left in the fallopian tubes can block the progress of sperm and embryos. Animals contract venereal infections too, but the effects on fertility are rarely so severe and never as common as in our species. Likewise, ectopic pregnancy is almost unheard of in animals, whereas up to 1 in 30 human pregnancies is affected in some parts of the world where pelvic infection is common.

Another hazard of reproduction that divides animals and humans is the birth process itself. We now take a happy outcome very much for granted in the West but, up to the turn of the century, fifty times more women died during or shortly after labour than do today. Many were victims of haemorrhage or fever, until new drugs and aseptic methods made these largely things of the past. The first day of life is more hazardous than any other, and delivery is riskier than in any other primate. A human baby has to turn to allow its large head and shoulders to pass safely through the mother's birth canal; if the baby gets stuck, it and its mother are in danger. Apes and monkeys use their hands to help deliver their own baby, but it is difficult and dangerous for a woman to attempt this unaided. That is why midwifery may be the oldest profession of all.

Numerous other afflictions and hazards of human reproduction could be mentioned, but they are more appropriate for other books and better-qualified writers. The biologist is more interested in the general issues than in particular syndromes and infectious diseases which vary from place to place. The quality of the germ cells holds a particular fascination because they are the pivots upon which the life cycle turns. No matter how efficient subsequent events in the reproductive process may be, they can never compensate for a poor egg or sperm in the first place.

• A Curate's Egg

Human germ cells are rather like the curate's egg – good in parts. Most of them are of such poor quality that they will never succeed in meeting a partner and making an embryo, and the outcome for those that do is often in doubt. Researchers who have watched human embryos growing in a Petri dish know that they are very fussy about culture conditions and that their quality is much more mixed than that of mouse embryos.

The odds against an individual sperm making a conquest are huge because an average man makes a couple of trillion in his lifetime (2×10^{12}). It is a case of 'many are called, but few are chosen'. Teeming numbers of these tiny cells are needed to storm the comparatively vast reaches of space in the vagina, uterus and fallopian tubes. This marathon competition to reach the egg helps to weed out poor cells which fall by the wayside, improving the chances that the best will succeed and make a good embryo. Many sperm are imperfectly formed, either because they carry an abnormal set of chromosomes or because they are structurally defective. Defects are relatively easy to spot under the microscope because the swimming motions betray any weaknesses. A sperm that cannot swim well is like an injured athlete and cannot win or even finish a race.

Rather more is known about the quality of sperm than of eggs because they are far more abundant and easier to obtain. If men were lined up for testing the quality of their semen, like prize bulls for an artificial insemination service, most would be rejected by the vet and sent for slaughter. A beakerful of semen coaxed out of a boar displays wonderful wave motions resulting from the coordinated activities of billions of individual sperm cells. By contrast, a man's offering is a pitiful two or three millilitres, looking as lifeless as a catarrh specimen.

Under the microscope, human sperm look comparatively puny. Fewer than half are strong enough to complete the first stage of the swim through a woman's cervix. Weird forms are common: some have two heads or no head at all, others have two tails and flap about in aimless circles. The products of the human testis are wanting not only in quality but in quantity too. Virtually every other mammal produces about 25 million sperm per gram of testis each day from a production line in the organs which is a model of efficiency. By contrast, men produce only 4 million for the same amount of tissue, and then in a rather less-organized fashion. Were it not for the fact that we are sexually active the year round and our womenfolk have up to thirty-five years for reproduction, our species might never have lasted as long as it has.

Testes are vulnerable organs, for not only does their location invite injury, but they receive a barely adequate blood supply at the best of times. They dangle precariously, physiologically speaking, between the risk of receiving insufficient oxygen and nutrition from the bloodstream and the dangers of getting overheated and generating too many free radicals. It is easy to imagine how the balance tips when blood flow is seriously compromised by narrowed and hardened arteries. Healthy organs then metamorphose into fibrotic balls of little more than decorative value, though still dearly cherished by their owners. There can be little doubt that the state of sexual health says a good deal about a man's circulation and general well-being.

There is little insulating fat in scrotal skin, and the superficial blood vessels help to keep the testes cool. Why these organs are kept in a scrotum rather than safe within the main body cavity and several degrees warmer is still a mystery. Perhaps the lower temperature reduces the number of mutations and the risk of cancer, and this is why it is important for a boy's testes to have descended by birth; if they have not, hormonal or surgical assistance will be necessary. These advantages might be sufficient explanation for the evolution of a scrotum but for the fact that not all animals keep their organs in one. Most of the exceptions are puzzling, though it is understandable that hedgehogs are more comfortable keeping their tender members tucked away inside.

If human testicles fail to descend, the chances of infertility are high because sperm cannot tolerate the higher temperature. Likewise, heating the testes in a hot bath, tight jeans or even by long hours of driving is said to diminish sperm production. Samuel Pepys suspected as much for he advised couples wanting to have children to wear cool holland drawers. Even after sitting cross-legged for twenty minutes the scrotum gets overheated, so loose clothing, or even a kilt, is not necessarily a guarantee of male fertility. Decorum and a northern climate prevent us going naked to minimize the problem, but we can at least be thankful that our testosterone production is unaffected by high temperature.

While the interminable debate about the best diet rages on, few now disagree that unwise consumption can harm our health and our fertility. We have become inured to the idea that anything enjoyable carries a price tag, and relentless bashing of recreational habits by the biomedical establishment reinforces the sense of guilt. To the better-known ills of smokers' lung and heart can be added 'smokers' testicles', for tobacco products reduce the quality of sperm. They evidently harm eggs too because heavy smokers can on average expect a menopause some two years earlier than others. Alcohol is also harmful to sperm and eggs, though it carries the safeguard that, when taken to excess, it drowns sexual capacity and so its actions become self-limiting. These effects stretch across the length of pregnancy – from chromosome abnormalities in germ cells and embryos to morbid effects on foetuses nearer to term. Even as far back as Old Testament times, warnings were given about the dangers of alcohol – and by no less an authority than an angel. Samson's mother, who had been barren, was told 'Now therefore beware, I pray thee, and drink not wine nor strong drink, and eat not any unclean thing: for, lo, thou shalt conceive, and bear a son'.

There have been fewer studies of the effects of illegal recreational drugs on fertility and sexual performance, though they generally point to the dangers of abuse. One of the first people to bring this to attention was Edward Tilt, a pioneer of menopause research. During a foreign tour in the 1850s, he noticed a higher incidence of impotence than back at home in Britain, but he refused to accept conventional Victorian wisdom that it was due to sexual overindulgence:

> This impotence, in comparatively young men, is always attributed to great abuse of the sexual gratifications; but if it be more observable in Constantinople and Cairo than in Paris and Vienna, I attribute the fact, not so much to immoral practices, equally frequent in most towns, but to the constant use of opium and hashish, which have a decided anaphrodisiac effect.

The manufacture of sperm and egg cells is among the most complex processes in the body and is open to mistakes at many stages. Germ cells are at least as sensitive to poisons as other cells, if not more so. Occupational exposure to the heavy metals, lead, cadmium and mercury, and to certain pesticides has been found to cause infertility in miners and farm-workers. A soil-dressing, DBCP (dibromochloropropane), was the first substance to be banned in the USA because of its reproductive toxicity, and others have followed. Household products such as paints, varnishes and even plastic wrappings have come under the spotlight in recent years because harmful effects on sperm production have been suspected. No doubt there are other dangers lurking in our pantries and garages that need to be uncovered and relabelled accordingly.

A principle which generally holds true is that the earlier damage is inflicted, the more serious the effects will be. This is obviously true of the ovary since eggs that are damaged in the foetus or child cannot be replaced later on. Sperm may seem to be better off since stem cells for making new ones are present throughout life. But their nurse cells are formed before birth and cannot be renewed, and so any fall in number can lead to a lower rate of sperm production.

There is growing evidence that human sperm production has been in decline for a generation or two in several countries. The Danish andrologist Niels Skakkebaek found that the average sperm count has fallen from 113 million per millilitre of semen in 1940 to only 66 million in 1990. Also, the subjects were ejaculating a volume of 3.4 millilitres formerly compared with 2.75 now. This fall has recently been confirmed in Belgium and France where the quality as well as the quantity was found to be reduced. This is a drop of 40 per cent over fifty years. If these figures are representative of whole populations and the trend continues, in another fifty years time sperm numbers will fall below the critical 20 million per millilitre needed for fertility. At that point, most conceptions would need medical assistance. The proportion of infertile couples in the population has not yet shown signs of rising, so this bleak scenario is unlikely to materialize. Still, any further drop in sperm numbers is worrying as it compromises the fertility of the least well-endowed individuals, including many older ones.

Infertility is not regarded as a blight by everyone, but even those who are content to remain childless may have cause to worry. Fewer sperm could be an early warning of something harmful in our lifestyle. Problems with fertility do not stand alone but are often ominous forebodings of other problems lurking nearby. It may be no coincidence that abnormalities of the genital organs in young men have been increasing in recent years and that testicular cancer is now the commonest cancer in young men. The hunt is on for the causes.

One of the prime candidates is oestrogen because, although small amounts of this hormone may be important in men, more is definitely undesirable. Not only does it feminize the body, it also harms the nurse cells needed for sperm function, and these can themselves turn cancerous. If some reports are to be believed, our environment is awash with oestrogens and our bodies are overexposed from dietary and medical sources.

A foetus is normally protected from the high levels of oestrogens in its mother's blood by the placenta which has a powerful battery of enzymes to inactivate any hormones trying to make the crossing. Stilboestrol, the synthetic oestrogen formerly used to prevent recurrent miscarriage, can pass across the placenta with dire consequences for the future health and fertility of the baby, whether a boy or a girl. It has been banned for over twenty years, but there are plenty of other unnatural sources of oestrogen to which we are all exposed. Some household cleaning agents have oestrogenic potency and, together with hormones excreted by contraceptive pill users, penetrate water-purification systems to contaminate public drinking supplies. Remarkable stories have emerged lately about sex changes in male fish inhabiting British inland waters. Oestrogen levels in tap water are not high enough to raise concern, but we need to be vigilant about our water sources and methods of food production. Regrettably, ecotoxicology has often had to struggle to gain attention against commercial opposition and indifference.

Lest we become paranoid about oestrogen contamination, we must remember that we consume small amounts of natural oestrogens in soya and other vegetable products as well as in dairy products, and these have not been shown to harm us. Cows' milk is highly nutritious, but it is not a natural food after infancy and the milk taken from pregnant animals is seventy-fold richer in oestrone sulphate than that from others. Whether this matters is uncertain, and it may even be beneficial for menopausal women who need the hormone and the extra calcium. At least it is reassuring to know that oestrogen activity is lost during the processing of baby formula milk powder.

Whatever damage may accrue from environmental or dietary

influences, it pales beside the drastic effects of some cancer treatments on the gonads. It is not yet possible to target chemotherapy and radiation with sufficient precision to kill only the malignant cells: healthy cells in the bone marrow, gut, hair follicles and gonads are all susceptible too, especially when they are in a state of growth. Some patients experience a lull in sperm production or suspension of menstrual cycles for a few months after treatment, whereas others become irreversibly sterilized and their testes or ovaries shrink. The only comfort for men is that they usually recover testosterone levels and are able to resume a normal sex life. As a precaution against sterility, young men can deposit semen specimens in a sperm bank before treatment, to give them a chance of fathering children later on. The ovaries of a young woman whose eggs are destroyed cannot regenerate, and she will suffer an abrupt menopause, even as early as her teens. These sacrifices may seem a small price to pay for the chances of survival, which have been rapidly improving for *some* leukaemias, lymphomas and solid tumours. Even so, a few patients refuse the best treatment if it has the worst prognosis for future fertility. Some victims of the radioactive blow-out at Chernobyl in April 1986 have suffered anxiety and depression to the point of suicide because of worries about their fertility and sex life. Their fears, sometimes unfounded, underline the priority that many people set on reproduction, and emphasize the importance of research into the prevention of early sterility.

To all intents and purposes, anything that destroys germ cells speeds up the rate of ageing of the gonads, but there is more to it than just the disappearance of cells – there are changes in the quality of gametes too. Given the differing ways in which eggs and sperm are made, it is not surprising that each has a distinctive set of problems.

Sperm are the end-products of a long history of cell divisions, and the greater the age of a man the more rounds that the cells will have been through. Every time a cell divides into two, the genes are copied and there is a chance of errors creeping in – so the older the man the greater the risk of a mutation in his sperm. This is why children born to older fathers are five times more likely to have skeletal abnormalities such as achondroplasia in which the bones are unresponsive to growth hormone and the limbs are unnaturally short. Fortunately the risks are still low.

There are fewer gene mutations in eggs than in sperm and the frequency does not rise with age; nor is there a bigger risk in children born to women who have undergone radiotherapy or chemotherapy before pregnancy. This is all very reassuring, but what accounts for the egg's privilege? Unlike a sperm, it has completed all the divisions it will ever have and has become dormant before the baby girl is born, so there are fewer opportunities for errors. Being the most important cell in the body, it may have especially good repair mechanisms, but the usually healthy outcome at childbirth also depends on weeding out bad eggs and embryos in the mother's body. This certainly ties in with the natural wastage of human embryos, which is higher in former cancer patients and older women.

An important distinction is sometimes overlooked between errors in single genes and the grosser ones which affect the number of chromosomes. The first is more a feature of an old sperm and the second of an old egg. An egg with an extra or missing chromosome has a serious problem because it is over- or underendowed to the tune of thousands of genes. An abnormal number of chromosomes always handicaps the baby in some way – if it survives at all, which most don't.

Perhaps the greatest fear for an older mother is that her baby will have Down's syndrome. In fact the majority of affected babies are born to young mothers simply because they are more reproductively active, but an older one is at much greater risk. This birth defect results from an extra copy of chromosome 21 and has effects sufficiently well known that they do not need to be described here. Like other chromosome errors that originate at or shortly before fertilization, the tragedy is that it is inherited by every cell in the body. The embryos often survive because they get off relatively lightly from the effects of an additional small chromosome compared with other chromosome errors, though the baby is always born mentally handicapped and is unlikely to enjoy full health throughout life.

The risk of a Down's baby is low in young women but it rises quickly after age thirty, strengthening the ovary's dubious honour of being the most rapidly ageing organ in the body (excepting the placenta). Only one in every two to three thousand pregnancies is affected in mothers in their twenties, but by the forties the risk has risen almost 100-fold. Despite better and earlier antenatal tests for Down's syndrome, we still have little idea why it occurs or how to prevent it. Ageing of the egg is the main problem, though occasionally a sperm may carry the extra chromosome. With the current trend towards deferred births and a growing opposition to pregnancy termination in America, we can expect to see more Down's children in coming years. If abortion is discouraged on moral grounds, then it behoves a nation to ensure that one perceived evil is not substituted by another – namely, the neglect of children needing special care.

Concern about birth defects has mostly focused on mutations in the nucleus, and comparatively little attention has been paid to the genes in the mitochondria. That is understandable because there is only a handful of genes in these tiny organelles compared with the 70,000 or so in the nucleus. Yet their importance is out of proportion to their number, for they are at the heart of energy generation and have a particularly high risk of mutation.

The spiral mitochondria in the mid-piece of the sperm provide energy for propelling it towards the egg. Not only are sperm very active, they are also the products of an energetically expensive process which takes three months to complete. It would not be surprising, therefore, if their mitochondrial genes were shot full of mutations from free-radical action, or that the sperm of older men were the most affected. Trials are currently under way to test whether the antioxidant vitamin E can improve the quality of sperm by quenching radicals generated by the life processes in the mitochondria.

Once a sperm finds its target and the egg is fertilized, the state of its mitochondria is of no further significance. The male mitochondria and sperm tail are lost – rather like the jettisoning of booster rockets by a spaceship leaving the earth's atmosphere. Only the eggs bequeath mitochondria to the embryo, so we inherit these organelles in the same way as people inherit Jewishness – from their mothers. This rule is all the more remarkable for being almost universal in nature (the redwood tree is one of the rare exceptions), and awaits an explanation.

Quality assurance of the mitochondria in the eggs is therefore crucial because mutations prove devastating later on. A low energy output from these cellular power stations will have the most severe effects on tissues with the highest energy demands, such as the eyes and brain, where neurological problems may result. Luckily, the mitochondrial legacy from our mothers is usually of high quality and such diseases are rare. It helps that mitochondria are present in the egg in their thousands, in contrast to the few in the sperm cell.

Evolution may have favoured inheritance of our mother's mitochondria over our father's because the egg lies dormant for much of its life and fewer free radicals are generated while a cell is resting. According to the British biologist Roger Short, this precaution could be the explanation for stockpiling a store of eggs at the beginning of life. Once a sperm makes contact, like Prince Charming kissing the Sleeping Beauty, the egg springs into activity, having aged hardly at all during its long slumber.

We shall have to await the results of further research to find out whether this neat theory holds water. Eggs are not excused from ageing, and, as we shall see, their fertility actually deteriorates rather quickly. A build-up of mitochondrial mutations, however slow, seems inevitable because even resting cells generate some free radicals. If the lower fertility of old eggs is a problem of energy generation, we may yet overcome it by injecting healthy mitochondria from young eggs. This falls far short of cloning human beings but, since it involves the transfer of mitochondrial DNA into a germ cell, the practice would be bound to be controversial.

• Never Too Late?

There are many understandable reasons why a woman might delay motherhood until her late thirties or early forties – a demanding career, financial commitments, a health problem, finding the right partner. It may never have occurred to her that reproductive options are running out as her eggs age and the ovaries drift towards menopause. How late dare she wait? Even if her menstrual cycles are still regular, she may find it difficult or even impossible to conceive. And her plight may not receive the sympathy she deserves. Most people approve of helping couples to have children, but opinion is divided on the question of when it is just too late. Aristotle recommended that 'marriage be set for girls at eighteen, for men at thirty-seven or somewhat less' because these were the ages he thought produced the finest offspring. It is difficult to peep behind the veils of contraception and cultural taboos that conceal the time when a woman is optimally fertile, but the tapestry of human behaviour is so rich that there is usually a community somewhere which sheds light on our biology.

The Hutterites are an exclusive Anabaptist sect founded by fewer than a hundred refugees from Europe who emigrated in the 1870s to an area centred around South Dakota. To this day, they choose to remain separate from the rest of society and they proscribe all forms of fertility control. Unlike communities in undeveloped parts of the world where contraception is lacking, the Hutterites are prosperous and enjoy a high standard of housing, diet and health care. Hence their fertility could realize its full potential were it not for marrying in their twenties and not earlier. The first detailed studies in the 1950s showed that Hutterite women were, on average, delivering eleven babies during the course of a lifetime. The rate is somewhat lower today – whether because of inbreeding or a relaxation of the contraceptive code is difficult to say – but their fertility still tops the world league table. Until about thirty years of age, Hutterite women become pregnant approximately every two years because they wean their babies from the breast early. The interval between deliveries to increase after thirty, as does the rate of miscarriage. The last confinement occurs at about age fifty, shortly before the normal age of menopause. This should be a warning to the rest of us that fertility cannot be considered to be extinguished until the last cycle is definitely past.

According to the Hutterite records, human fertility starts to decline long before the erratic and often infertile cycles preceding the menopause appear on the scene. The records don't reveal when the peak occurs, and the most we can say is that it must be somewhere between a few years after puberty and age thirty, but it is unlikely that fertility varies much in these years. Just as we don't worry about having slightly moved up the mortality slope by our early thirties, we need not be overly concerned about the effects of ageing on our fertility until a few years later, though women must be prepared to wait a little longer to get pregnant. Another decade on, however, it is a different story. The female reproductive system ages faster than the body as a whole and, by age forty-five can be said to be in the state that a woman's other organs have reached after eighty. Time is running out for motherhood, but what of her partner?

Many fertility tests are available, but the only unequivocal indicator that matters is the birth of a healthy baby. Since this is the product of a conjugal act, it is often not obvious whether a fertility problem lies with one partner or both. Fertility is a joint affair, and a man is as often responsible for infertility as his wife – at least while she is still young. It is largely a myth that he is able to impregnate a younger mate equally well at any age, though there are a few exceptions. Record books cite the case of a North Carolina farmer of ninety-three who had no teeth and a leathery skin but succeeded in winning a twenty-seven-year-old bride who bore him a child. It is difficult to rule out the possibility that he was cuckolded, though this would not appear to be the case for an Englishman who fathered a child at the same age in 1994. Sperm production can continue until the end of life, so paternity at such an age is not beyond the bounds of possibility, even if it is near the limits of credibility.

This was borne out in a study by Eberhard Nieschlag of German grandfathers in the pink of health. Their sperm counts, like their testosterone levels, were similar to their sons'. The motility of sperm was reduced in some of the older men, but this was thought to be due to sexual abstinence because cells become stale if they linger in the tubes for a long time. Not all older men are as well endowed, and usually there is a wide range of semen quality – some specimens with high sperm counts and others below the 20 million per millilitre mark and probably infertile. Normally 90 per cent of seminiferous tubules in the testes of thirty-year-olds are manufacturing sperm, but this can fall to 10 per cent or less in ninety-year-old men. Summing up the general picture, Caleb Finch has said that 'the evidence to date indicates a gradual trend for a decrease in sperm production with age, but with considerable intersubject variability, which shows that there is no age limit in male fertility analogous to menopause'. Other things being equal, men who were good producers when they were young are likely to be better equipped to thwart the effects of time than those who were less advantaged.

In laboratory animals, the respective contributions of maternal and paternal ageing have been revealed by mating old females with young male mice, and vice versa. Older sires have more sexual inertia but, after overcoming it, they are able to impregnate young females as efficiently as youngsters which show more gusto. When the experiment is reversed the effects of female age are striking, and their litters are much diminished compared to those of young mothers, whether the sire is young or old.

Investigating the female factor in humans is difficult, but studies of donor insemination (AID) where a husband is sterile and his wife is in apparently good reproductive health are close to the ideal experiment. Donors recruited by fertility clinics are young men and proven producers of good-quality sperm. In 1982, the CECOS organization which coordinates AID programmes in France published the results of 2,000 cases which showed beyond any reasonable doubt that a woman's age affects the outcome of treatment, if only a little at first. Women over thirty-five required more than twelve successive monthly insemination attempts to become pregnant, compared with six tries for women under thirty. This decline is similar to that in women conceiving in the time-honoured way. Like most other age changes, loss of fertility is gradual, but its effects grow stronger by the year, and by the age of forty-five the ovaries of 1 in 20 women will have packed up for good. At this stage, nature may need a little help.

Nowhere is the age factor more evident than in clinics offering *in vitro* fertilization (IVF) services. This technique was originally developed by Robert Edwards and Patrick Steptoe in Oldham, Lancashire, for women who had healthy ovaries but blocked fallopian tubes. So versatile has it proved to be since the birth of the first IVF baby, Louise Brown, that many other types of infertility have been overcome as well. IVF has been able to shed fresh light on reproductive ageing as well as enabling a few women to snub the menopause by using eggs from young donors.

For many infertile couples IVF offers the best hope of pregnancy, but is not guaranteed to be successful. Take-home baby rates – the only yardstick that matters to hopeful parents – vary from clinic to clinic and rarely exceed a 30 per cent chance per treatment cycle for a woman in her twenties. Most patients in their early forties can still produce eggs which can be fertilized *in vitro*, but when the embryos are transferred to the uterus they seldom lead to a successful pregnancy. So poor are the results with their own eggs that patients older than forty-two attending centres in America are often automatically offered more vigorous eggs from young donors. In the UK, where donated eggs are scarce, women of this age are usually turned away. The success of egg donation confirms that it is not only the number but the quality of eggs that limits the fertility of older women. More eggs are available in America because donors are paid a tidy sum for their time, discomfort and the slight risk involved. Provided there is not a colour mismatch between donor and recipient, egg donation scarcely raises an eyebrow in the ethnic melting-pot of California where genetic origins count for less than elsewhere. Where it is important to be able to trace one's lineage back for generations, as in Japan (and the British Royal Family), donation of either egg or sperm from an anonymous person is anathema, but this reduces the options for individuals who are sterile.

The British authorities allow a maximum of three embryos, whether her own or from donors' eggs, to be transferred to a woman's womb at any one time, even though a greater number would increase the prospect of a pregnancy. The UK position is a compromise between giving a good chance of success and risking a multiple pregnancy which might require terminating some of the embryos to ensure that some grow normally. There is an argument for a sliding scale to compensate for the effects of ageing. To give the same chance of a singleton pregnancy to a mother of, say, forty compared to one of thirty, five embryos may be needed instead of three if she is using her own eggs. If she is using donor eggs the scale is less appropriate, because they stand a better chance of success.

Artificial insemination was pioneered by John Hunter, and it took another 150 years until the first successful egg donation to a young woman took place. A few years later women past fifty were being helped. Egg donation is more successful than we had dreamt, and the middle-aged uterus is more receptive than we had assumed. A short course of oestrogen and progesterone puts reproductive ageing into reverse in the postmenopausal woman and prepares her womb for pregnancy using donor eggs fertilized in the test-tube. Even after years without monthly periods this organ is not seriously disadvantaged, and a history of hormonal inactivity may even contribute to successful child-bearing.

Back in the early 1970s when my interest in the effects of ageing on reproduction was germinating, the subject was widely regarded as little more than an irrelevant backwater of eccentric speculation. Now it is at centre stage. Fending off the problems of ageing is given a higher priority as more people postpone their family or decide to have another baby with a new partner. While pregnancies after menopause are becoming sufficiently frequent that they no longer command newspaper headlines, there is still no agreement whether an upper age limit should be set and, if so, what it should be.

Apparently, biology does not set an upper age limit. In deciding whether a mature couple should have fertility treatment, a balanced and sensible position would seem to be to consider the combined ages of the couple in the interests of the child. Perhaps a combined age of a hundred would be a reasonable limit for the present, but it is best to leave these sensitive decisions to the individuals concerned, in consultation with their doctors and counsellors.

The thought of having a baby is likely to fill most women over fifty with horror. One of the compensations of the menopause is that it is nature's permanent and assured contraceptive. But there will always be a few individuals who missed the chance of fertility treatment when they were younger, or leave matters until is too late. Sarah's pregnancy was regarded as a miracle, and established her as the mother of a nation. Those in our own day who look for fulfilment of the biblical prophecy 'they still bring forth fruit in old age, they are ever full of sap and green' would have to look hard to find better examples than some recent cases of very late motherhood. The odd practitioner seems willing – some say recklessly – to try to push the record ever higher, and it currently stands at sixty-three for an Italian woman.

Gynaecologists used to regard any first-time mother over the age of thirty-five as an 'elderly primigravida'. No particular year is any more of a biological watershed than another as far as egg donation is concerned, but age still sends alarm bells ringing in doctors' heads. The older the mother, the greater the risk of high blood pressure, diabetes and complications during labour. But a woman at sixty can be as vigorous as another at forty, and could outlive the younger one. Different rates of biological ageing are the usual justification for offering fertility services to women who are not just postmenopausal but even past the record for natural child-bearing, which is about fifty-six. These are not typical women, though, and they have to undergo rigorous health checks and counselling before treatment is approved. If carefully selected, the results can be remarkably good by the standard of much younger women. Out of the first fourteen patients between fifty and fifty-nine years old that were treated by

Mark Sauer at the University of Southern California, nine became pregnant and only one miscarried.

Despite the new opportunities, pregnancy past fifty is likely to remain exceptional, and the more important social change is the demographic drift towards later motherhood. The trend is slight as yet, and the difference in the age of women sitting in the waiting-rooms of antenatal clinics is unlikely ever to become obvious. Still, national statistics show that the numbers of births in the twenty-to-twenty-five age bracket have been slowly falling for several decades in the UK, and those between thirty and forty are rising. A shift is more marked in the prosperous parts of the USA and resembles what happened during the Great Depression, though the domestic and economic causes are quite different. The proportion of women having their first child between the ages of thirty to thirty-four has doubled, and the number of women still childless at thirty-four had gone up from 18 to 28 per cent. It remains to be seen how many of them are choosing to stay childless or are deferring their families until after their prime years.

We ought to applaud the greater seriousness with which repro-ductive decisions are taken by people today, but attitudes to late motherhood are disappointing. The birth of a late child is still treated as a joke, and older mums are still frowned upon and fear being mistaken for granny at the school gate. Needless to say there is an element of hypocrisy older fathers wear their achievements with pride. We have seen that women in middle age are biologically younger and fitter than they used to be. Lifespans are still increasing while the age of menopause remains stationary at around fifty. If surveys are anything to go by, the experiences of older parents and their children are generally positive. These couples are likely to be highly committed, wiser and better able to provide for the needs of a child than many younger people.

Changing social attitudes towards reproduction, coupled with high expectations of living longer and better, are setting some of the key priorities for biomedical research, and will continue to do so in the next century. The questions that are coming to the fore are these.

Given that women now have the option to choose when to become pregnant and how often, what is the best state for the reposing reproductive system in between times? And, if people are increasingly deferring births, what more can technology do to help them if their reproductive systems fail before they are ready? Such questions will no doubt keep researchers busy for many years to come.

CHAPTER 12

Brave New Age?

> The true aim of science is the discovery of all operations
> from immortality (if it were possible) to the meanest
> mechanical practice.
>
> Francis Bacon

In one of Oscar Wilde's more psychological works a handsome young man sits for a portrait by one of his friends. When Dorian Gray's eyes fall on the finished work, he murmurs:

> How sad it is! I shall grow old, and horrible, and dreadful. But this picture will remain always young. It will never be older than this particular day of June ... If it were only the other way! ... For that – I would give everything! Yes, there is nothing in the whole world I would not give! I would give my soul for that!

The Picture of Dorian Gray was published in 1891, two years after Brown-Séquard had publicized his rejuvenation experiments. A century later, we are only marginally better at stopping the bloom of youth from fading, but our chances of a longer life have increased dramatically. Improved public health and advances in medicine have almost doubled life expectancy in the prosperous parts of the world. Warmer and drier homes, cleaner water, better nutrition in the womb and afterwards, vaccination and drugs to combat diseases all add up to a safer life than ever before. Not that health has been shared out equitably or that the social gap is narrowing.

The better off are leaving the poor behind not only in material advantages but also in years to enjoy them. And, if there is a long way to go to close the gap at home, the task is even more daunting in the developing parts of the world. The priority for those living in poverty is to eke out a day-to-day existence, with fewer cares for tomorrow. The rest of us take our better prospects for granted and are growing ever more concerned about the personal and social ills of chronic disability and dependence in our declining years.

Some fifteen years ago a Stanford doctor, James Fries, published a paper in the *New England Journal of Medicine* which offered a remarkably optimistic forecast for the future. He pointed out that the survival curve from birth to old age is getting closer to a rectangle. That means that almost everyone will live out a full span and then suddenly pass away. Imagine a swarm of human lemmings migrating the eighty miles from London to Dover, a mile for every year of life. If the dangers on the roads and from predators were eliminated, virtually every rodent would manage to reach the coast, whereupon they would heave themselves over the cliffs together.

According to Fries, the consequence of making life safer for ourselves is that the average lifespan is being pushed towards its biological limit. Most people will die within a year or two of age eighty-five, though there will always be a few privileged individuals who run a longer course. Diseases and disabilities will be compressed into this terminal period, so future generations can look forward to a longer span of full mental and physical vigour. Senescence will be staved off for longer, even if it triumphs in the end. Rather like the 'one-hoss-shay' in the wonderful story by Oliver Wendell Holmes, everything will keep going almost to the end – when it suddenly falls apart.

If only that were true. Most evidence is to the contrary, and it is nonsense to separate the underlying ageing process from its manifestations. If anything, we are currently gaining more years of disability than of vigour. We can do little about this at the moment, except to give children as good a start in life as possible and tackle problems later on one by one as they arise. Controlling infectious diseases like tuberculosis has lowered mortality at all ages, but the tide of degenerative diseases continues to rise as we get older. Life is less risky for a man of, say, fifty than it was for his great-grandfather, but the chances of dying doubled every eight years for them both. Ageing stands undefeated and, until the root causes can be treated, we cannot dodge its problems, only try to soften its blows.

If the rate of ageing has not changed, neither has the maximum lifespan. Setting aside the mythical longevity of Methuselah and other Old Testament worthies, no one has lived much longer than about 120 years. True, we are seeing more centenarians than ever before, and Mme Jeanne Calment will not hold her longevity record for long. But the explanation is simply that there have never been so many old people around who stand a chance of a place in the *Guinness Book of Records*. Overall, we are no further forward than *Homo erectus*, because the genes which set the upper limits to life a million or so years ago are still with us today. *Homo economus* has succeeded in creating a safer environment and in removing the hurdles that used to trip people up early in life, such as plague, smallpox and tuberculosis. But as we grow older the hurdles come thicker and faster, and if we don't stumble at one we will at another. Medical scientists have yet to find a way of putting back the finishing line, and few of them even contemplate it.

Cardiovascular diseases and cancer have become the dominant hurdles for us, but future generations may have to face a different set of hazards. Much to everyone's surprise, we have been chipping away at heart disease, and its death rate after adjusting for age now stands over 34 per cent lower in the USA than in the 1960s. But even if heart disease were stamped out completely, our life expectancy would rise by only fifteen years, no more.

Any progress against diseases that cut people down in their prime is desirable, yet I wonder whether total abolition of cardio-vascular disease would be so welcome. When a group of Canadian doctors were asked how they would like to go when their time came, they chose a heart attack. They apparently agreed with the novelist Kingsley Amis, who is reputed to have said that 'No pleasure is worth giving up for the sake of two more years in a geriatric home at Weston-super-Mare.' Most people would agree that there are fates worse than death. If today's major killers could be treated as successfully as yesterday's, something else would be lurking in the wings to take their place – kidney disease or different kinds of cancer, for example. Even the lucky survivors of all these threats will sooner or later run into the biological buffers. People are now beginning to worry as much about how they will die as when, and calls to legitimize euthanasia are rising in consequence.

The globe is growing greyer almost everywhere as more people complete their full span. The significance of this demographic transition is difficult to overestimate and is without parallel in any other species or era on earth. Population ageing could soon come to supplant population growth as the chief concern for public policymakers. The fuse for this socio-economic time bomb was lit when birth rates started to drop and lifespans to lengthen dramatically. The baby-boom years following the Second World War have provided us with a breathing-space to take in the implications before our generation retires in earnest after the year 2010.

The impact is going to be greatest in countries which have seen birth rates fall the most. Before long, there will be more people in Japan over sixty-five than under fifteen. The one-baby policy in the world's most populous country will eventually change China from being a predominantly young population into an old one. At present, only 6 per cent of Chinese are older than sixty-five, but this is set to rise to 20 per cent or 270 million people by the year 2050 – which is more than the entire population of the USA. Such huge shifts will shake existing institutions – political, social, economic and domestic. Hopefully, the recent gains against age discrimination will not be reversed and society will not so much dwell on the costs of caring for older people as rediscover the unique contributions that they can make. Elders provide some of the greatest examples of moral and creative leadership – Nelson Mandela, Mother Theresa, Artur Rubinstein and, closer, to home, Patrick Steptoe, who pioneered two revolutions in fertility treatment near the end of his career.

Most very old people are only too keen to share the secrets of a long life, even if some of their recommendations are a little idiosyncratic. We hear of the benefits of walking and natural yoghurt at the same time as the merits of the local whisky and chewing tobacco. Government authorities are concerned about the costs of providing for an ailing population, and dispense plenty of dietary advice. There is no denying that, in a sense, we are what we eat. The British are currently recommended to eat five portions of fresh fruit and vegetables every day. For some, this is preaching to the converted, because there is already a groundswell of interest in good eating habits.

Vegetarianism is increasingly popular, and domestic refrigerator shelves sag under the weight of organically grown foods, 'alternative' medicines' and a bevy of vitamin tablets and capsules – at least in the homes of the comfortably-off. We are targeted at every turn by advertisers of dietary supplements and foods that are low-calorie, high-fibre, or low-fat, high-vitamin or combinations of them. The virtues are said to be an improved circulation, less cancer, and quenching of free radicals, and we find the products more attractive for being natural, even if recommended in unnatural amounts. We are easy victims of simple slogans denying the adequacy of what we used to think was a wholesome diet. But if we take nutrition seriously and search the literature assiduously, we invite even greater confusion because even the experts do not always agree. As Peter Medawar once quipped, nutrition is 'kitchen science'.

There is no end in sight to arguments about the natural diet for our species, how much stress we can take or exercise we should take, or how much weight we dare gain and lose. This is frustrating, but while researchers argue we can at least toast their efforts. A recent paper from Sir Richard Doll, the Oxford doyen of epidemiology, makes a fairly convincing case that alcohol – taken *in moderation* – actually reduces mortality. Less contentious is his great achievement in proving, against resistance at first, that smoking is harmful to health. In his latest paper on the subject he has shown that a half of regular smokers will shorten their lives as a direct result of their habit.

Except for those who begin at the back of a book, as I sometimes do, readers will now know that this one is a description of living systems rather than a prescription for a long life. I will not venture to say anything more specific about a healthy diet and lifestyle. My own view, for what it is worth, is that we should heed our evolutionary roots in searching for optimum living conditions. Our ancestors who took up farming about 500 generations ago would hardly recognize modern lifestyles, though our genes and physiology have changed hardly at all. In the blinking of an eye in evolutionary time, we have altered our habits and the environment to which our species had become attuned, and we are no doubt paying a price. But our primeval state was never an idyll of health and harmony, and no one in their right mind would really want to exchange their lot for the life of a hunter-gatherer, unless perhaps they are unlucky enough to inhabit the alienated housing estates of the West or the slums of the Third World. We take our chances in our modern world, and ward off the harmful side-effects as best we can.

In choosing which is the most prudent course to take, a balance has to be struck between what we know about our origins and the evidence of science and our own experience. Generally speaking, what is good for us when we are young will probably turn out good for old age, but not necessarily so. Senescence is one of the oversights of nature because evolutionary selection has not fitted us for long life. The wholesome diet, exercise and hormone levels that were good for us in youth are a guide to old age – no more. Only by trial and experiment will we discover what is best for our brave new age.

The reasons for the larger numbers of old people in society today are more social than biological, rather like the dental improvements over the years. Better oral hygiene, fluoridation of water and orthodontic dentistry have helped to keep teeth in better shape for longer than ever before, but they still wear down in the end. The equivalent of slowing the ageing process would be to grow a third set of molars. Since this would require cells to be genetically reprogrammed, and is not remotely possible yet, gerontology has been regarded as the most hopeless of the life sciences. On the contrary, we should remember that not so long ago people scoffed at the idea of eliminating smallpox and that of fertilizing human eggs in the test-tube.

The much-publicized interventions in the reproductive process have produced some of the more dramatic signs of how the limits of biological time can be rolled back. Nobody doubts that a woman of sixty can be helped to become pregnant, though many question its wisdom. Reproduction is admittedly a special case because the sex organs are not vital in the way that the heart and kidneys are. Our lifespan is not suddenly cut short by castration or menopause, although the rest of the body is far from indifferent to the withdrawal of sex hormones.

If pregnancy provides some of the clearest evidence that the effects of ageing are not written in tablets of stone, it is because reproduction is so dependent on hormones. The rejuvenators thought that sex hormones were panaceas for all ills, but the facts of old age cannot be reconciled with a deficiency of just one hormone, however important it may be. The role of hormones in ageing has sometimes been overplayed, but they do have one great virtue: we don't have to put up with the levels that nature dictates, and what we deem to be insufficient can easily be made good. Gene therapy will have to go a long way before it supersedes hormone therapy in efficiency, and for the foreseeable future we are stuck with our genes for better or worse. But if we shrewdly control our hormone levels we can play nature's wild cards in such a way as to win a few more tricks and stay healthy a little longer.

Replacement of oestrogen and testosterone in older people immediately spring to mind, but these are not the only hormones we can adjust. Hopes of a new hormone to cure all the mysterious ills of age spring eternal, but it is more likely that we shall first discover new applications for old ones, such as growth hormone.

Growth hormone was one of the first pituitary hormones to be discovered because it is stored in much larger quantities than the rest. Dwarfism was quickly recognized as a consequence of its deficiency, and injections of growth hormone dramatically increase the stature of small children. There was never enough growth hormone to go round while it still had to be extracted from cadavers, but it has recently been produced industrially from genetically engineered bacteria and there is now sufficient to treat people of all ages.

Growth hormone is released by the adolescent pituitary in large pulses during sleep. The amounts diminish in some people more than others, but many will lose 10–15 per cent every decade, and it is cleared more quickly from the blood in older people. The net result is that levels fall further by old age than those of any other hormone except the sex steroids. Naturally winding down production after puberty may seem a wise economy, but is it?

Lower hormone levels result in less lean muscle and more fat, particularly of the unhealthy male variety. The extra body weight aggravates the hormone deficit, setting up a vicious cycle encouraging even more fat to be deposited. Leaving matters to nature is not always the best policy because our vital interests may not be served at every age. Boosting growth hormone is as unnatural as HRT, but in an older person who is deficient it improves strength and increases leanness. Some say it even gives them a mental tonic, though it is not addictive. If its reputation for switching metabolism from amassing fat to accumulating protein is borne out, older folk will not be the only ones clamouring for it. But extra hormone does not have to come down the barrel of a needle. Menopausal women who are taking HRT are already enjoying a bonus because oestrogen boosts growth hormone release from the pituitary gland – even from an old one. Testosterone has the same effect in men.

Growth hormone is not the only hormone treatment for ageing in the news. An adrenal steroid, dehydroepiandrosterone (DHEA for short), and melatonin from the pineal gland have both been advocated. Such 'discoveries' follow a predictable course which is reminiscent of the first hormonal remedies manufactured a century ago from testicle extracts. Volunteers are recruited and injected with purified hormones and are tested by hopeful researchers. The results are usually mixed, because of the nature of human variation, but some benefits are usually reported, even for those receiving the placebos. Anyone acquainted with the history of rejuvenation science will smile at news of simple cures, though we ought to keep an open mind until all the evidence is in. We must also beware of the fallacy that every hormone deficiency later in life needs to be treated, even if the benefits of extra growth hormone and sex steroids are undeniable.

We are so accustomed to the idea that a penalty has to be paid for thwarting nature that people are surprised about good news. The pill is now respected not only for its high contraceptive efficiency but for a serendipitous health bonus. The low-oestrogen formulations reduce not only heavy periods and anaemia, as expected, but also the risks of uterine and ovarian cancer. Even benign lumps in the breasts are less common. Suppressing ovulation for long stretches at a time is not as unnatural as we may think. Originally the norm for our species was a series of pregnancies interspersed with long intervals of breast-feeding, when fertility and oestrogen levels were low. This is still the pattern in a few communities, as it is in our primate cousins, the great apes. The epidemic of female cancers now ravaging the West has probably a lot to do with the greater number of ovulations and exposure to oestrogen in modern women. Matters are made worse by an earlier puberty and possibly a slightly later menopause nowadays. Putting the ovaries into a resting state now looks like a healthy option, and one that even celibate women would do well to consider.

There is no reason why women must have lunar cycles and the high levels of oestrogen that go along with them. The hormone levels needed for reproduction are far higher than those required for keeping osteoporosis, heart attacks and the other deficiency symptoms at bay. By suppressing the ovaries' own hormones by using a progestogen combined with a low level of oestrogen, a woman is protected on every count. However, the pill still contains more oestrogen than is required to keep healthy, low though the level may be. In theory, a safer contraceptive tactic would be to shut down the ovaries with one drug and give HRT, since this provides the minimum amount a woman needs to safeguard health.

At the University of Southern California, Malcolm Pike is testing this theory in clinical trials. His aim is to provide 100 per cent protection against pregnancy while further reducing the risk of dreaded breast cancer, which strikes 1 in 7 women in some parts of the state. The trial volunteers take a drug to stop the release of FSH and LH from the pituitary gland by inhibiting the hypothalamic gonadotrophin-releasing hormone, GNRH. A little oestrogen is added to counter the effects of chemical castration. A progestogen is not protective against breast cancer but it is taken every four months to eliminate the risk of uterine cancer by allowing menstruation to occur. The longer interval between periods is welcomed by some women as a respite from the monthly 'curse'. A little androgen is added to protect the bones, and this may help the libido too.

So far the results are encouraging. The contraceptive is both effective and reversible, and, what is more, breast tissue is healthier under the low-oestrogen regime. The hormone cocktail is too complex to become widely accepted as it stands but, if presented in another form, it could be attractive for women at risk of breast cancer. Whether men will ever enjoy the advantages of reducing their risks of prostate disease at the same time as taking a male contraceptive pill is more doubtful. They are less eager to experiment than their wives, and, if they are willing to accept the dangers of smoking and dangerous sports it seems unlikely that they will worry about a possible backlash from testosterone in the distant future.

Nowadays more people want to keep their reproductive options open into mid-life, if not later. The numbers of sterilization operations for both sexes are at an all-time high, but so are requests for reversals. Even the menopause is no longer seen as a one-way door. With the advent of egg donation there is a chance – no more – that a woman of any age can become pregnant with a little help from hormone replacement therapy. This may seem remarkable enough, but the revolution in what is called assisted reproductive technology still has some way to run. It may sound like a flight of fancy, but cold storage of ovaries for after the menopause looms as a distinct possibility.

Freezing ovarian tissue is already presenting a ray of hope for young cancer sufferers who face infertility as a result of treatment. On top of the shock of being told they have a dreaded disease, they learn that life-saving treatment may include sudden and permanent sterilization. This is because the chemotherapy or radiotherapy destroys developing eggs and sperm along with cancer cells – as it were speeding up the ageing process. Anyone who has discussed these matters cannot fail to be touched by the poignancy of a young person's fierce hope of becoming a parent one day even while his or her life is being shaken like a straw in the wind.

A female patient may choose to have IVF treatment and frozen storage of her embryos if she has a partner and there is time before her cancer treatment begins. This is rarely possible, however, and the chance of storing part of the ovary is more attractive because it can be done immediately and keeps open her options for choosing a partner for her eggs. Whether as eggs or embryos, her reproductive potential should be safe if committed to tanks of liquid nitrogen at a temperature of nearly −200°C. This is sufficiently cold for life to stand still indefinitely.

If she becomes menopausal meantime, her thawed embryos stand a chance of implanting in her womb after priming with HRT. Some people feel happier with the idea of ovary storage because it does not hold embryos as hostages to fortune. What happens to them, and who decides, if the mother dies? Since a whole ovary cannot be frozen because of ice-crystal damage, only the outer 'skin' containing most of the egg store is used. The tissue can be returned to its original site in due course, rather like a skin graft. So far only a few patients have deposited tissue in freezer banks, and it will be several years before they retrieve it. When they do, we hope they will be able to resume their menstrual cycles after stopping a decade or two before. It is too early to give any assurances but, if lambs conceived from frozen eggs are anything to go by, it will be possible to rekindle the life of an ovary.

Other women may want to try this technology if it is proven reliable. Whether it is advisable is another matter. If breast cancer patients want to deposit an ovary in the bank 'just in case', they must accept that there is a risk that restoring oestrogens and becoming pregnant might inflame the old disease. Healthy women too might consider storage of ovarian tissue as an insurance policy against infertility, particularly if they have a family history of early menopause or if egg donation is unacceptable. The eggs would stay as young and fresh as the day they were frozen, though the authorities will doubtless want to set a shelf-life for them.

Women seem to have drawn the short straw in reproductive treatments, considering the time, trouble and expense of the various technologies needed to establish a pregnancy. A man can deliver his gametes for frozen storage at will. But a man with cancer may have difficulty producing a specimen and, even if he can, it may be so poor that he had better not count on it. He is also more likely to worry about the shrunken state of his gonads after chemotherapy, even if he has something stored down at the freezer bank. Are there any other options for him?

Testicles like it cool but, like the ovaries, they are too large to be frozen whole with any hope of recovery. A much better prospect is to collect their stem cells in a testicular biopsy, rather like the routine storage of bone marrow for some cancer patients. Returning test-icular cells to their original tubules when it is safe is likely to be much more difficult than injecting marrow cells but, if this proved success-ful, the patient would regain his fertility and his old pride in his organs.

Cancer treatment may obliterate sperm production, but luckily it has no more than a passing effect on testosterone. But some older men do suffer waning hormone levels even without the hazard of chemotherapy, and may need a boost. This can be provided simply with an implant of testosterone, but the natural solution is to top up the Leydig cells in the organs. If suitable donors could be found (which would not be easy), the cells should evade rejection by the immune system and thrive, provided there is a good blood supply. The testis is one of the few organs that will accept implanted foreign tissues, and could harbour other hormonal grafts too. If pancreatic islet cells could happily survive there, diabetics would no longer need insulin injections.

When it comes to using cells from unrelated donors, the ovary is disadvantaged because it is not so immunologically privileged as the testis. Some women who desperately want a child would leap at the chance of an ovarian graft as a way of skirting long waiting-lists for donor eggs. There is also the dividend that a graft is cheaper than egg donation, and a single operation might keep menstrual cycles going for decades, making the menopause a thing of the past. This is because the pituitary gland stands up well to ageing and produces enough gonadotrophins to stimulate ovarian grafts into deep old age.

All this may sound dangerously avant-garde, but the concept is far from novel. In fact 1995 marked the centenary of the first attempt to transplant ovaries, by Robert Morris in New York. A prematurely menopausal woman was said to have had a successful pregnancy after receiving a graft from another woman. Once it was realized that foreign organs are usually rejected by the host's immune system, Morris's claims were thrown into doubt and were not followed up. Today the problem can be overcome by suppressing the immune system with steroids and drugs. The risks are worth taking for a life-saving heart or bone-marrow transplant, but difficult to justify for someone who is sterile but otherwise healthy.

This technology is therefore waiting for a breakthrough in immunology. Once the immune system can be coaxed into accepting a foreign graft without having to disarm its ability to fight infections and malignant cells, we may see more of the ovarian graft. Only one major obstacle will then remain. If close relatives are unable or unwilling to donate an organ, who will? The criteria have to be rather more stringent than for hearts and kidneys: the donors must be young and female and match the physical characteristics of the host. Since there will be few volunteers, applications will depend on post-mortem donors. The largest source of eggs that currently goes to waste is the ovaries of aborted foetuses, but their use for infertility treatment was outlawed in Britain in 1994 before it had even been tested. That leaves tissue recovered from accident victims, which has been approved at least in principle if the deceased was over eighteen.

Opponents of reproductive medicine may imagine the spectre of consumers choosing transplant organs like meat from the supermarket freezer, but their fears are needless. Those who store ovarian tissue will do so for their own needs, and egg donation will continue to be the mainstay for treating sterility. A graft may be a natural remedy for hormone deficiency, but is not a particularly healthy alternative to HRT because it prolongs exposure to oestrogens at full strength. If only protection against oestrogen deficiency is required, HRT is still the best treatment.

The larger issues sometimes get lost behind bizarre and sensational stories about new ways of having a baby. Women are having their babies later than their mothers did, and this is beginning to have an impact on the priorities set for fertility services. Certainly we shall see more mutations from older fathers and more Down's syndrome from older mums, but do older parents offer any genetic benefits to posterity? Mike Rose showed with fruit flies that, when a population is bred only from older mothers, each successive generation ages more slowly and lives a little longer than the last. Are we engaged in a rather similar experiment at this stage in our history?

I doubt it very much. Looking back over the century, reproductive trends have been fickle and in the next generation we may well see a reversal of the trend to postpone families. Child-bearing is, by and large, treated as an inalienable human right, and we all hope that reproduction will never become as regimented for humans as it was for Rose's flies. Even then, longevity would creep up only very slowly. A woman's ability to ovulate is curtailed by the early onset of menopause, whereas flies keep breeding until they drop. Our window of reproductive opportunity is comparatively narrow. Finally, as social beings, we are likely to dilute any inborn biological advantage as soon as it emerges. For greater longevity to take hold on the population, the offspring of older mothers would have to produce children of their own and choose partners with a similar background. In practice, people who start late usually have smaller families, and there are, as

301

always, so many unpredictable factors affecting the choice of mates that any kind of breeding bias is unlikely.

Being what we are, our concerns for the future do not stretch much beyond the next generation or two. We cannot, and perhaps dare not, hope that longevity is going to be extended in our time. Prevention of disease rather than cure of ageing is our formula for getting the most out of our physiology. By jockeying the genes we may one day beat the ageing process, but this is a tall order even for the remarkable and expectant era in biology and molecular medicine that we live in. We can expect more progress against the problems of age, but not yet against its cause. Whereas treatment with hormones and drugs has held sway in this century, gene therapy will come to pre-eminence in the next. Increasingly, it will be possible to substitute beneficial genes and knock out harmful ones, and even revolutionize treatments that we had thought were reaching perfection.

Spare-part surgery has come a long way in the treatment of organ collapse since the pioneer days of Alexis Carrel, but it is set for further strides to overcome donor shortages. Pigs are already being reared from embryos that were genetically engineered to produce organs tolerated by the human body after transplantation. The first human heart transplants in South Africa caused uproar because of the sentimental and traditional associations this organ. How much more fuss will we see when a pig's organ beats in a man's chest? And what are the chances of a porcine heart exceeding the thirty-year quota in the original species? The doors of biology and medicine open into the unknown, and we can only say that new medical uses will be found for more and more parts of the animal – short of its squeal. There will be horrified reactions, but an animal that saves a human life surely has more dignity than one ending up as the Sunday roast.

Everyone agrees that it would be better if animals were not needed for research and treatment, but science often solves the very problems that it has created. One day, small repair jobs should be possible using human cells tailored to order in the Petri dish. Each of our cells still holds the same uncorrupted genetic code that we inherited on the day we were conceived. In theory, replacement cells and organs might be made if the genetic program could be run again. Sacrificing one cell, say from the skin, to make another, say a muscle cell for patching up the heart, seems eminently attractive. Admittedly, changing one cell type into another is one of the more intractable problems of biology and, even if it is cracked, there will be the worry that tampering could provoke a malignant change. It is like driving north through a one-way system and discovering that you should have gone south, with the consequent risk of getting lost on the way back. It would be better to start the journey from the beginning with fresh embryonic stem cells (ES cells) because they can be grown continuously *in vitro* after harvesting from 'spare' embryos donated by infertility patients. Since they have not been committed to any particular fate, the cells might be genetically coaxed into making bone marrow, nerves or other cells needed for implanting in the body.

The first fruits of molecular genetics in plants and animals are giving a fillip to hopes of treating patients who inherit one of the several thousand genetic diseases. Genes transferred into crops can improve their shelf-life and their resistance to disease, and encourage nitrogen-fixing ability. This could reduce the need for chemicals to be spread on the land, which should be welcomed by everyone. New varieties of fruit and vegetables have already reached the supermarkets in America, including the famous tomato which softens more slowly because a gene involved in ethylene production has been knocked out. Would that our own overripening could be cured as easily!

The creation of novel heritable changes in animals requires transferring genes into eggs or embryos and is called germ-line technology. This is showing some success in the laboratory but has no place in medicine for the present because genes cannot be targeted to a precise part of a chromosome and attempts might lead to disaster. The more acceptable side of gene technology is somatic gene therapy because it aims to treat the symptoms of genetic diseases such as cystic fibrosis, Huntington's disease and muscular dystrophy. Unfortunately the patients can still pass a mutant gene down to their children, however, and the only safeguard that can be offered is antenatal diagnosis of the embryo or foetus and the possibility of pregnancy termination.

Sifting through the haystack of human DNA to find the needles responsible for genetic diseases is an immense task, but each month more and more of the genetic code comes to light and the results of new gene therapy trials are reported. How to transfer the genes remains a major problem, and no doubt we shall come to regard the first hit-or-miss attempts as rather crude. Microscopic fat bubbles or liposomes are currently favoured because they can be inhaled to treat the lungs of cystic fibrosis sufferers but, since most of the DNA does not reach the nucleus of the lung cells, it goes to waste. Some viruses responsible for bronchial illnesses are more attractive vehicles because they can shuttle genes directly into the lining of the lung – as long as they don't bring the whole family down with a cold! The technology is still at the blunderbuss stage and a long way from the magic bullet.

Far more people are affected by cancer and cardiovascular disease than by inborn genetic diseases, but these too will benefit from knowledge of the genes concerned. Understanding the environmental triggers of cancer has come a long way since Dr Percival Pott made a connection between soot and scrotal cancer in London chimney-sweeps at the end of the eighteenth century. For a long time it was thought that chance dictated why one person and not another contracts cancer after exposure to the same hazardous material, but we now know better. Some people have loaded dice. Breast cancer, for instance, occasionally runs in families, and two genes account for 5 per cent of all cases, especially the younger ones. When one of my male colleagues first suggested that a prophylactic mastectomy should be offered to those at most risk, the press created a hullabaloo, but the sense of this radical course is now accepted. Unfortunately, mass screening for these genes is looking to be a prohibitively expensive process.

Cancer treatment too could be revolutionized by gene therapy because cancers are rooted in the genetic machinery. A series of changes in a single rogue cell affecting genes involved in growth or death enables it and all of its descendants to grow and spread carelessly around the body like barbarian invaders. The cells may also become more resistant to killing by drugs and radiation and by the immunological watchdog cells of the body. If the faults can be corrected, the tumours will shrink without the miseries of chemotherapy, radiotherapy and surgery.

But is all this new technology going to help us to hold back the tide of ageing? In the next ten years it will be possible to read the human DNA code from end to end on a CD-ROM. This will enable doctors to predict, diagnose and treat genetic diseases, but it is difficult to see how the ageing process can be modified. Tackling single mutations is challenging enough, but is child's play compared with the intricacies of ageing. Perhaps the syndromes of premature ageing will be more tractable for being due to single genes, though conquering them will be no easy task. George Martin estimates that the mutation of any one of 1,000 genes can produce symptoms of premature ageing.

Molecular biology has come a long way in forty years but is still a young science, and discovering the multitude of genes involved in setting our lifespan will take some effort. Many are daunted by the prospect, but there are also optimists such as Caleb Finch who says, 'many aspects of senescence should be strongly modifiable by interventions at the level of gene expression'. Progress will not come easily, though. We will be lucky if something as 'simple' as knocking out a few gerontogenes or transferring beneficial genes provides more than a temporary respite. The idea of refreshing our cells with an infection of youthful mitochondria also takes some swallowing, but it is at least poetically attractive as a recapitulation of early life on earth.

No one but a crank would say that a cure for ageing is just around the corner. Fortunately for the planet, progress on this last and most challenging of biological problems will be slow, giving society time to adjust to its consequences. Futurology is not a science, let alone an exact one, and it is hard to predict where and when breakthroughs will be made. But science is as full of surprises as nature, and progress often comes unexpectedly. A hundred years of hormone research have now been completed, and the next few decades will undoubtedly see even more dramatic progress in molecular genetics. I share Finch's conviction that we need not accept the inevitability of senile decline. There are magnificent examples of defiance of ageing by the human spirit, but if mounting mind over matter was our only option I would be more pessimistic. Biology gives us hope of organic improvement, and plenty of food for thought. Not all creatures are subject to senescence. Decay is not a necessary fact of life, and rates of deterioration vary enormously. Besides, we already have dramatic examples of how ageing can be defeated, at least for a time.

One of the dangers is that an ambitious quest breeds triumphalism. Longevity may not be a forbidden fruit, but we should beware of the price that may have to be paid for winning more years. Closing the door on today's diseases and disabilities could open another to let in a new pack of devils. Senescence is much more complicated than the simple accumulation of a few genetic scars and warts. Many of the genes involved are probably beneficial to us at some time or another, particularly when we are young. Would we choose greater longevity if the price was to be infertile or ugly in youth? I doubt that Dorian Gray would have volunteered. Anyway, we must remember that additional years cannot be guaranteed because even biologically perfect beings can be struck by lightning or a hansom cab.

Quack remedies for ageing have never come cheap, and the real thing is likely to be expensive. Those who question the use of human and financial resources to explore the far reaches of biology have a point. Vaccination of the world's children is a higher priority, but gerontology is better than Trident submarines. The promise of defeating ageing has always been immensely attractive and profitable, and there lies a danger. Some people will pay $150,000 to have their mortal remains frozen in the hope of being revitalized later – which only goes to show that there is one born every minute.

To be realistic, no major venture is likely to succeed on idealism alone, and private and corporate investment will be needed. We hear a good deal about partnerships being struck between academic researchers and industry. The pursuit of profit lies behind these agreements, and the secrecy which is often demanded poses a threat to traditional scientific openness. Can you imagine the rush to the patent office if a gene which could hold back the tide of ageing were found? The worst fears of science fiction writers would soon be realized, and the trophy would be tarnished. Scientists have sometimes been portrayed as bogeymen, but Mammon is more often the enemy of the people.

A little over a century ago, Brown-Séquard thought he had found a remedy for ageing. His cure was worthless, except as the spark that ignited research into the sex hormones and HRT, but we ought to pause and reflect on his example. Contrary to newspaper hyperbole of the time, he made no extravagant claims; nor did he keep his formula secret or patent it. He even offered free samples of his 'elixir'. Late in the next century, our descendants may see the conquest of time, but I wonder if we shall see his like again.

Further Reading

Chapter 1: Mating Madness

Lee, A. K. & Cockburn, A., *Evolutionary Ecology of Marsupials*
(Monographs in Marsupial Biology) (Cambridge University Press,
Cambridge, 1985)

Renfree, M. B., 'Diapausing dilemmas, sexual stress and mating madness
in marsupials.' In K. E. Sheppard, J. H. Baublik & J. W. Funder
(eds), *Stress and Reproduction* (Serono Symposium No. 86),
pp. 347–60 (Raven Press, New York, 1992)

Chapter 2: A Dog's Life

Brooke, M. & Birkhead, T. (eds), *The Cambridge Encyclopedia
of Ornithology* (Cambridge University Press, Cambridge, 1991)

Calder, W. A. III, *Size, Function and Life History* (Harvard University
Press, Cambridge, Mass., 1984)

Comfort, Alex, *The Biology of Senescence*, 3rd edn (Churchill Livingstone,
Edinburgh, 1979)

Davies, Paul, *God and The New Physics* (J. M. Dent, London
& Melbourne, 1983)

Dunnet, G. M., 'Population studies of the fulmar on Eynhallow, Orkney Islands', *Ibis* **133**, Supplement 1, 24–7 (1991)

Finch, C. E., *Longevity, Senescence and the Genome* (University of Chicago Press, Chicago, 1990)

Finch, C. E., Pike, M. C. & Witten, M., 'Slow increases in the Gompertz mortality rate during aging in humans also occur in other animals and in birds', *Science* **249**, 901–4 (1990)

Fraser, J. T., *Time: The Familiar Stranger* (University of Massachusetts Press, Boston, 1987)

Lindstedt, S. L. & Calder. W. A. III, 'Body size and longevity in birds', *Condor* **78**, 91–4 (1976)

Masters, P. M., 'Stereochemically altered noncollagenous protein from human dentin', *Calcified Tissue International* **35**, 43–7 (1983)

Sacher, G. A., 'Relation of lifespan to brain weight and body weight in mammals', in G. E. W. Wolstenholme & M. O'Connor (eds), *The Lifespan of Animals* (Ciba Foundation Colloquia on Ageing, Vol. 5), pp. 115–33 (Churchill, London, 1959)

Sacher, G. A., 'Life table modification and life prolongation', in C. E. Finch & L. Hayflick (eds), *Handbook of the Biology of Aging*, pp. 582–638 (Van Nostrand Reinhold, New York, 1977)

Schrodinger, E., *What is Life? The Physical Aspect of the Living Cell* (Cambridge University Press, Cambridge, 1951)

Chapter 3: Old Father William

Abbot, M. H., Abbey, H., Bolling, D. R. & Murphy, E. A., 'The familial component in longevity – a study of offspring of nonagenarians', III. Intrafamilial studies, *American Journal of Medical Genetics* **2**, 105–20 (1978)

Baker, G. T. & Sprott, R. L., 'Biomarkers of aging', *Experimental Gerontology* **23**, 223–39 (1988)

Barker, D. J. P., Winter, P. D., Osmond, C., Margetts, B. & Simmonds, S. J. 'Weight in infancy and death from ischaemic heart disease', *Lancet* **ii**, 577–80 (1989)

Bean, W. B., 'Nail growth: Thirty-five years of observation', *Archives of Internal Medicine* **140**, 73–6 (1980)

Doty, R. L., Shaman, P., Applebaum, S., Giberson, R., Sikorski, L. & Rosenberg, L., 'Smell identification ability: changes with age', *Science* **226**, 1441–3 (1984)

Finch, C. E., *Longevity, Senescence and the Genome* (University of Chicago Press, Chicago, 1990)

Gompertz, B., 'On the nature of the function expressive of the law of human mortality, and on a new mode of determining the values of life contingencies', *Philosophical Transactions of the Royal Society of London* **115**, 513–85 (1825)

Jones, Hardin B., 'Mechanism of aging suggested from study of altered death risks', in J. Neyman (ed.), *Proceedings of Fourth Berkeley Symposium on Mathematical Statistics and Probability*, Vol. 4, pp. 267–92 (1962)

Kallman, F. J. & Sander, G., 'Twin studies on aging and longevity', *Journal of Heredity* **39**, 349–57 (1948)

Katzman, R., Terry, R., DeTeresa, R., Brown, T., Davies, P., Fuld, P., Renbing, X. & Peck, A., 'Clinical, pathological, and neurochemical changes in dementia: a subgroup with preserved mental status and numerous neocortical plaques', *Annals of Neurology* **23**, 138–44 (1988)

Kohn, R. R., 'Cause of death in very old people', *Journal of the American Medical Association* **247**, 2793–7 (1982)

Lack, D., *Population Studies of Birds* (Clarendon Press, Oxford, 1966)

Orentreich, N. & Sharp, N. J., 'Keratin replacement as an aging parameter', *Journal of the Society of Cosmetic Chemists* **18**, 537–47 (1967)

Rees, T. S. & Duckert, L. G., 'Auditory and vestibular dysfunction in aging', in W. R. Hazzard, R. Andres, E. L. Bierman & J. P. Blass (eds), *Principles of Geriatric Medicine and Gerontology*, 2nd edn, pp. 432–44 (McGraw-Hill, New York, 1990)

Rosen, S., Bergman, M., Plester, D., El-Mofty, A. & Satti, M. H., 'Presbycusis study of a relatively noise-free population in the Sudan', *Annals of Oto-Rhino-Laryngology* **71**, 727–43 (1962)

Schneider, E. L. & Rowe, J. W., *Handbook of the Biology of Aging*,
    3rd edn (Academic Press, New York, 1990)
Smith, D. W. E., 'Is greater female longevity a general finding among
    animals?', *Biological Reviews* **64**, 1–12 (1989)
Weindruch, R. & Walford, R. L., *The Retardation of Aging and Disease
    by Dietary Restriction* (C. C. Thomas, Springfield, Illinois, 1988)

Chapter 4: Programmed Senescence

Abbott, M. H., Abbey, H., Boling, D. R. & Murphy, E. A., 'The familial
    component in longevity – a study of offspring in nonagenarians',
    III. Intrafamilial studies, *American Journal of Medical Genetics* **2**,
    105–20 (1978)
Adelman, R., Saul, R. L. & Ames, B. N., 'Oxidative damage to DNA:
    relation to species metabolic rate and lifespan', *Proceedings of the
    National Academy of Sciences of the USA* **85**, 2706–8 (1988)
Alpha-Tocopherol, Beta Carotene Cancer Prevention Study Group,
    'The effect of vitamin E and beta carotene on the incidence of lung
    cancer and other cancers in male smokers', *New England Journal
    of Medicine* **330**, 1029–35 (1994)
Burness, G. *The White Badger* (George G. Harrap, London 1970)
Carrel, A., *Man, the Unknown* (Harper & Bros, New York, 1935)
Dexter, T. M., Raff, M. C. & Wyllie, A. H. (eds), 'Death from inside
    out: the role of apoptosis in development, tissue homeostasis and
    malignancy', *Philosophical Transactions of the Royal Society Series B*
    345, 231–333 (1994)
Finch, C. E., *Longevity, Senescence and the Genome* (University of Chicago
    Press, Chicago, 1990)
Gelman, R. E., Watson, A. L., Bronson, R. T. & Yunis, E. J., 'Murine
    chromosomal regions correlated with longevity, *Genetics* **118**,
    693–704 (1988)
Goldstein, S., 'Replicative senescence: the human fibroblast comes
    of age', *Science* **249**, 1129–33 (1990)

Goodrick, C. L., 'Life span and the inheritance of longevity in inbred mice', *Journal of Gerontology* **30**, 257–63 (1975)

Halliwell, B. & Gutteridge, J. M. C., *Free Radicals in Biology and Medicine* (Clarendon Press, Oxford, 1985)

Harman, D., 'Free radicals in aging', *Molecular and Cellular Biochemistry* **84**, 155–61 (1988)

Hayflick, L. & Moorhead, P. S., 'The serial cultivation of human diploid cell strains', *Experimental Cell Research* **25**, 585–621 (1961)

Johnson, T. E., 'The increased life-span of *age–1* mutants in *Caenorhabditis elegans* results from lowering the Gompertz rate of aging', *Science* **249**, 908–12 (1990)

Kleiber, M., *The Fire of Life* (Wiley, New York, 1961)

Lane, D. P., '*p53*, guardian of the genome', *Nature* **358**, 15–16 (1992)

Leaf, A., 'Long-lived populations (extreme old age)', in W. R. Hazzard, R. Andres, E. L. Bierman & J. P. Blass (eds), *Principles of Geriatric Medicine and Gerontology*, 2nd edn, pp. 142–5 (McGraw-Hill, New York, 1990)

Martin, G. M., 'Genetic syndromes in man with potential relevance to the pathobiology of aging', in D. E. Harrison (ed.), *Genetic Effects on Aging, Birth Defects* (Original Article Series, Vol. 14), pp. 5–39 (Alan R. Liss, New York, 1978)

Masoro, E. J., Yu, B. P. & Bertrand, H. (1982), 'Action of food restriction in delaying the aging process', *Proceedings of the National Academy of Sciences of the USA* **79**, 4239–41 (1982)

Metchnikoff, E., *The Prolongation of Life* (Putnam's Sons, New York, 1910)

Pearl, R., *The Rate of Living* (Knopf, New York, 1928)

Pereira-Smith, O. M. & Smith, J. R. (1983), 'Evidence for the recessive nature of cellular immortality', *Science* **221**, 964–6 (1983)

Rubner, M. (1908), *Das Problem der Lebensdauer und seine Beziehungen zu Wachstum und Ernährung* (Munich and Berlin, 1908)

Rusting, Ricki L., 'Why do we age?' *Scientific American*, pp. 86–95 (December 1992)

Takata, H., Susuki, M., Ishii, T., Sekiguchi, S. & Iri, H., 'Influence of major histocompatibility complex region genes on human longevity among Okinawan-Japanese centenarians and nonagenarians', *Lancet* **ii**, 824–6 (1987)

Tolmasoff, J. M., Ono, T. & Cutler, R. G., 'Superoxide dismutase: correlation with lifespan and specific metabolic rate in primate species', *Proceedings of the National Academy of Sciences of the USA* **77**, 2777–81 (1980)

Vaziri, H., Dragowska, W., Allsopp, R. C., Thomas, T. E., Harley, C. B. & Lansdorp, P. M., 'Evidence for a mitotic clock in human hematopoietic stem cells: loss of telomeric DNA with age', *Proceedings of the National Academy of Sciences of the USA* **91**, 9857–60 (1994)

Wallace, D. C., 'Mitochondrial DNA sequence variation in human evolution and disease', *Proceedings of the National Academy of Sciences of the USA* **91**, 8739–46 (1994)

Chapter 5: The Great Trade-Off

Austad, S. N., 'Retarded senescence in an insular population of Virginia opossums (*Didelphis virginiana*)', *Journal of Zoology* **229**, 695–708 (1993)

Calow, P., 'The cost of reproduction – a physiological approach', *Biological Reviews* **54**, 23–40 (1979)

Charlesworth, B., *Evolution in Age-Structured Populations* (Cambridge University Press, Cambridge, 1980)

Darwin, C., *On the Origin of Species by Means of Natural Selection*. 6th edn (John Murray, London, 1876)

Desmond, A. & Moore, J., *Darwin* (Michael Joseph, London, 1991)

Eisenberg, J. F., *The Mammalian Radiations* (University of Chicago Press, Chicago, 1981)

Haldane, J. B. S., *New Paths in Genetics* (Allen & Unwin, London, 1941)

Hamilton, W. D., 'The moulding of senescence by natural selection', *Journal of Theoretical Biology* **12**, 12–45 (1966)

Kirkwood, T. B. L., 'Comparative life spans of species: why do species have the life spans they do?' *American Journal of Clinical Nutrition* **55**, 1191S–1195S (1992)

MacArthur, R. H. & Wilson, E. O., *The Theory of Island Biogeography* (Princeton University Press, Princeton, 1967)

Maynard Smith, J. (1958), 'The effects of temperature and of egg-laying on the longevity of *Drosophila subobscura*', *Journal of Experimental Biology* **35**, 832–42 (1958)

Medawar, P. B., *An Unsolved Problem in Biology* (H. K. Lewis, London, 1952)

Medawar, P. B., *Memoir of a Thinking Radish* (Oxford University Press, Oxford, 1986)

Orr, W. C. & Sohal, R. S., 'Extension of life-span by overexpression of superoxide dismutase and catalase in *Drosophila melanogaster*', *Science* **263**, 1128–30 (1994)

Partridge, L. & Barton, N. H., 'Optimality, mutation and the evolution of ageing', *Nature* **362**, 305–11 (1993)

Pianka, E. R., 'On *r* and *K* selection', *American Naturalist* **104**, 592–7 (1970)

Promislow, D. E. L. & Harvey, P. H., 'Living fast and dying young: a comparative analysis of life-history variation among mammals', *Journal of Zoology* **220**, 417–37 (1990)

Rose, M. R., *The Evolutionary Biology of Aging* (Oxford University Press, Oxford, 1991)

Rose, M. & Charlesworth, B., 'A test of evolutionary theories of senescence', *Nature* **287**, 141–2 (1980)

Stearns, S. C., 'Life-history tactics: a review of the ideas', *Quarterly Review of Biology* **51**, 3–47 (1976)

Tuttle, M. D. & Stephenson, D., 'Growth and survival of bats', in T. H. Kunz (ed.), *Ecology of Bats* (Plenum Press, New York, 1982)

Weismann, A., 'The duration of life', in E. B. Poulton, S. Schonland & A. E. Shipley (eds), *Essays upon Heredity and Kindred Biological Problems*, pp. 1–66 (Clarendon Press, Oxford, 1889)

Williams, G. C., 'Pleiotropy, natural selection and the evolution of senescence', *Evolution* **11**, 398–411 (1957)

Williams, G. C., *Adaptation and Natural Selection: A Critique of Some*

Current Evolutionary Thought (Princeton University Press, Princeton, 1966)

Chapter 6: Brown-Séquard's Elixir

Aminoff, M. J., *Brown-Séquard. A Visionary of Science* (Raven Press, New York, 1993)

Borell, Merriley, 'Organotherapy and the emergence of reproductive endocrinology', *Journal of the History of Biology* **18**, 1–30 (1985)

Brown-Séquard, C. E., 'Du rôle physiologique et thérapeutique d'un suc extrait de testicules d'animaux d'après nombre observés chez l'homme', *Archives de physiologie normale et pathologique* (5e sér.) **1**, 739–46 (1889)

Olmsted, J. M. D., *Charles-Edourd Brown-Séquard: A Nineteenth-Century Neurologist and Endocrinologist* (Johns Hopkins Press, Baltimore, 1946)

Ranke-Heinemann, Uta, *Eunuchs for Heaven: the Catholic Church and Sexuality*, trans. John Brownjohn (André Deutsch, London, 1990)

Chapter 7: The Gland Grafters

Carson, Gerald, *The Roguish World of Doctor Brinkley* (Reinhardt & Co., Inc., New York & Toronto, 1960)

Gosden, R. G. & Aubard, Y., *Transplantation of Ovarian and Testicular Tissues* (R. G. Landes Co., Austin, Texas, 1996)

Hamilton, J. B., *The Monkey Gland Affair* (Chatto & Windus, London, 1986)

Lydston, G. F., 'Sex gland implantation: Additional cases and conclusions to date', *Journal of the American Medical Association* **66**, 1540–3 (1916)

Marshall, F. H. A., et al., *Report on Dr Serge Voronoff's Experiments on the Improvement of Livestock* (Ministry of Agriculture and Fisheries, Board of Agriculture for Scotland) (HMSO, London, 1928)

Medvei, V. C., *The History of Clinical Endocrinology* (Parthenon Press, Carnforth, Lancashire, 1993)

Morris, R. T., 'A case of heteroplastic ovarian grafting, followed by pregnancy, and the delivery of a living child', *Medical Record, New York* **69**, 697–8 (1906)

Stall, S., *What a Man of Forty-Five Ought to Know* (Vir Publishing Co., Philadelphia, 1929)

Steinach, E., *Sex and Life: Forty Years of Biological and Medical Experiments* (Viking Press, New York, 1940)

Voronoff, Serge, 'Can old age be deferred?', *Scientific American*, pp. 226–7 (October 1925)

Chapter 8: Hormones Come of Age

Bardin, C. W., Swerdloff, R. S. & Stanten, R. J., 'Androgens; risks and benefits'. *Journal of Clinical Endocrinology and Metabolism* **73**, 4–7 (1991)

Colditz, G. A., Willett, W. C., Stampfer, M. J., Rosner, B., Speizer, F. E. & Hennekens, C. H., 'Menopause and the risk of coronary heart disease in women', *New England Journal of Medicine* **316**, 1105–10 (1987)

Djerassi, C., *The Pill, Pygmy Chimps and Degas' Horse* (Basic Books, New York; HarperCollins, London, 1992)

Grossman, C. J., 'Interactions between the gonadal steroids and the immune system', *Science* **227**, 257–65 (1985)

Gwei-Djen, L. & Needham, J., 'Medieval preparations of urinary steroid hormones', *Medical History* **8**, 101–21 (1964)

Hamilton, J. B. & Mestler, G. E., 'Mortality and survival: a comparison of eunuchs with intact men and women in a mentally retarded population', *Journal of Gerontology* **24**, 395–411 (1969)

Parkes, A. S., 'The rise of reproductive endocrinology, 1926–1940', *Journal of Endocrinology* **34**, xix–xxxii (1966)

Pincus, G. & Thimann, K. V., *The Hormones. Physiology, Chemistry and Applications* (Academic Press, New York, 1948)

Royal College of General Practitioners, 'Mortality among oral contraceptive users', *Lancet* **ii**, 727–31 (1977)

Stampfer, M. J., Willett, W. C., Colditz, G. A., Rosner, B., Speizer, F. E. & Hennekens, C. H., 'A prospective study of postmenopausal estrogen therapy and coronary heart disease', *New England Journal of Medicine* **313**, 1044–9 (1985)

Stevenson, J. C., Crook, D. & Godsland, I. F., 'Influence of age and menopause on serum lipids and lipoproteins in healthy women', *Atherosclerosis* **98**, 83–90 (1993)

Chapter 9: The Meaning of Menopause

Bancroft, John, *Human Sexuality and its Problems*, 2nd edn (Churchill Livingstone, Edinburgh, 1989)

Brecher, E. M., *Love, Sex and Aging: A Consumer's Union Report* (Little, Brown, Boston, 1984)

Brindley, G. S., 'Pilot experiments on the actions of drugs injected into the human corpus cavernosum', *British Journal of Pharmacology* **87**, 495–500 (1986)

Dennerstein, L., Burrows, G. D., Wood, C. & Hyman, G., 'Hormones and sexuality: effect of estrogen and progestogen', *Obstetrics and Gynecology* **56**, 316–22 (1980)

Faddy, M. J., Gosden, R. G., Gougeon, A., Richardson, S. J. & Nelson, J. F., 'Accelerated disappearance of ovarian follicles in mid-life – implications for forecasting menopause', *Human Reproduction* **7**, 1342–6 (1992)

Featherstone, M. & Hepworth, M. (1985), 'The history of the male menopause, 1848–1936', *Maturitas* **7**, 249–57 (1985)

Goodall, J., *The Chimpanzees of Gombe: Patterns of Behavior* (Belknap Press of Harvard University Press, Cambridge, Mass., 1986)

Gosden, R. G., *Biology of Menopause: The Causes and Consequences of Ovarian Ageing* (Academic Press, London, 1985)

Gow, S. M., Turner, E. I. & Glasier, A., 'Clinical biochemistry of the menopause and hormone replacement therapy', *Annals of Clinical Biochemistry* **31**, 509–28 (1994)

Greer, Germaine, *The Change: Women, Ageing and the Menopause* (Penguin, 1991)

Hallström, T., 'Sexuality of women in middle age: the Göteborg study', *Journal of Biosocial Science*, Supplement 6, 165–75 (1979)

Harman, S. M. & Tsitouras, P. D., 'Reproductive hormones in ageing men. 1. Measurement of sex steroids, basal luteinizing hormone and Leydig cell response to human chorionic gonadotropin', *Journal of Clinical Endocrinology and Metabolism* **51**, 35–40 (1980)

Judd, H. L., Judd, G. E., Lucas, W. E. & Yen, S. S. C., 'Endocrine function of the postmenopusal ovary: concentrations of androgens and estrogens in ovarian and peripheral vein blood', *Journal of Clinical Endocrinology and Metabolism* **39**, 1020–4 (1974)

Kinsey, A. C., Pomeroy, W. B. & Martin, C. E. (1948), *Sexual Behavior in the Human Male* (W. B. Saunders, Philadelphia, 1948)

Kinsey, A. C., Pomeroy, W. B., Martin, C. E. & Gebhard, P. H., *Sexual Behavior in the Human Female* (W. B. Saunders, Philadelphia, 1953)

Masters, V. H. & Johnson, V. E., *Human Sexual Response* (Little Brown, Boston, 1966)

Neaves, W. B., Johnson, L., Porter, J. C., Parker, Jr., C. R. & Petty, C. S. (1984), 'Leydig cell numbers, daily sperm production, and serum gonadotropin levels in aging men', *Journal of Clinical Endocrinology and Metabolism* **59**, 756–63 (1984)

Nesheim, B. I. & Saetre, T., 'Changes in skin blood flow and body temperatures during climacteric hot flushes', *Maturitas* **4**, 49–55 (1982)

Tenover, J. S., 'Effects of testosterone supplementation in the aging male', *Journal of Clinical Endocrinology and Metabolism* **75**, 1092–8 (1992)

Tilt, E. J., *The Change of Life in Health and Disease*, 3rd edn (Churchill, London, 1870)

Treloar, A. E., Boynton, R. E., Behn, B. G. & Brown, B. W. (1967), 'Variation of the human menstrual cycle through reproductive life', *International Journal of Fertility* **12**, 77–126 (1967)

Vermeulen, A., 'Sex hormone status of the postmenopausal woman',
  Maturitas 2, 81–9 (1980)
Whitehead, M. & Godfree, V., *Hormone Replacement Therapy – Your
  Questions Answered* (Churchill Livingstone, Edinburgh, 1992)

Chapter 10: The Shape of Steroid Action

Albright, F., Smith, P. H. & Richardson, A. M., 'Postmenopausal
  osteoporosis', *Journal of the American Medical Association* 116,
  2465–74 (1941)
Bardin, C. W. & Catterall, J. F., 'Testosterone: a major determinant
  of extragenital sexual dimorphism', *Science* 211, 1285–94 (1981)
Barker, D. J. P., Hales, C. N., Fall, C. H. D., Osmond, C., Phipps, K.
  & Clark, P. M. S. (1993), 'Type 2 (non-insulin-dependent)
  diabetes mellitus, hypertension and hyperlipidaemia (syndrome X):
  relation to reduced fetal growth', *Diabetologia* 36, 62–7 (1993)
Christiansen, C., Riis, B. J. & Rødbro. P., 'Prediction of rapid bone loss
  in postmenopausal women', *Lancet* i, 1105–7 (1987)
Darwin, C., *The Descent of Man and Selection in Relation to Sex* (John
  Murray, London, 1871)
Fraser, D., Padwick, M. L., Whitehead, M. I., Coffer, A. & King, R. J. B.
  (1991), 'Presence of an oestradiol receptor-related protein in the
  skin: changes during the normal menstrual cycle', British Journal
  of Obstetrics and Gynaecology 98, 1277–82 (1991)
Hartz, A. J., Rupley, D. C. & Rimm, A. A., 'The association of girth
  measurements with disease in 32,856 women', *American Journal
  of Epidemiology* 119, 71–85 (1984)
Jones, B. M., 'Surgical treatment of male pattern baldness,' *British
  Medical Journal* 292, 430 (1986)
Kissebah, A. H. & Krakower, G. R., 'Regional adiposity and morbidity',
  Physiological Reviews 74, 761–811 (1994)
Lees, B., Molleson, T., Arnett, T. R. & Stevenson, J. C., 'Differences in

proximal bone density over two centuries', *Lancet* **341**, 673–5 (1993)

Reaven, G. M., 'Role of insulin resistance in human disease', *Diabetes* **37**, 1595–1607 (1988)

Tanner, J. M., *Foetus into Man: Physical Growth from Conception to Maturity*. 2nd edn (Castlemead Publications, Ware, Hertfordshire, 1989)

Vague, J., 'The degree of masculine differentiation of obesities: A factor determining predisposition to diabetes, atherosclerosis, gout and uric calculous disease', *American Journal of Clinical Nutrition* **4**, 20–34 (1956)

Chapter 11: A Very Infertile Species

Berryman, J. C. & Windridge, K., 'Having a baby after 40: II. A preliminary investigation of women's experience of motherhood', *Journal of Reproductive and Infant Psychology* **9**, 19–33 (1991)

Bond, D. J. & Chandley, A. C., *Aneuploidy* (Oxford Monographs on Medical Genetics, No. 11) (Oxford University Press, Oxford, 1983)

Carlsen, E., Giwercman, A., Keiding, N. & Skakkebaek, N. E., 'Evidence for decreasing quality of semen during past 50 years', *British Medical Journal* **305**, 609–13 (1992)

Cummins, J. M., Jequier, A. M. & Kan, R., 'Molecular biology of human male infertility: links with aging, mitchondrial genetics, and oxidative stress?' *Molecular Reproduction and Development* **37**, 345–62 (1994)

Fédération CECOS, Schwartz, D. & Mayoux, N. J., 'Female fecundity as a function of age. Results of artificial insemination in 2193 nulliparous women with azoospermic husbands', *New England Journal of Medicine* **306**, 404–6 (1982)

Meldrum, D. R., 'Female reproductive aging – ovarian and uterine factors', *Fertility and Sterility* **59**, 1–5 (1993)

Menken, J., Trussell, J. & Larsen, U. (1986), 'Age and infertility', *Science* **233**, 1389–94 (1986)

Navot, D., Bergh, P. A., Williams, M. A., Garrisi, G. J., Guzman, I., Sandler, B. & Grunfeld, L., 'Poor oocyte quality rather than implantation failure as a cause of age-related decline in fertility', *Lancet* **337**, 1375–7 (1991)

Ober, W. B., 'Reuben's mandrakes: infertility in the Bible', *International Journal of Gynecological Pathology* **3**, 299–317 (1984)

Paulson, R. J. & Sauer, M. V., 'Pregnancies in post-menopausal women', *Human Reproduction* **9**, 571–2 (1994)

Sharpe, R. M. & Skakkebaek, N. E., 'Are oestrogens involved in falling sperm counts and disorders of the male reproductive tract?' *Lancet* **341**, 1392–5 (1993)

Silber, S. J., *How to Get Pregnant with the New Technology* (Warner Books, New York, 1990)

Tietze, C. (1957), 'Reproductive span and rate of reproduction among Hutterite women', *Fertility and Sterility* **8**, 89–97 (1957)

Wallace, D. C. (1992), 'Mitochondrial genetics: a paradigm for aging and degenerative diseases?' *Science* **256**, 628–32 (1992)

Winston, Robert M. L., *Infertility*, rev. edn (Optima, London, 1994)

Chapter 12: A Brave New Age

Brinster, R. L. & Zimmermann, J. W., 'Spermatogenesis following male germ-cell transplantation', *Proceedings of the National Academy of Sciences of the USA* **91**, 11298–302 (1994)

Corpas, E., Harman, S. M. & Blackman, M. R., 'Human growth hormone and human aging', *Endocrine Reviews* **14**, 20–39 (1993)

Doll, R., Peto, R., Hall, E., Wheatley, K. & Gray, R., 'Mortality in relation to consumption of alcohol: 13 years' observations on male British doctors', *British Medical Journal*, **309**, 911–18 (1994)

Doll, R., Peto, R., Wheatley, K., Gray, R. & Sutherland, I., 'Mortality in relation to smoking: 40 years' observations on male British doctors', *British Medical Journal* **309**, 901–10 (1994)

Eaton, S. B., Pike, M. C., Short, R. V. et al., 'Women's reproductive cancer in evolutionary context', *Quarterly Review of Biology* **69**, 353–67

Fries, James F. & Crapo, Lawrence M., *Vitality and Aging: Implications of the Rectangular Curve* (W. H. Freeman & Co., Oxford, 1981)

Gosden, R. G. & Aubard, Y., *Transplantation of Ovarian and Testicular Tissues* (R. G. Landes Co., Austin, Texas, 1996)

Gosden, R. G., Baird, D. T., Wade, J. C. & Webb, R., 'Restoration of fertility to oophorectomised sheep by ovarian autografts stored at −196%C', *Human Reproduction* **9**, 597–603 (1994)

Henderson, B. E., Ross, R. K. & Pike, M. O. (1993), 'Hormonal chemoprevention of cancer in women', *Science* **259**, 633–38 (1993)

Medawar, P. B., *Memoir of a Thinking Radish* (Oxford University Press, Oxford, 1986)

Olshansky, S. J., Carnes, B. A. & Cassel, C. K., 'The Aging of the Human Species', *Scientific American*, pp. 18–24 (April 1993)

Paulson, R. J. & Sauer, M. V., 'Pregnancies in post-menopausal women', *Human Reproduction* **9**, 571–2 (1994)

Short, R. V., 'The evolution of human reproduction', *Proceedings of the Royal Society of London* **195**, 3–24 (1976)

GLOSSARY

Adenosine triphosphate (ATP): molecules that store energy for use in metabolism

Adipose tissue: fat cells

Adrenal gland: a small gland lying beside each kidney that produces a variety of hormones, including corticosteroids (q.v.) and adrenalin

Amino acid: one of a group of twenty molecules that are the building blocks of proteins

Anabolic: growth-promoting

Androgen: a generic term of male sex hormones (e.g. testosterone (q.v.))

Antechinus: a genus of Australian marsupial 'mice'

Atherosclerosis: narrowing of the arteries

Basal metabolic rate (BMR): the rate at which energy is released within the whole body under conditions of minimal activity

Catalase (CAT): an enzyme that combats free radical (q.v.) production

Cholesterol: a lipid (q.v.) molecule that is needed for making parts of the cell fabric as well as steroid (q.v.) hormones but which, if deposited in artery walls, leads to atherosclerosis (q.v.)

Chromosome: a thread-like structure within the nucleus (q.v.) which carries the genes (q.v.) in linear array

Climacteric: a phase of one or two years either side of the menopause (q.v.) associated with symptoms of oestrogen deficiency (e.g. hot flushes and sweating, vaginal dryness)

Corpus luteum: a structure forming from a collapsed follicle (q.v.) after ovulation which produces progesterone in the second half of the menstrual cycle.

Corticosteroid: steroid (q.v.) hormones produced by adrenal glands (q.v.)

Corticosteroid binding globulin (CBG): a protein produced in the liver which binds corticosteroids (q.v.) secreted from the adrenal gland (q.v.) into the blood stream and tempers their effects on cells

Corticotrophin (adrenocorticotrophin, ACTH): a pituitary hormone that stimulates corticosteroid (q.v.) production by the adrenal glands (q.v.)

Cryptorchidism: the state of undescended testicles

Cytoplasm: the fabric of the cell except the nucleus (q.v.)

Dihydrotestosterone: a derivative of testosterone (q.v.) that is more potent, molecule for molecule, but does not act on all androgen-sensitive tissues (e.g. brain)

Endocrinology: the science of hormone production, action and control

325

Enzyme: a protein which converts a molecule to a different product rapidly and with high specificity

Fallopian tube (oviduct): a tube that conveys eggs and sperm between the ovary and uterus (q.v.)

Fibroblast: a fibre-producing cell that is widely distributed in tissues

Follicle stimulating hormone (FSH): a pituitary gonadotrophin (q.v.) that causes ovarian follicles (q.v.) to grow and secrete oestrogen

Follicle: a ball of cells within the ovary producing oestrogen and containing a single egg cell

Free radical: an often highly reactive agent that can damage the cell fabric and other molecules

Gene: the heritable unit of cells – there are about 70,000 different genes in human cells, each being represented by a stretch of the enormously long DNA molecules of the chromosomes (q.v.)

Germ cell: the egg or sperm cell

Gerontogene: any gene which has, among other actions, the ability to increase the rate of ageing

Gonad: the ovary or testis (testicle)

Gonadotrophin: a protein hormone produced by the pituitary gland (q.v.) or placenta that affects the growth and secretion of hormones by follicles (q.v.) and corpora lutea (q.v.) in the ovary or the production of testosterone (q.v.) and sperm from testes. There are three gonadotrophins – follicle stimulating hormone, luteinizing hormone and human chorionic gonadotrophin (q.v.)

Haemoglobin: the red pigment in blood cells that carries oxygen and carbon dioxide

Hormone replacement therapy (HRT): a chemical formulation of oestrogen (q.v.) or oestrogen and progesterone (q.v.) for treating postmenopausal women

Human chorionic gonadotrophin (HCG): the hormone used in pregnancy testing which is produced by the placenta and acts on the ovaries

Hypophysectomy: surgical removal of the pituitary gland

Hypothalamus: the part of the brain that, *inter alia*, controls the pituitary gland

Iteroparity: a life-history (q.v.) pattern characterized by a series of breeding attempts

Leydig cells: the cells in testes responsible for testosterone secretion (q.v.)

Life history: the timetable of development and ageing for each species (e.g. puberty, menopause and longevity in humans)

Lipid: fat molecule

Longevity: maximum lifespan recorded for the species

Luteinizing hormone (LH): a pituitary gonadotrophin (q.v.) that causes follicles (q.v.) to ovulate, corpora lutea (q.v.) to secret progesterone and Leydig cells (q.v.) to secrete testosterone

Melatonin: a hormone produced by the pineal gland (q.v.) during the hours of darkness that affects diurnal body rhythms

Menopause: the final period ('menses') in the lifespan

Mitochondrion: a sausage-shaped organelle within cells which is responsible for generating most of the energy in the form of adenosine triphosphate (q.v.)

Nucleus: the sac within each cell that contains the chromosomes (q.v.)

Oestrogen: the female sex hormone, which is mainly produced by ovaries

Oestrus: the day of the fertility cycle when an animal is sexually receptive

Ovariectomy (oophorectomy): surgical removal of both ovaries

Pheromone: an airborne product of one individual that influences the sexual or reproductive activity of another

Pineal gland: a small gland attached to the brain that is responsible for melatonin (q.v.) secretion and hence physiological responses to dark and light

Pituitary gland: a pea-sized gland under the brain which produces a number of hormones, including luteinizing hormone and follicle stimulating hormone.

Pleiotrophy: more than one effect

Progestogen: a steroid hormone produced mainly by the ovaries and placenta which is needed to prepare for and maintain pregnancy

Prostate gland: a gland in the lower abdomen of men which contributes to the formation of seminal fluid

Protoplasm: the cell substance including the nucleus (q.v.) and cytoplasm (q.v.)

Semelparity: a life-history (q.v.) pattern characterized by a single burst of reproductive activity: and rapid ageing

Senescence: the biological characteristics of ageing

Sex hormone binding globulin (SHBG): a protein produced in the liver which binds most sex hormones in the bloodstream and tempers their effects on cells

Somatic cell: any cell except a germ cell (q.v.)

Stem cell: a self-renewing type of cell that also produces differentiated products (e.g. red blood corpuscles from bone marrow stem cells)

Steroid: a family of lipid (q.v.) molecules including cholesterol and the sex hormones, oestrogen (q.v.) and testosterone (q.v.)

Superoxide dismutase (SOD): an enzyme that combats free radical (q.v.) production

Telomere: a cap on the end of chromosomes (q.v.) which does not contain a genetic code for proteins but has a protective function.

Testosterone: the male sex hormone which is mainly produced by testes

Thyroid gland: a gland found in the lower neck which produces the hormone thyroxine that can increase the basal metabolic rate (q.v.)

Uterus: womb

INDEX